Guide to Client/Server Databases, Second Edition

Guide to Client/Server Databases, Second Edition

Joe Salemi

Ziff-Davis Press
Emeryville, California

Copy Editor	Stephanie Raney
Technical Reviewer	Mark Streger
Project Coordinator	Cort Day
Proofreaders	Carol Burbo and Nicole Clausing
Cover Design	Regan Honda
Book Design	Paper Crane Graphics, Berkeley
Technical Illustration	Cherie Plumlee Computer Graphics & Illustration
Word Processing	Howard Blechman
Page Layout	Tony Jonick
Indexer	Ted Laux

Ziff-Davis Press books are produced on a Macintosh computer system with the following applications: FrameMaker®, Microsoft® Word, QuarkXPress®, Adobe Illustrator®, Adobe Photoshop®, Adobe Streamline™, MacLink®Plus, Aldus® FreeHand™, Collage Plus™.

If you have comments or questions or would like to receive a free catalog, call or write:
Ziff-Davis Press
5903 Christie Avenue
Emeryville, CA 94608
1-800-688-0448

ISBN 1-56276-310-5

Manufactured in the United States of America
10 9 8 7 6 5 4 3 2 1

To Nancy. Thanks for still believing in me.

■ Contents at a Glance

■ Table of Contents

■ Acknowledgments

My thanks to all who helped in the process of updating this book for the second edition. I'd especially like to thank Stephanie Raney for her copy editing, and Mark Streger for his technical editing.

This second edition wouldn't exist if it weren't for all the folks at Ziff-Davis Press who helped make the first edition a success. Thanks!

Finally, I'd like to thank my wife and my friends for constantly reminding me that there is a life beyond computers.

■ Introduction

The Client/Server market has experienced enormous growth since the first edition of this book was published in 1993. New database servers have become available, and the number of high-quality, high-power front-end applications has doubled (and almost tripled). There's no sign that this growth will slack off anytime soon.

As I said in the introduction to the first edition, the Client/Server market is a mine field for the unwary. If you haven't joined the Client/Server revolution yet, you can use this book as your guide. If you're running a C/S system (and perhaps have a copy of the first edition), you'll find this book contains a wealth of information on the latest C/S technology.

■ Who Is This Book For?

This book is designed as a guide for navigating through the Client/Server market. It's written for the business managers, information system managers, technical support personnel, and application developers whose bosses complained, "Okay, now that we've spent all this money on LANs—what the heck do we do with them?" While the casual PC or database user may benefit from the information presented here, the very nature of the technology assumes that those who are considering a move toward the Client/Server architecture are already familiar with some of the basic concepts of database design and computer networking.

■ A Quick Tour of the Contents

You may be tempted to skip over the first three chapters and dive into the chapters that cover specific products. But I urge you not to. These first chapters cover concepts essential to a complete understanding of the capabilities and features of systems addressed throughout the book.

Chapter 1 presents a broad overview of the current database technology, including the different types, models, architectures, and programming languages available. Chapter 2 begins the discussion of the Client/Server technology and covers the foundation of the architecture, the types of systems it runs on, and the networking and communications needed to create a Client/Server system. Chapter 3 explains and shows you how to use the Decision Tree that's bound into the back of this book. The Decision Tree is a map designed to guide you through the basic questions that will help you identify which systems and products may meet your needs and which direction to move in next.

Chapters 4 through 7 describe the products available for each of the four major Client/Server platforms: PCs, RISC and UNIX systems, minicomputers, and mainframes. Each chapter opens with an overview of the products and the platform, discussing their advantages and disadvantages, things to consider before deciding to base your system on the platform, and some advice and tips that I and my colleagues have gathered from years of experience. The balance of each chapter examines the particular products that run on the platform, including information about their features, hardware and software requirements, native languages, and the front-ends provided. Each section closes with a discussion of the product's advantages, disadvantages, my recommendations, and a chart that summarizes its primary features. Bear in mind that the Client/Server market is rapidly evolving; many of the features listed will change over time.

Chapter 8 provides an overview of a new class of C/S products known as groupware. Groupware covers the range from on-line discussion products to document management systems. You'll find information on both dedicated C/S groupware products and third-party groupware C/S add-ons in this chapter.

Chapters 9 and 10 provide an overview of some of the client (front-end) applications available for accessing data stored in a Client/Server database, with emphasis on PC-based clients. Chapter 9 describes how front-ends work, identifies the different types available, and covers two of the four types of front-ends (add-ons and query/reporting tools). Chapter 10 covers the remaining front-ends (application development and data analysis tools) and offers tips on choosing the right one for your needs. Chapter 10 closes with a chart that links front-end applications with the particular databases they support.

Chapter 11 considers the future of database technologies and also takes a look back at some of the predictions I made in the first edition. The opinions in this chapter are my own; however, I hope you'll find them useful as a starting point for your own explorations of where the technology is going and how it will affect your long-term plans.

The remainder of the book contains a glossary of the terms used throughout the book and three appendices. Appendix A brings together the quick summary charts of all the products in Chapters 4 through 7 to make it easy to compare the many products and platforms described in these chapters. In Appendix B, you'll find the names, addresses, and phone numbers for all the vendors covered in the book, along with their products. The Client/Server field combines several different technologies, and no one book can cover all of them, so Appendix C offers some suggestions for further reading about databases, SQL, and networks. It's my sincere hope that you will find this book a useful guide to Client/Server databases. Use it as a reference point and foundation for your own explorations of this exciting and revolutionary technology.

- *What Is a DBMS?*
- *DBMS Models*
- *DBMS System Architectures*
- *Database Application Programming Languages*

1

An Overview of Database Management Systems

COMPUTERS ARE DESIGNED TO MANIPULATE INFORMATION IN THE form of data—but to a computer, data is nothing more than random bits of electricity. We give structure and meaning to the data we put into our computers through the use of data files, which contain numbers, text, or both. These data files are accessed by familiar applications such as spreadsheets, word processing programs, and databases.

A *database system* gives us a way of gathering together specific pieces or lists of information that are relevant to us in our jobs or our lives. It also provides a way to store and maintain that information in a central place. The first commercial computers were really nothing more than dedicated database machines used to gather, sort, and report on census information. To this day, one of the most common reasons for purchasing a computer is to run a database system.

A database system consists of two parts: the *Database Management System* (DBMS), which is the program that organizes and maintains these lists of information, and the *database application*, a program that lets us retrieve, view, and update the information stored by the DBMS. Databases are everywhere: a company's personnel system (the application) written in dBASE (the DBMS) on a PC; an inventory system (application) of the parts in a warehouse maintained in Rdb/VMS (DBMS) on a DEC VAX; or patient records (application) stored in DB2 (DBMS) on an IBM mainframe.

It's common for both the DBMS and the database application to reside and execute on the same computer; in many cases the two are combined in the same program. Most of the database systems available today are designed this way. However, a lot of attention is now focused on one of the latest stages in the evolution of DBMS technology—*Client/Server* (C/S) database technology.

A Client/Server database increases database processing power by separating the DBMS from the database application. The application runs on one or more user workstations (which are usually PCs) and communicates over a network with one or more DBMSs running on other computers. C/S Database Systems make the best use of today's powerful computers, and they can also be very complex. In order to fully understand how they function, and the advantages and disadvantages of the many different types available, we will first explore the historical evolution of methods of storing, accessing, and manipulating data. Along the way, we'll encounter many terms that are either specific to the world of databases or used in ways that conflict with how they're used elsewhere.

This chapter covers the basic terms used to describe what a database is, the different methods of storing the data, and the many ways of accessing and manipulating the data. I'll be defining these terms as we go along, and they'll also be covered in the glossary. Later chapters will cover the theory and practice of Client/Server databases, what's needed to set one up, and the specific C/S systems available.

■ What Is a DBMS?

The data stored in a database can be thought of as a *population* of information. When used this way, population doesn't just describe a group of people that live in the same geographical area; it means any group or class of items or objects that we can define. When we create a database, the population we're interested in is the specific one we need to keep track of, which becomes the foundation of the database. For example, the populations of the previously mentioned database examples are the employees of the Acme Submarine Company, the parts in the company's warehouse, or the patients in FeelGood Hospital.

As Figure 1.1 demonstrates, the population of Acme Submarine's personnel database is the company's employees; each *record* in the database stores the information about one member of this population. The *fields* in each record store important details about that member. In Figure 1.1, a single record contains four fields of information (First Name, Last Name, Social Security Number, and Salary) for each member of the population.

Figure 1.1

The elements of a
database

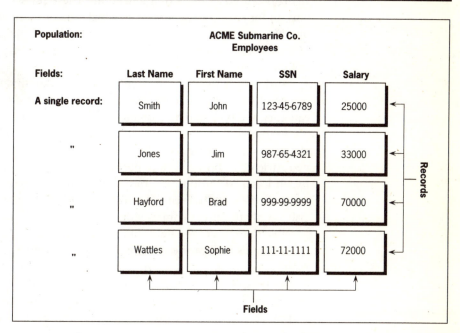

In order to store the population of data on a disk the DBMS has to provide some type of data definition services to define the records and fields in the database. It also needs an internal mechanism that maintains the data on disk and knows where each particular element resides.

Of course, we want to do more than just store data; we also need a way to enter or insert data into the database, sort it, retrieve all or portions of it, and maintain it by adding, updating or deleting records from the database. The DBMS is responsible for providing some or all of these data manipulation services to the user.

We also need a way to display the data, either on a terminal or PC screen, or as a printed report. The DBMS may provide these display services, or they may be provided by the database application. If the DBMS doesn't provide any of these services, it's commonly referred to as a *database engine*.

However, just having the data on disk and getting it back when we want it isn't any good if we can't trust that the data is accurate. The DBMS has to provide some type of *data integrity* services to ensure that the data isn't corrupted through outside means, such as disk crashes or power outages. It also has the more difficult job of protecting the database against unintentional changes caused by users or applications. These services are particularly important for *multiuser databases*, in which one or more users can be updating the same data at the same time. The DBMS has to make sure that only one of the changes actually takes place, and it should notify other users about the change made.

A database can store any type of information that the user wants, but to be useful, the data has to be stored according to its *domain*. A domain is the category and type of data elements allowed in a particular field—for example, a set of alphabetical (text) characters, all the words in the English language, or only integers. A domain is usually represented as a set and can also be restricted to only a certain portion of a set, such as positive integers between 1 and 20. Various programming techniques can even use *data lookups* from another database or file to restrict a field's domain to something as precise as only the street names within a particular city. Table 1.1 outlines some possible domains of the fields in the sample employee database.

Responsibility for ensuring that the data entered fits the field's domain is a data integrity service that can be left entirely up to the DBMS or can be split between the user application and the DBMS. Overall, providing this service is the most important job a DBMS can have; the more responsibility it has for providing it, the better the data integrity of the whole database system.

Table 1.1

The Domains in the
Sample Employee
Database

FIELD NAME	DOMAIN
Last Name	[A...Z,a...z,-] Upper- and lowercase letters, and the hyphen; or, all names containing only these elements.
First Name	[A...Z,a...z] Upper- and lowercase letters only; or, all names containing only these elements.
Middle Initial	[A...Z,.] Uppercase letters and the period.
SS Number	[0...9,-] Integers and the hyphen; or numbers in the "999-99-9999" format.
Salary	["0.00"..."99,999.99"] Positive decimal numbers between 0 and 99,999.99.

To pull it all together, a Database Management System (DBMS) provides the following services:

- *Data definition* provides a method of defining and storing a data population.

- *Data maintenance* maintains the population using a record for each item in the population, with fields containing particular information that describes that item.

- *Data manipulation* provides services that let the user insert, update, delete, and sort data in the database.

- *Data display* optionally provides some method of displaying the data for the user.

- *Data integrity* provides one or more methods of ensuring that the data is accurate.

■ DBMS Models

The Database Management Systems available today can be grouped into four different types, or as they're commonly called, models: the File Management System, Hierarchical Database System, Network Database System, and Relational Database Model. A newer type of DBMS called Object-Oriented

Databases (OODBMS) has started to see widespread use in the last two years, primarily in C/S groupware applications. However, there is as yet no standard model for Object-Oriented Databases, and each vendor has its own description for what it is and how to imnplement it. I'll be covering OODMBSs in greater detail in Chapter 11. Each database model is a conceptual description of how the database works. Specifically, it describes how the data is presented to the user and programmer for access.

A database model also describes the relationships between different items; for example, in the sample employee database each item of information, such as salary or Social Security number, is related to the particular employee that the whole record describes. That particular employee's record may also be related to other items in the database, such as the employee's supervisor or department. Note that the relations between the different data items are separate and distinct from the Relational Database Model described later in this chapter—this is one of those circumstances where meaning depends on context.

With the one exception addressed below, the database models don't describe how data is stored on disk. These details are worked out by the designers of the DBMS. However, in some circumstances, a model may indirectly place constraints on how the data is stored if the DBMS is to meet all the requirements that comprise that particular model. These constraints (where applicable) are covered in the descriptions of the models that follow.

It's interesting to note that historically, the Relational model was the first description of a database model to precede development of such a DBMS; the other three models were defined after the fact to describe database systems that had already been in use for several years. The actual evolution of these database systems followed the path from File Management to Hierarchical to Network to Relational.

File Management Systems

The File Management System (FMS) is the easiest database model to understand, and it is the only one that describes how the data is stored on disk. In the FMS model, each field or data item is stored sequentially on disk in one large file. As with a word processing program, in order to find a particular element (word), the application starts at the beginning and checks each item until it finds a match.

The File Management System was the first method used to store data in a computerized database, and simplicity is its only advantage. Today, about the only DBMS products built on this model are the low-end, "flat-file" databases, such Borland's *Reflex*. Figure 1.2 demonstrates how the sample employee database would look if it were stored on disk in an FMS database.

Figure 1.2

The File Management
System model

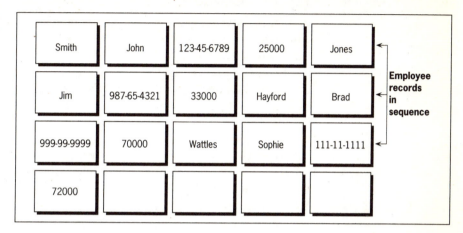

When you look at Figure 1.2, the disadvantages of the FMS become clear. First, there's no indication of the relationship between the various items other than the storage sequence. The programmer, and sometimes the user, has to know exactly how the data is stored in the file in order to manipulate it.

This complicates the task of data access by requiring knowledge of how the computer's operating system physically stores the data on disk. There's too much room for error when these details have to be handled by each application that accesses the database.

Second, the FMS creates problems with data integrity; all field values have to be checked by the application program prior to being stored on disk. The same database can be accessed by different applications, and each one can allow slightly different values for each field. The different applications have to be manually coordinated to ensure that they're defining each field's domain in the same way.

Third, there's no way to find a particular employee's record quickly; every search starts from the beginning of the file, examining each and every record. At best the DBMS can keep a *pointer* (a logical or physical indicator on the disk) to the last data item retrieved, so that searches for more occurrences of the same data type don't have to start again from the beginning of the file.

In addition, the only way to sort the data is by reading the entire file and rewriting it in the new order. This can be solved through the use of an *index file*—a subset of the data file based on one or more fields—that contains pointers to each record in the database. Index files can also quicken searches; however, they add a level of complexity to the database and must be constantly updated as the database changes.

Finally, the biggest disadvantage of the FMS is that it doesn't allow easy changes to the database structure. For example, adding the department name to each employee's record would require the DBMS to read each record, write it to a temporary file, and add the new information after the last field of each record. After scanning the whole file and writing the new one, it would delete the original file and rename the temporary file. This whole procedure occurs even if the programmer simply wants to change the size of a field to store more data. The system overhead involved in making structural changes is enormous, opening many opportunities for errors which might corrupt the entire database.

The need for a better way to describe *one-to-many relationships* among different records, as well as an easier and faster way to conduct searches, led to the development of the next database model, the Hierarchical Database System.

Hierarchical Database Systems

The next logical development in database models is the Hierarchical Database System (HDS). In this model, data is organized in a tree structure that originates from a *root*. Each class of data is located at different levels along a particular branch that stems from the root. The data structure at each class level is called a *node*; if no further branches follow, the last node in the series is considered a *leaf*.

The diagram of an HDS structure presented in Figure 1.3 resembles something that's familiar to just about all of us—the ubiquitous organization chart. In database terms, the tree structure of the HDS defines the "*parent-child*" and "*sibling*" relationships between the various items in our database, and it clearly shows the advantages over the File Management System model for defining one-to-many relationships. It also demonstrates how the hierarchical structure makes it easier, and faster, to search for data; for example, if a user wants to find the information that's in field 1B1, the DBMS doesn't have to search the entire file to find the data it wants. It examines the request, breaks it down into its components, and follows the B branch down to 1B, and then down one more level to the 1B1 field. As in the FMS, an index can be used to speed up searches even further, though in the case of a Hierarchical DBMS, the index would be on a particular class (level) of data instead.

In an HDS, there's always one and only one *root node*, which is usually "owned" by the system or DBMS. Pointers from the root lead down to the level 1 nodes (the children of the root node), where the real database begins. The level 1 nodes represent a particular class of data—in our sample database, that class could be the departments in the Acme Submarine Company (Figure 1.4). Each level 1 node can have one or more level 2 children, which would represent the employees assigned to each department (identified by a unique

Figure 1.3

The Hierarchical
Database System model

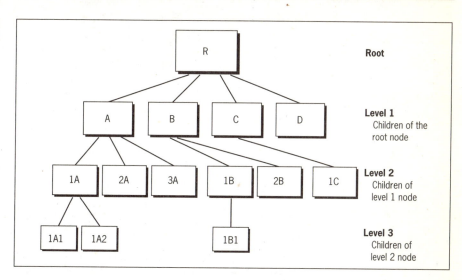

identifier, such as their SSN). The children of the employee identifier class
would then consist of the fields that contain the information about individual
employees. In Figure 1.4, the structure of the level 3 nodes differs slightly from
Figure 1.3 in order to show the sibling relationship between the different
fields. The path between level 3 fields consists of a chain of pointers from one
leaf node to the next; for example, from last name to first name to salary.
Any or all of the different levels in an HDS can be clearly diagrammed with
such a path. Also note that in this model, each child can have pointers to
numerous siblings, but only one pointer to the parent, preserving the one-to-
many relationship in a single direction.

The physical structure of the data on the disk doesn't matter under the
HDS model; the DBMS can (and usually does) store the data as a linked list
of fields, with pointers that go from parent to child and from sibling to sibling, ending in a null or *terminal pointer* at the last leaf. It quickly becomes
obvious that this design makes it easy to add new fields at any level, as the
DBMS only has to change the terminal pointer to point to the next sibling
node in the list. On the other hand, the HDS diagram doesn't quite show
which fields comprise a particular record. For convenience, we can define a
record as a parent and all its children; in the sample database, each employee's
record starts at the SSN class level and includes all the leaves that describe
that employee. However, we can also start the record at the department class
level and define a record as all the information about the employees in that
department. While this model provides a great deal of flexibility, it's not without its drawbacks.

Figure 1.4

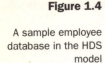

A sample employee
database in the HDS
model

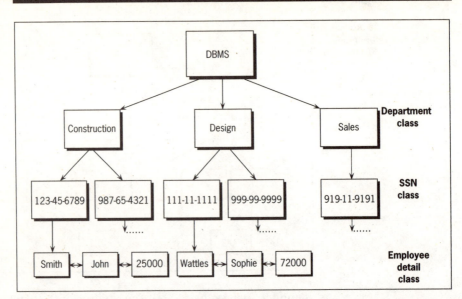

The first problem arises from the initial structure of the database, which
is arbitrary and must be defined by the programmer when the database is
created. From that point on, the parent-child relationship can't be changed
without redesigning the whole structure. Continuing with our example, suppose that Acme decides to open a branch office and moves the sales division
to it. The database must now have another level between the root and the
department class that contains the office identifiers. In order to make this
change, the programmer must first create an entirely new structure to identify the new parent-child relationships, and then copy the data over from the
original database to the proper locations in the new one.

Alternatively, the programmer could also simply add another field to each
of the employees' records to identify their office assignments. However, adding an office field duplicates data, which wastes disk space. It also results in
slowing a search for all the employees assigned to a particular office, since every
branch has to be searched to the last leaf to check for the office identifiers.

Another problem created by the rigidity of the HDS structure is that it's
not easy to change the definition of the class levels. Suppose the company
decides to use employee numbers instead of Social Security numbers to identify each employee; the programmer would have to recreate the structure
with the new employee number class replacing the SSN class, and then move
the SSN information to the employee detail level.

The most significant drawback to the Hierarchical Database System model is that it provides no easy method of defining cross or many-to-many relationships. An example of a *cross-relationship* is when an employee is also a manager; in order to identify which employees report to which supervisors, the database would have to incorporate another level between the department name and the Social Security numbers to contain an identifier for every manager. Since each manager is also an employee under that department, this would create the slightly illogical situation in which a parent-child relationship exists between a manager and herself. Taking another approach, each employee's record could contain a field that identifies that employee's manager—but this method is inefficient, due to the duplication and slow search problems mentioned earlier.

The *many-to-many relationship* problem would also arise in an inventory database that (for example) tracked the parts of Acme's submarines and the suppliers of those parts. It's entirely possible that more than one vendor sells the same part and that the same vendor also sells different classes of parts. Under the Hierarchical model, the common solution to this problem is the highly inefficient one of storing multiple copies of the same data at multiple levels.

Another approach to solving the many-to-many relationship problem is adding secondary parent-child and sibling pointers to the hierarchical structure. This method creates numerous circular relationships; as these relationships become more complex, the database architecture gradually evolves into the next model.

Network Database Systems

Though the concepts behind the Network Database System model originated in the 1960s, the first written specifications were released in 1971 by the Conference on Data System Languages (CODASYL). DBMSs based on the Network model are still sometimes referred to as CODASYL databases. Note, however, that the name "network" has nothing to do with the physical medium that the database actually runs on—the Network model conceptually describes databases in which many-to-many (multiple parent-child) relationships exist. The relationships between the different data items are commonly referred to as "sets" to distinguish them from the strictly parent-child relationships defined by the Hierarchical model.

A Network Database System (NDS) relies on either straight-line or cyclical pointers to map out the relationships between the different data items. Take the example of Acme Submarine Company's inventory database; in many cases, Acme deals with multiple vendors that sell the same product. Figure 1.5 illustrates a simple straight-line form of an NDS inventory, showing the various relationships between parts and suppliers. An Acme manager can find out who sells propellers by having the DBMS search the parts set and then following the pointers back to the two vendors that supply them. Conversely, if this manager wants to know what Acme buys from Santa Fe Office Supplies, the DBMS can search the vendor set and follow the pointers from Santa Fe to the two items that they sell. This approach is very flexible, as the DBMS can also treat the combination of a particular vendor and the parts the vendor sells as a purchase set, as shown in Figure 1.5 by the circle around Mason's Metal Works and the rivets and propellers they sell.

Figure 1.5

A simple Network
Database System model

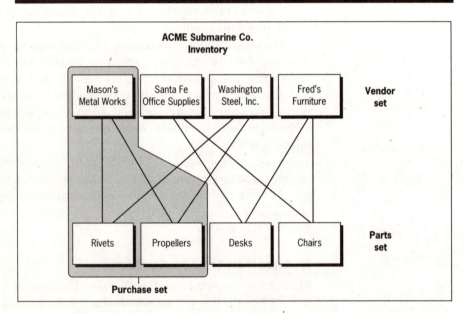

The Network model can be used to describe even more complex relationships, as shown in Figure 1.6. Suppose an Acme manager wants to know not only who sells a particular part, but what they charge for it. Through the addition of a set called "prices," the DBMS can now trace a cyclical pattern from vendor to part to price. Again, the search can start at any of the defined sets. The Acme manager can decide that they need more rivets, and then can follow the pointers around to the vendor and to the price the vendor charges (or conversely, to the price and then the vendor who sells it at that price).

The flexibility of the Network Database System model in showing many-to-many relationships is its greatest strength, though that flexibility comes at a price. The interrelationships between the different sets can become extremely complex and difficult to map out. (Imagine Figure 1.6 with a hundred vendors, thousands of different parts, and multiple price ranges based on the quantity

Figure 1.6

A complex Network
Database System model

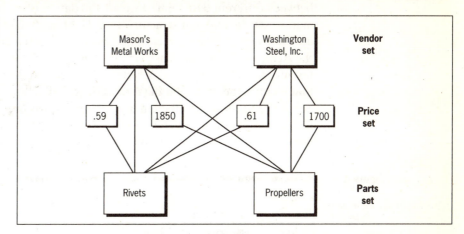

purchased.) This can become a severe problem, as most NDS databases require the programmer to write the application code that traces out the different data paths. Like Hierarchical databases, Network databases can be very
fast, especially through the use of index pointers that lead directly to the first
item in a set being searched. The NDS also goes a long way toward eliminating duplicated data.

However, the Network model also suffers from the same structural problems mentioned in the description of the HDS. The initial design of the database is arbitrary. Once it's set up, any changes to the different sets require
the programmer to create an entirely new structure. The NDS does make it
simpler to add new data items to the database or to change existing ones.
The programmer only has to define a new set and adjust the various pointers
to put the new set in the proper relationship with the rest of the data.

You'll have noticed by now that the descriptions of the previous three
database models have constantly referred to the "relationship" between the
different data items in the database. Thinking about the relationships between
data led one IBM scientist to create an entirely different model for database
design, the Relational Database Model.

Relational Database Models

In 1969, Dr. E.F. Codd published the first paper to define a model for databases based on the mathematical concept of relational sets. The Relational
Database Model (RDM) has been constantly refined since then, most notably in Dr. Codd's 1985 paper that laid out the "12 Rules" for relational databases, and in his 1990 book that defines Version 2 (RV/2) of the Relational
model through 333 rules that are subsets and expansions of the original 12.

The Relational model abandons the concept of parent-child relationships between different data items. Instead, the data is organized in logical mathematical sets in a tabular structure. In a RDM, each data field becomes a column in a table, and each record becomes a row in the table. Figure 1.7 shows the Acme inventory database arranged in relational form. Notice that the different sets under the complex Network model here become different tables that identify the particular data items by the column names in the first row. All the vendors are grouped in one table, the parts and prices in other tables. Different relationships between the various tables are defined through the use of the mathematical set functions, such as JOIN and UNION.

Figure 1.7

The Relational Database
Model

VENDORS

V#	Vendor_Name	Contact
M1	Mason's Metal Works	Nigel Mason
S1	Santa Fe Office Supplies	Mike Michaels
W1	Washington Steel Inc.	Jane Austin
F1	Fred's Furniture	Fred Johnson

PARTS

P#	Part_Description	V#
1001	Rivets	M1
5204	Desks	S1
3333	Propellers	W1
3333	Propellers	M1
5210	Chairs	F1
5204	Desks	F1
1001	Rivets	W1
5210	Chairs	S1

PRICES

P#	V#	Price	Min_Quan
1001	M1	0.59	10
1001	M1	0.61	1
3333	W1	1700.00	1
3333	M1	1850.00	1
1001	W1	0.61	1

You'll notice that each table has one or more columns with the same name as that in another table. It's these common column names that are used to relate the different tables; however, the column names don't have to be identical in the Relational model, so long as the data in the common columns is of the same type and in the same domain.

In order to find a particular part from a particular vendor, the DBMS searches the PARTS table for the part name, finds the vendor number in the V# column and relates it to the similar data in the V# column in the VENDORS table to find the vendor's name and contact person. To find the price of the item, the P# and V# columns in the PARTS table are related to the same-named columns in the PRICES table. These separate relationships can also be combined: A user can ask the DBMS to display the vendor, part name, price, and minimum quantity at that price, and the DBMS will look up both relations described previously and display the information.

The Relational model has a number of clear advantages over the Hierarchical and Network models, the most important of which is its complete flexibility in describing the relationships between the various data items. The programmer defines the database by creating the tables and deciding which columns the tables will be related on. From that point on, users can query the database on any of the individual columns in a table or on the relationships between the different tables. Changing the structure of the database is as simple as adding or deleting columns from a table, which doesn't affect the other tables in any way. New tables can be created from scratch or as projections (subsets) of existing tables, and old tables can be removed at will. Not having to rebuild the entire database structure to make changes also represents an increase in the preservation of data integrity.

The major decision for a Relational database designer is the table definitions. The process of breaking down the data to be stored into subsets for the tables is called normalization. While the concepts behind normalization are beyond the scope of this book, in simple terms the RDM defines five levels of *normalization,* in which each level reduces the complexity of the structure of the previous level and also reduces the amount of duplicated data in the database. For an example of normalization, look at the PARTS table in Figure 1.7. You'll notice that even though the P# and Part Description columns contain some duplicated information, each row of data is unique because the values in the V# column are different for each row. This table can be taken to the next level of normalization by splitting up the V# column into multiple columns, as shown in Figure 1.8. This reduces the amount of space required to store the parts information even further (though it slightly increases the amount of storage needed for the PRICES table, as the V# column has to be replaced with V1 and V2). It's important to note that these changes in no way affect the data or structure of the VENDORS table.

Figure 1.8

The PARTS table after further normalization

PARTS			
P#	Part_Description	V1	V2
1001	Rivets	M1	W1
5204	Desks	S1	F1
3333	Propellers	W1	M1
5210	Chairs	F1	S1

In a properly designed Relational DBMS, the information on the structures that comprise the database is held in a separate set of tables, commonly called the *system tables* or *database dictionary*. This information consists of data elements such as the names of the database's tables, the names of the columns in those tables, and the type of data stored in each column. The DBMS treats these system tables just like any other data tables, so the programmer can query them to find out the names of the tables in a database or the names of the columns in each table.

The primary goal of the Relational Database Model is to preserve data integrity. To be considered truly relational, a DBMS must completely prevent access to the data by any means other than queries handled by the DBMS itself. While the Relational model (like the Hierarchical and Network models) says nothing about how the data is stored on the disk, the preservation of data integrity implies that the data must be stored in a format that prevents it from being accessed from outside the DBMS that created it.

The Relational model also requires that the data be accessed through programs that don't rely on the position of the data in the database. This is in direct contrast to the other database models, where the program has to follow a series of pointers to the data it seeks. A program querying a Relational database simply asks for the data it seeks; the DBMS performs the necessary searches and provides the information. The details on how the search is done are specific to the DBMS and vary from product to product. Searches can be sped up by creating an index on one or more columns in a table; however, the index is again under the control and use of the DBMS. The programmer simply asks the DBMS to create the index, and the index will be maintained and used automatically from that point on.

The emphasis on data integrity makes the Relational model ideal for transaction processing systems, and thus for Client/Server databases. In the other database models, changes have to be made directly to the data itself, which can cause conflicts when multiple users are updating the same records. A Relational DBMS treats every change (or group of changes) to the data as a transaction, which it executes on a temporary copy of the table being altered. Changes don't become permanent until the user or application commits the change to the database itself. Under this system, the DBMS itself controls conflicting changes to the data and can arbitrate between them. The disadvantage comes in the form of increased system and computational overhead; a trade-off is made between speedy access to the data and assurance that the data is accurate.

 Until recently, the extra overhead involved in running a Relational DBMS meant such databases were only run on the largest mainframe and minicomputers. This lead to the phenomena of a number of DBMS packages (particularly those designed for PCs) implementing only portions of the Relational model. These databases, now known as semirelational databases, trade off portions of the model for increased speed or better data access by the programmer. It's only since 1987, with the increase in PCs based on the powerful Intel 80386, 80486, and Pentium CPUs, that DBMSs which more closely adhere to the Relational model have moved down to microcomputers. This move of relational databases to microcomputers has led to the development of Client/Server systems, which are the subject of the rest of this book.

■ DBMS System Architectures

The type of computer systems that databases run on can be broken down into four broad categories or platforms: centralized, PC, Client/Server, and distributed. The four differ the most in where the actual data processing occurs. The architecture of the DBMS itself doesn't necessarily determine the type of computer system that the database has to run on, though certain architectures are more suited (or more common) to some platforms than others.

Centralized Platforms

In a centralized system, all programs run on a main "host" computer, including the DBMS, the applications that access the database, and the communications facilities that send and receive data from the users' terminals.

The users access the database through either locally connected or dial-up (remote) terminals, as shown in Figure 1.9. The terminals are generally "dumb," having little or no processing power of their own, and consist of only a screen, keyboard, and hardware to communicate with the host. The advent of microprocessors has led to the development of more intelligent terminals in recent years, where the terminal shares some of the responsibility for handling screen drawing and user input. While mainframe and minicomputer systems are the primary platform for large corporate database systems, PC-based systems can also communicate with centralized systems through hardware/software combinations that emulate (imitate) the terminal types used with a particular host.

All the data processing in a centralized system takes place on the host computer, and the DBMS must be running before any database applications can access the database. When a user first turns on a terminal, he usually sees a log-in screen; the user enters a log-on ID and password to gain access to the host's applications. When the database application starts up, it sends the appropriate screen information "down the wire" to the user's terminal and responds with different actions based on the user's subsequent keystrokes. The application and the DBMS, both running on the same host, communicate through shared memory areas or application task areas that are managed by the host's operating system. The DBMS is responsible for moving

Figure 1.9

A typical centralized
database system

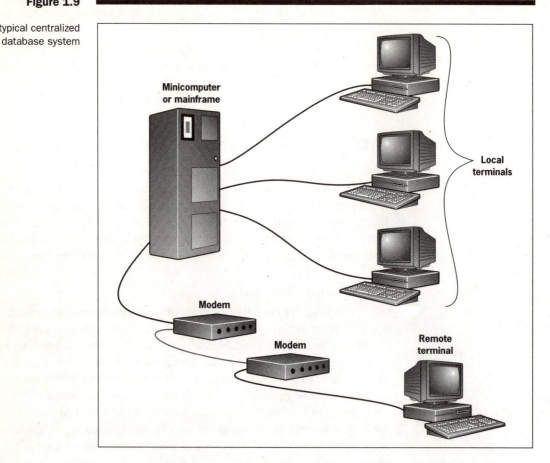

the data to and from the disk storage systems, using the services provided by
the operating system. Figure 1.10 represents one possible way these applications interact: The applications communicate with the users at the terminals
and with the DBMS; the DBMS communicates with the storage devices
(which may be, but aren't limited to, hard disks) and with the applications.

The DBMS that runs on the host system can be based on any of the four
models, though the Hierarchical and Relational models are the most common.
On mainframes, the DBMS is usually based on IBM's IMS, a Hierarchical
database. In recent years, however, more and more mainframes are running
DBMSs based on the Relational model, most notably IBM's DB2.

Minicomputers are the traditional home of DBMSs based on the Network model, databases such as the early DBMS-10 from Digital Equipment
Corporation (DEC), the Image/1000 and Image/3000 from Hewlett-Packard

Figure 1.10

Database processing on
a centralized system

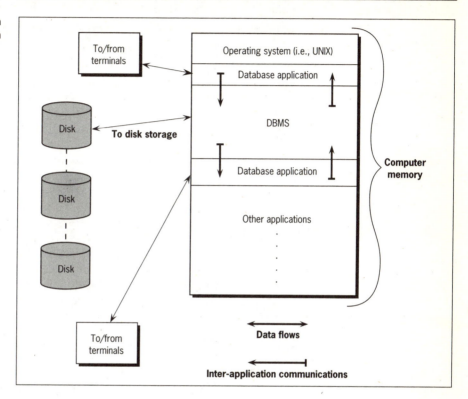

(HP), and the UNIFY DBMS from Unify Corporation. Since the early 1980s,
a number of companies have produced Relational databases that run on minicomputers (under either UNIX or DEC's VAX/VMS), databases such as
INGRES from Ingres Corporation, Rdb/VMS from DEC, and ORACLE
from Oracle Corporation.

   The principal advantages of a centralized system are centralized security
and the ability to handle enormous amounts of data on storage devices. Centralized systems can also support numerous simultaneous users; it's not uncommon for a database on an IBM mainframe to support over 1,000 users at
once. The disadvantages are generally related to the costs of purchasing and
maintaining these systems. Large mainframe and large minicomputer systems
require specialized support facilities, such as the fairly common data center
with raised floors, water-cooling systems, and very large climate-control systems. A highly trained staff of operators and system programmers is usually
necessary to keep the system up and running, which adds considerable personnel costs. Finally, the purchase price of hardware for large centralized

systems often runs well into the millions of dollars, and maintenance costs run high as well.

In recent years, companies have increasingly opted for department-sized minicomputers, such as DEC's MicroVAX and IBM'S AS/400, which don't cost as much to purchase or support as centralized systems, and generally don't require a special environment to run in. These systems are best suited for smaller companies with fewer users (not more than 200) or for database applications that are of interest to only one particular department in a large company (that is, a minicomputer that runs engineering applications may only be of interest to a design department). These smaller computers may also be networked to other minicomputers and mainframes, so that all the computers can share data. These "distributed" systems will be covered later in this chapter.

Personal Computer Systems

Personal computers (PCs) first emerged in the late 1970s and began a revolution in how we view and use computers. One of the earliest successful operating systems for PCs was Digital Research's CP/M (Control Program for Microcomputers). The first successful PC-based DBMS, Ashton-Tate's dBASE II, ran under CP/M. When IBM released the first MS-DOS–based PC in 1981, Ashton-Tate ported dBASE over to the new operating system. dBASE has since spawned newer versions, compatibles and look-alikes, and competing DBMSs that have proven to the data processing community that PCs can perform many of the same tasks that the large systems do.

When a DBMS is run on a PC, the PC acts as both the host computer and the terminal. Unlike the larger systems, the DBMS functions and the database application functions are combined into one application. Database applications on a PC handle the user input, screen output, and access to the data on the disk. Combining these different functions into one unit gives the DBMS a great deal of power, flexibility, and speed, though usually at the cost of decreased data security and integrity.

PCs originated as stand-alone systems; however, in recent years many have been connected to Local Area Networks (LANs). In a LAN, the data and usually the user applications reside on the File Server, a PC running a special Network Operating System (NOS) such as Novell's NetWare or Microsoft's Windows NT Advanced Server. The File Server manages the LAN users' shared access to data on its hard disks and frequently provides access to other shared resources, such as printers.

While a LAN enables users of PC-based databases to share common data files, it doesn't significantly change how the DBMS works; all the actual data processing is still performed on the PC running the database application. The

File Server only searches its disks for the data needed by the user and sends that data across the network cable to the user's PC. The data is then processed by the DBMS running on the PC, and any changes to the database require the PC to send the whole data file back to the File Server to be stored again on disk. This exchange is shown in Figure 1.11. Though multiuser access to shared data is a plus, the most significant disadvantage of a LAN-based DBMS is that regardless of how fast or powerful the File Server is, its performance is limited by the power of the PC running the actual DBMS. When multiple users are accessing the database, the same data files have to be sent from the File Server to every PC accessing them; this increased traffic can cause the network to slow down.

Figure 1.11

A database on a PC-based LAN

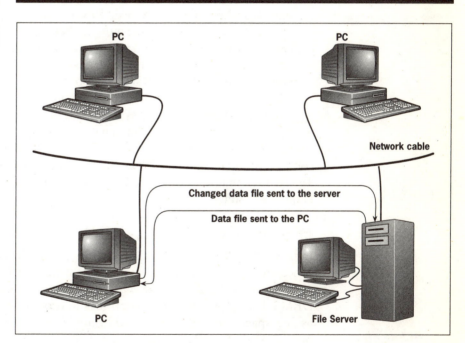

The only enhancement needed by a multiuser DBMS over a single-user one is the ability to handle simultaneous changes to the data by multiple users. This is usually accomplished by some type of locking scheme, in which the record or data file that a user is updating or changing is locked to prevent other users from also changing it. Most LAN-based DBMSs available today are simply multiuser versions of common stand-alone database systems, though the types of locking schemes vary widely and can significantly affect the performance of a multiuser database.

The majority of PC-based DBMSs are designed on the Relational model, though the fact that the DBMS isn't separated from the database application means that many (if not most) of the relational principles aren't implemented. The most notable missing components are those that address data integrity. Most PC databases allow direct access to the data files outside of the DBMS that created them. This creates a situation in which changes can be made to the data files that violate the rules by which the database application ensures data integrity. Such a violation can even cause the data file to be unreadable by the DBMS. For this reason, PC databases based on the Relational model are more accurately described as semirelational. Some of the more common semirelational PC databases available today include Microrim's R:Base, Borland's dBASE IV and its many "clones" such as Microsoft's FoxPro, Borland's Paradox, DataEase International's DataEase, and Revelation Technologies's Advanced Revelation.

As mentioned previously, the more limited flat-file PC databases are commonly based on the File Management System model. There are also PC-based DBMSs that derive from the Network model, such as Data Access Corporation's DataFlex and Raima Corporation's db_Vista III.

Most PC-based multiuser database systems handle the same number of users as the smaller centralized systems. However, the problems of handling multiple simultaneous transactions and increased network traffic, and the limits to the processing power of the PCs running the DBMS cause increasing complexity and performance degradation as the number of users multiplies. The solution that was developed for these limitations is the Client/Server Database System.

Client/Server Databases

In its simplest form, a Client/Server (C/S) database splits the database processing between two systems: the client PC which runs the database application, and the database server which runs all or part of the actual DBMS. The LAN File Server continues to provide shared resources, such as disk space for applications, and printers. The database server can run on the same PC as the File Server, or (as is more common) on its own computer. The database application on the client PC, referred to as the *front-end system*, handles all the screen and user input/output processing. The *back-end system* on the database server handles data processing and disk access. For example, a user on the front-end creates a request (query) for data from the database server, and the front-end application sends the request across the network to the server. The database server performs the actual search and sends back only the data that answers the user's query, as shown in Figure 1.12.

Figure 1.12

A Client/Server system

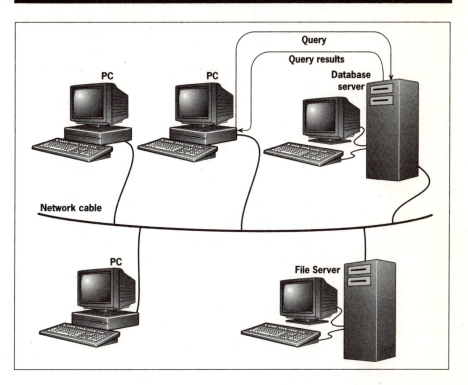

The immediate advantage of a C/S system is obvious; splitting the processing between two systems reduces the amount of data traffic on the network cable. Chapter 2 will discuss the other advantages (and disadvantages) of Client/Server systems and will describe the system architecture in more detail. Typical platforms for C/S systems will also be discussed.

In one of the typically confusing cases of different meanings for the same term that we sometimes encounter in the computer field, the definition of Client/Server is apparently reversed on UNIX-based systems running the graphical interface X-Windows. The split in processing is the same as on a PC-based C/S system; however, the front-end is called the server under X-Windows, as it provides the display and user interface services. The back-end system, on which the DBMS runs, is referred to as the client of the services provided by the front-end system.

The number of C/S systems is growing rapidly—new ones are being designed and released almost monthly. While the client systems generally run on PCs, the database server can run on anything from another PC to a mainframe. Chapters 4 through 7 will cover the various Client/Server DBMSs available today. Chapter 8 will cover Client/Server-based groupware applications like

Lotus Notes. More and more front-end applications are coming out as well, including those that extend the reach of the traditional PC-based DBMSs to database servers. Chapters 9 and 10 will give an overview of representative front-end systems.

The greatest disadvantage of the database systems described so far is that they require the data to be stored on a single system. This can be a problem for large companies, which may have to support database users scattered over a wide geographical area or which need to share portions of their departmental databases with other departments or a central host. Some way of distributing the data among the various hosts or sites is needed, which has led to the development of distributed processing systems.

Distributed Processing Systems

A simple form of distributed processing has existed for several years. In this limited form, data is shared among various host systems via updates sent either through direct connections (on the same network) or through remote connections via phone or dedicated data lines. An application which runs on one or more of the hosts extracts the portion of data that's been changed during a programmer-defined period, and then transmits the data to either a centralized host or other hosts in the distributed circuit. The other databases are then updated so that all the systems are in sync with each other. This type of distributed processing usually occurs between departmental computers or LANs and host systems; the data goes to a large central minicomputer or mainframe host after the close of the business day.

While this system is ideal for sharing portions of data among different hosts, it doesn't address the issue of users' access to data not stored in their local host. Users must change their connections to the different hosts to access different databases, remembering which database is where. Combining data from databases that exist on different hosts also presents some serious challenges for both users and programmers. There's also the issue of duplicated data; although disk storage systems have declined in price over the years, providing numerous disk systems to store the same data can be expensive. Keeping all the duplicate sets of data in sync adds additional complexities to the system.

The solution to these problems is emerging in the technology of "seamless" data access called *distributed processing*. Under a distributed processing system, a user requests data from the local host; if the local host makes the determination that it doesn't have the data, it goes out over the network to get it from the system that does. It then passes the data back to the user without the user ever knowing that the data was retrieved from a different system, except, perhaps, for a slight delay in getting the data. Figure 1.13 illustrates one form of a distributed processing system. First, the user creates and sends a data query to the local database server. The database server then sends the request for data it doesn't have over the network to the mainframe (possibly through a gateway or bridge system that joins the two networks together). It gets back a response answering the query. The local database server then combines those results with the data found on its own disks and sends everything back to the user.

Figure 1.13

A distributed processing system

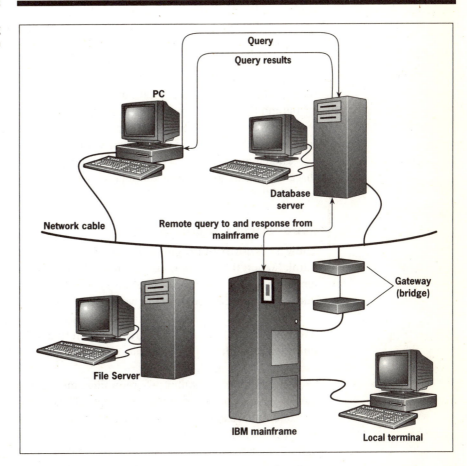

Ideally, this distributed system can also work the other way: Terminal users connected directly to the mainframe can access data that exists on remote database servers. The design and implementation of distributed processing systems is a very new field; many pieces aren't in place yet, and existing solutions are not always compatible with each other. I'll mention some of the existing solutions when I cover Client/Server DBMSs in later chapters, and I will discuss the future of distributed processing in Chapter 11.

■ Database Application Programming Languages

A sophisticated DBMS doesn't do anyone a bit of good if the users don't have a way of accessing the data. I've mentioned database applications throughout this chapter; now it's time to explore exactly what a database application is and how it communicates with the DBMS.

A database application is simply a computer program that allows users to enter, change, delete, and report on the data in a database. Applications, traditionally written by programmers, are written in one or more general or specialized programming languages. However, there has been a trend in recent years toward user-oriented database access tools that simplify the process of using a DBMS and eliminate the need for custom programming.

While the topic of actually programming a database is well beyond the scope of this book, an understanding of some of the languages and mechanics behind the programming will make it easier to understand the topics that will be covered in upcoming chapters. Appendix C lists other books that cover programming databases in more detail if you want to pursue this topic further.

The languages used to create database applications can be grouped into three broad categories: procedural languages, SQL (and SQL-like) languages, and all other languages.

Procedural Languages

The vast majority of programming languages can be described as "procedural." When the programmer creates a database application in one of these languages, he or she has to write the application's code as a series of procedures. Each procedure does the work of one portion of the application, such as a procedure to query the database or a procedure to update data in the database. The different procedures are then tied together through other user-interface procedures (for example, a menu system) and run at the appropriate points in the application.

The standard computer programming languages, such as Pascal, COBOL, BASIC, and C, are procedural languages. These languages can be used to create database applications through the use of an *Application Programming Interface* (API), which consists of a standard set of functions (or calls) that extend the language to give it access to the data on the DBMS. The API functions are usually contained in "libraries" that are included in the application when it's compiled. Most DBMS vendors have these libraries available as part of the DBMS package or as an extra-cost option. Some DBMS file types (such as the .DBF files used by dBASE) are so common, or the structure of the file so well documented, that it's possible to create database applications to access the data without having to use an API library. All these high-level languages, which can also be used to create nondatabase applications, are generally referred to as "third generation languages" (3GLs).

Some procedural programming languages are specific to one particular DBMS. These languages are commonly referred to as "fourth generation languages" (4GLs) to distinguish them from the general-use 3GLs. The most common example of a database-specific procedural language is the dBASE language, available in different products from a number of vendors. Other examples of database-specific languages are PAL (Paradox Application Language) used by Paradox, and the R/BASIC language used by Advanced Revelation.

Structured Query Language (SQL)

The Structured Query Language (SQL) was initially designed as a database language to explicitly access DBMSs based on the Relational model. The initial version of the language first appeared as SEQUEL in the mid-1970s and was developed by IBM as the standard language for accessing an early Relational database that ran on IBM mainframes. By the late '70s, the name had been shortened to SQL, though there are those that still pronounce it "sequel" out of habit.

SQL is more properly described as a sublanguage, since it doesn't contain any facilities for screen handling or user input/output. Its main purpose is to provide a standard method for accessing databases, regardless of the language the rest of the database application is written in. It's designed for interactive queries of a database (and referred to as dynamic SQL) or as part of an application written in one of the procedural languages (and referred to as embedded SQL).

Since it was originally created, SQL has been revised several times. In the early '80s, an attempt was made by the American National Standards Institute (ANSI) to standardize the SQL language, which led to the release of the ANSI-86 SQL specifications and later on to the ANSI-89 SQL and ANSI-92 SQL specifications. IBM has been at the forefront of expanding the SQL language, working particularly to extend the capabilities of their DB2 relational mainframe database. For this reason it's become common to see the SQL implementations from other DBMS vendors described as "ANSI SQL with DB2 extensions." Attempts are underway to incorporate many of these extensions into the SQL2 specifications, which are due out from ANSI sometime in the next few years, though such releases are difficult to predict. However, don't assume that one vendor's SQL implementation can talk to another's. Every DBMS vendor adds their own extensions to the SQL standard, and these extensions can make the various SQL versions incompatible with each other.

It's important to note that while SQL is primarily used with databases based on the Relational model, no hard-and-fast rule says that a database that "understands" SQL has to be relational, or for that matter, that a Relational database has to understand SQL. The Relational model doesn't address the subject of languages, other than that the language used to access the DBMS has to preserve data integrity. There are numerous DBMSs that use SQL on the market, yet they are only semirelational or based on one of the other database models.

When you're evaluating a DBMS for use in your business, don't assume that it's a Relational database just because it understands SQL; make sure that the underlying database is actually based on the Relational model, if that's what you want. This is an important issue that will be addressed throughout the rest of this book, particularly in the chapters that cover specific C/S databases.

Other Languages

Into this group fall the languages that don't neatly fit into the previous two categories. The most common of these other languages are the *Object Oriented Programming* (OOP) languages such as Modula-2 or C++. OOP languages represent an entirely different approach to programming, where actions are defined as taking place on "objects," instead of as a series of procedures. The use of OOP languages for database applications is growing and I'll cover them more fully in Chapters 10 and 11.

Another type of language that's used with databases is a *macro* (or script) language. Macro languages aren't full programming languages; they're actually a list of the keystrokes that a user manually enters into an application to automate certain tasks. Highly specific to a particular application, macro languages are commonly found in the low-end DBMS packages or in the front-ends for database servers.

A language specifically designed for accessing relational databases, QUEL was developed by Ingres Corporation for their VAX-based INGRES Relational database. Unfortunately, QUEL didn't catch on with other Relational DBMS vendors and has been superseded by SQL as the de facto standard relational language.

Finally, there's *Query-By-Example* (QBE). QBE is not strictly a language; it's an interface that presents the user with one or more blank tables that correspond to the tables in the database. The user then picks and chooses the columns to be included in the query through keystrokes, and defines any search conditions for the query by filling the conditions into the appropriate columns. The DBMS then translates the QBE into the actions necessary to fulfill the user's request.

Figure 1.14 represents a possible QBE screen for the Acme Submarine Company's inventory database. The column names of the PARTS table appear in the first row of the QBE table; then the user is directed to choose the columns that are to appear in the query answer (the check-marks in row 2) and the search conditions (the =1001 in row 3). This QBE screen would then produce a smaller table that shows the part number and description of the part that matches P# 1001. Currently, the most popular example of a QBE interface is found in Borland's Paradox DBMS. Some vendors are also starting to include QBE screens in their front-end applications for accessing C/S databases.

Figure 1.14

A sample Query-By-Example screen

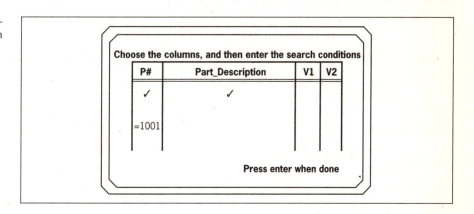

- *Capabilities*
- *Platforms*
- *Communications*

CHAPTER

2

Client/Server Database Technology

NOW THAT WE'VE COVERED THE BASICS OF A DBMS, IT'S TIME TO examine the specifics of Client/Server technology. This chapter will cover the reasons for selecting a C/S system, and the hardware and software you need to run one. We'll also cover the network technologies used to connect the various systems.

3

If you want to start a heated debate, ask your colleagues to define Client/ Server computing and to identify Client/Server products. Of course, any local area network could be considered a Client/Server system, since the workstations (clients) request services such as data, program files, or printing from the server. However, "Client/Server" is now generally accepted to mean any system that splits its data processing between two distinct components.

By this definition, C/S systems aren't limited to database applications: Any application that has a user interface portion ("front-end") that runs locally on the client and a processing portion that runs on the server ("back-end") is a form of C/S computing. Examples of other C/S applications include such products as Lotus's groupware product Notes, DCA's OpenMind, and Novell's MHS (Message Handling Service) EMail system. Products such as these have a relatively easy-to-use front-end that lets the user enter, read, and reply to electronic mail and on-line discussions. The back-end application that runs on the server handles the storage and routing of the EMail until it reaches its final destination.

Currently the primary focus is on database applications. The reason for this is simple: Many corporations and businesses are reducing their computing costs by "downsizing" their databases to smaller, more manageable platforms. The idea behind downsizing is simple—moving corporate databases away from large and expensive centralized systems to smaller, less expensive systems that don't have as extensive support and maintenance requirements. Client/Server databases that run on the smaller systems are the primary means of handling the large amounts of data that these larger systems typically store and manipulate. The split in processing power that is the foundation of C/S computing makes it possible for the smaller systems to handle this data. We'll be covering the relative costs of the various systems in the discussions that follow.

Note that there's no such thing as a stand-alone C/S system. Vendors may provide single-user versions of their C/S software for developers, but a true Client/Server system needs some type of network with one or more interconnected workstations and servers. The workstations also have to have some type of CPU (central processing unit); diskless PCs would qualify as workstations, but dumb terminals need not apply for the job.

There's some debate about which software vendor first used the term to describe their product, though the honors generally fall to Microsoft, who co-wrote their SQL Server with Sybase for the OS/2 PC operating system. After Microsoft started using the term, other DBMS vendors such as Oracle and Ingres said, "Oh yes, we do that too," and the term Client/Server is now used to describe a whole class of products and applications.

4

■ Capabilities

How Client/Server systems are implemented depends on the platforms the front- and back-ends run on, and the degree to which the processing is split between the two. As yet, there's no standard way of classifying the different levels or implementations of C/S systems, so for the purpose of making comparisons between the different software and hardware platforms described later in this book, I'm proposing a classification system (Table 2.1). The C/S systems are ranked in class order; the most complete implementation is Class 1, the least complete is Class 5. While many products don't fit one category exactly (they may have elements of more than one class), it's easier to compare specific products as well as implementation solutions using a common ranking system.

The systems described later in this book can be categorized as Class 2, 3, or 4. Class 1 systems pretty much don't exist yet or exist only in limited form through a combination of the services provided by Class 2 and Class 3 systems. Class 5 systems have become virtually nonexistent, since these vendors decided to provide wide front-end access to their DBMSs in order to remain competitive. Note that the Class 2 through 4 systems don't rule out using a proprietary server (proprietary means that the DBMS software will only run on hardware provided by the same vendor), as long as the user and/or applications developer has a choice of front-ends to access it.

Advantages of Client/Server Databases

The primary advantages of a Client/Server system arise from splitting the processing between the client system and the database server. Since the bulk of the database processing is done on the back-end, the speed of the DBMS isn't tied to the speed of the workstation. As a result, the workstation need only be able to run the front-end software, effectively extending the life of many older or smaller PCs which don't have the horsepower needed to run a complex DBMS.

This division of work also reduces the load on the network connecting the workstations. Instead of sending the entire database file back and forth on the wire, the network traffic is reduced to queries to and responses from the database server. Some database servers can even store and run procedures and queries on the server itself, further reducing the traffic. On a large network with many workstations, this reduction in network traffic can more than offset the added cost of switching to a C/S system.

Another benefit of separating the client from the server is workstation independence; users aren't limited to one type of system or platform. In a C/S system, the workstations can be IBM-compatible PCs, Macintoshes, UNIX workstations, or a combination of these, and can run multiple operating

Table 2.1

Ranking of Client/Server
Systems and Platforms

RANK	DESCRIPTION	COMMENTS
Class 1: Full Distributed Processing	• Data resides on multiple systems and/or platforms. • User access is transparent: Users connect to one server, which accesses the other systems. • Server performs all DBMS functions and processing. • Users cannot access the data from outside the DBMS running on the server. • Multiple front-ends provide query, data modification, and reporting services.	Very limited implementation to date.
Class 2: Full Client/Server	• Data resides on one or more servers. • User or application makes explicit connections to each server. • Server performs all DBMS processing. • Users can only access the data via the DBMS running on the server. • Multiple front-ends provide query, data modification, and reporting services.	Most common type of C/S system today.
Class 3: Gated Client/Server	• Gateway systems and applications create a bridge between the user's front-end application and the DBMS running on the non-C/S system. • Gateway systems translate queries, data modifications, etc. into procedures and calls the database system can process. • The gateway supports multiple front-ends.	Commonly used between PC-based systems and DBMSs running on a mainframe or minicomputer, or as a link between a Class 2 system and a mainframe or mini.
Class 4: Limited Client/Server	• Server provides some DBMS functions, usually just data storage and indexing functions. • Server doesn't always prevent users from accessing the data from outside the DBMS running on the server. • Most processing takes place on client system. • Multiple front-ends are supported, though not as many as in a Class 2 system.	Systems of this type add server functionality to standard PC-based databases, using common file formats such as dBASE's .DBF.
Class 5: Proprietary Client/Server	• Requires a proprietary hardware platform and operating system. • Data can only be accessed through front-end software provided by the vendor of the DBMS.	Common in the early '80s; recently evolved into more open systems.

systems, such MS/PC-DOS, MS Windows, IBM OS/2, or Apple's System 7. A corollary to this is application independence; the workstations aren't required to use the same DBMS application software. Users can continue to use familiar software to access the database, and developers can design front-ends for a specific workstation or for particular users.

Another major advantage of a Client/Server system is the preservation of data integrity. Today, most database servers run a DBMS based on the Relational model, and users are prevented from accessing the data from outside the DBMS (Class 4 and some Class 3 systems are the exception to this). In addition, the DBMS can provide services that protect the data, such as encrypted file storage (the data is encrypted to prevent it from being viewed outside the DBMS); real-time backups to tape, which occur while the database is being accessed; disk mirroring, in which the data is automatically written to a duplicate database on another partition of the same hard disk; and disk duplexing, in which the data is automatically written to a duplicate database on a different hard disk. The DBMS can also provide transaction processing, which tracks changes to the database and helps correct errors in the database in case the server crashes.

Transaction processing is a method by which the DBMS keeps a running log of all the modifications made to the database over a period of time. It's primarily used for databases that are constantly being modified, such as an order-processing system, to ensure that the data modifications are properly recorded in the database. The log is used to restore the database (as much as possible) to a previous error-free state in the event the system crashes while modifications are being made. These capabilities make Client/Server systems ideal for large multiuser databases, particularly those which allow multiple simultaneous modifications to the data. The DBMS is responsible for handling the locks necessary to prevent multiple changes to the same record or field, and can provide better multiuser access through judicious use of those locks, for example, locking only a record or a field for update, instead of the whole file. Conflicts and deadlocks between users modifying the same record are significantly reduced when they're handled by a central DBMS.

Disadvantages of Client/Server Databases

The major disadvantage of Client/Server systems is the increased cost of administrative and support personnel who maintain the database server. On a small network (generally under 20 users), the network administrator can usually maintain the database server and user access to it, and support the front-end applications. However, as the number of users rises or as the database itself grows, a database administrator may be needed just to run the DBMS and support the front-ends. Training can also add to the start-up costs, since the DBMS may run on an operating system unfamiliar to support personnel.

There's also an increase in hardware costs. While many C/S databases run under the common operating systems (NetWare, OS/2, or UNIX), and most vendors claim that the DBMS can run on the same hardware side-by-side with the File Server software, the database server should run on its own dedicated machine to ensure performance and data integrity. This usually means purchasing a high-powered system with a large amount of RAM and hard disk space (at least 10 to 12Mb RAM and a 300Mb hard disk), as well as additional support equipment such as an uninterruptable power supply (UPS) to protect the server from power outages.

The overall cost of the software is usually higher than traditional PC-based multiuser DBMSs (though equivalent to or lower than the cost of most minicomputer and mainframe-based central systems). The cost-per-server for a C/S database can range from under $1,000 for five users to tens-of-thousands of dollars for unlimited users. Add to that the separate cost of the front-end applications or development tools, as well as the personnel costs for training programmers in the new system, and the difference in price over a traditional PC-based DBMS can be substantial.

There's also the issue of complexity. With so many parts comprising the entire C/S system, Murphy's Law can (and usually does) kick in—the more pieces that compose the system, the more pieces that can fail. It's also harder to track down problems when the system crashes. And it can initially take longer to get all the components set up and working together. All this is compounded by the general lack of experience and expertise of potential support personnel and programmers, due to the relative newness of the technology. As C/S systems become more common, this last problem should abate.

The C/S advantage of application independence also has a downside. Having multiple front-ends to the database increases the amount of programming support needed, because more and varied program code must be developed and maintained. Making a change to the structure of the database also has a ripple effect throughout the different front-ends. It becomes a longer and more complex process to make the necessary changes to the different front-end applications, and it's also harder to keep all of them in sync without seriously disrupting the users' access to the database.

Currently, there's also limited support for interconnectivity between different Client/Server DBMS systems. Most back-end systems can only share data with similar systems, and nearly all the available front-ends support only a select set of the many back-ends. Database vendors have designed standardized database access application programming interfaces (APIs), such as ODBC from Microsoft and IDAPI from Borland, to reduce this problem. I'll be covering these API's in more detail in Chapter 10. Setting up a C/S system can lock you into using the front-ends from only a few vendors and can limit the number of tools available for developing custom front-end applications. You may also find it tedious or nearly impossible to import existing databases into the C/S DBMS, and it's sometimes difficult to link a new C/S system with existing DBMSs. These problems are decreasing as Client/Server databases become more widespread; the vendors of front- and back-ends are also providing more support for accessing other systems.

■ Platforms

The platform is the hardware and software combination that the Client/Server DBMS runs on. There are four categories of platforms: PCs, UNIX (usually RISC) workstations, minicomputers, and mainframes. While the most common platform for C/S computing is a PC, all four have their advantages and disadvantages. I will cover these when I address the specific products that run on those platforms.

While hardware systems vary widely in features and capabilities, certain common features are needed for the operating system software. The operating system (OS) is the primary software that acts as an interface between the hardware and the applications that run on that hardware. Applications are usually written to run under a particular OS. Some common examples of OS software are MS/PC-DOS, OS/2, the many UNIX variants, DEC's VMS, and the MVS/XA that runs on IBM mainframes.

The primary OS feature needed for a C/S DBMS is *multitasking*—running numerous applications concurrently. Multitasking allows the DBMS software to properly handle the different user queries and requests without their interfering with each other by splitting (time-slicing) the CPU's processing time between the different tasks or processes. Multitasking operating systems can be *preemptive* or *nonpreemptive*. In a preemptive system, the OS controls the amount of CPU time for each task. Conversely, the application controls the CPU time in a nonpreemptive system, and only relinquishes it to other tasks when it's finished running its own tasks. Preemptive systems have a natural advantage for C/S databases, as they prevent any one task from dominating the entire system.

The operating system can also be *multiuser* (can support simultaneous users doing different tasks), particularly when dumb terminals are used to access the DBMS. A multiuser OS offers no particular advantage or disadvantage for a C/S DBMS.

Multithreading is a recent addition to commonly available preemptive multitasking OS software, though the concept dates back to the early '70s. This capability lets an application multitask within itself; for example, a multithreaded single-user DBMS can start a new thread (process or task) of execution to do a complex report in the background while the user is querying the system in the foreground. Multithreading has significant implications for the designing of complex Client/Server DBMSs, as it gives the application greater control over when a new task is started or stopped. The application can be designed with built-in intelligence to identify which process or task has a higher priority and should be given more CPU time than other tasks. For example, the DBMS can give slightly higher priority to data modifications over data queries, reducing the performance penalty that the more complex task incurs without significantly affecting the query speed.

No one platform suits every need or is right for every situation. How can you choose the right one for you? First examine your current DBMS systems, project their growth, and estimate how many users will access them at the same time. After reading this book, choose a couple of alternative platforms and DBMS systems, and talk to the vendors. To help you in this process, I've included a Decision Tree at the back of this book, which will be explained in detail in Chapter 3.

Personal Computers

Only in recent years have IBM-compatible PCs become an acceptable platform for Client/Server databases. The advent of high-powered 32-bit 80386, 80486, and Pentium systems, hard disks in the gigabyte (G, or one billion bytes) range, and stable multitasking operating systems make these PCs able competitors to the RISC workstations and minicomputers that have been the traditional platforms for resource-intensive DBMSs.

Hardware

While a PC based on a 80386 CPU can perform adequately as a database server, for sheer power and future growth potential, the best system to start with is one based on a 66Mhz 80486. Many of the newer PCs come with the CPU on a replaceable card, which makes it easier to upgrade the power of the system to a faster 486 or even a Pentium.

Your next decision will be how much RAM (random access memory) to acquire for the system. The bare minimum is 8Mb, and most of the PC-based DBMS vendors recommend at least 12Mb for adequate performance. Depending on the number of simultaneous users and the DBMS, I'd recommend 12 to 16Mb of RAM as the best starting point. Remember too, that many of the inexpensive 486 systems limit you to 16Mb of 32-bit memory. While this is fine for high-end workstation use, you definitely want the capability for at least 32Mb of RAM for a database server. Even if you don't need that much memory immediately, it pays in the long run to have the room to expand.

Also be aware that some systems limit the amount of RAM that can be put on the motherboard and require additional RAM to be put on a proprietary 32-bit add-in card. Avoid them. Instead, buy a system that lets you expand to the full 32Mb of RAM right on the motherboard, so you're not locked into one vendor when it's time to upgrade your servers.

Probably the most critical component for database performance is the hard disk subsystem, since the bulk of the DBMS's activities involve reading data from or writing data to it. Benchmark tests have shown that the best choice for speed and expandability is a hard disk based on the small computer system interface (SCSI) standard. A single SCSI board can support up to seven attached drives, each as large as 1.2G or more, giving you tremendous room to expand. The SCSI standard has its flaws, but most hard disk vendors make sure their drives are compatible with a wide variety of SCSI cards, again preventing your being locked into one vendor.

An interesting alternative to SCSI boards is the RAID (Random Access Independent Disk) technology. RAID lets you link a number of smaller drives together into what appears to the system to be one large hard disk. It also provides for increased data security, as the drives can be set up to automatically mirror data between themselves and to switch to the backup disk when the primary fails, all without administrator intervention.

Finally, the last decision you should make is what type of internal bus (data connection system for add-on cards) the server should have. The Industry Standard Architecture (ISA) bus is based on the original 16-bit bus that IBM designed for its PC-AT systems. As 32-bit processors became more common, the PC vendors saw the need for a 32-bit data bus—unfortunately, they couldn't agree on a standard. IBM proposed the Micro Channel architecture (MCA) standard and implemented it in their line of PS/2 computers. However, the otherwise technically excellent MCA bus had two problems to overcome: It wasn't backwards-compatible with ISA cards, and IBM originally demanded a large licensing fee from other PC vendors. Although they've since lowered the fees, the MCA bus hasn't spread much beyond IBM systems.

Compaq and a number of other PC vendors banded together and proposed an alternative 32-bit bus standard—Extended Industry Standard Architecture (EISA). The design of the EISA bus lets users continue to use ISA add-on cards, while supporting 32-bit EISA cards when needed. The number of PC vendors providing EISA systems has grown over the years, giving users a wide choice of systems.

Your decision of which bus standard to use should be based on factors besides speed, such as the availability of fast-disk subsystems and vendor support. Regardless of which standard you choose, go with a 32-bit bus for your database server. A full 32-bit bus will speed up both disk processing and network access when 32-bit interface cards are used, eliminating the most serious bottlenecks a server faces.

Multiprocessor (MPU) systems, an emerging technology in the PC world, may have a significant impact on the performance and capabilities of Client/Server databases in the future. However, at this time few MPU systems are available, and little (though growing) support for them exists among the various C/S products. It's a technology to watch for future developments.

Operating System Software

The first PC-based C/S databases were announced shortly after IBM and Microsoft announced their new protected-mode operating system (OS), called OS/2, in early 1987. OS/2 was the first full 16-bit preemptive multitasking, multithreaded OS designed expressly for PCs based on the 80286 (and higher) CPU. Though limited to accessing 16Mb of real RAM, OS/2 version 1.x provides superior capabilities over DOS for the resource-intensive database server software; its multitasking lets multiple services run on the same system, including both the LAN software and the DBMS. Multithreading means applications multitask within themselves, making it easy for software to support numerous users simultaneously running multiple tasks. Finally, it has native support for up to 512Mb of virtual memory (VM), which means that if an application runs out of RAM, the OS can swap portions of unused or idle data to the disk to free up working space. Vendors of UNIX-based DBMSs rushed to port their software to the new platform.

Novell countered the release of OS/2 with a 32-bit version of their network operating system (NOS), NetWare 3.0 (since upgraded to NetWare 3.2 and 4.1). NetWare 3.2 and higher provides access to up to 4G of RAM, though current hardware limitations usually restrict this to considerably less. It also has the ability to run applications on the File Server as NetWare Loadable Modules (NLMs) and provides nonpreemptive multitasking capabilities; however, it can only access the actual RAM present in the system. Early implementations of NetWare 3.x had problems running NLMs, but Novell quickly fixed this. With the release of 3.11 in 1991, a number of DBMS vendors created NLM versions of their OS/2 or UNIX software.

In April of 1992, IBM released their 32-bit version of OS/2, which ups the ante in the database server OS race. OS/2 2.0 increased the amount of real RAM support to 32Mb and continued support for virtual memory, multitasking, and multithreading. OS/2 3.0 is the latest version, and only a few DBMS vendors have announced support for it yet, but this will probably change quite soon.

Finally, some versions of UNIX run on 80386, 80486, and Pentium systems, and can be used as the OS for PC-based Client/Server databases. However, running UNIX on PCs isn't that common, and it's generally better to go with a hardware platform specifically designed for it if you must run C/S software that only comes in UNIX versions.

Some Client/Server DBMS vendors provide MS/PC-DOS or Windows 3.1 versions of their software, but other than for application development purposes, I don't recommend using them. There's a lot of system overhead involved in providing all the services of a C/S DBMS, and DOS and Windows aren't up to the task.

In 1993, Microsoft released Windows NT, a 32-bit, preemptive, multitasking, and multithreaded operating system. Version 3.5, with improved performance, was released in late 1994. Windows NT runs on multiple hardware systems, including both PCs based on the 80386 and higher CPUs, and a number of RISC CPUs. It has the potential to be the unifying OS between these disparate systems, and many DBMS vendors have ported their software to it. I'll be discussing the future of operating system advancements, and how they affect C/S computing, more fully in Chapter 11.

Which operating system is right for you? Currently, the number of C/S DBMS systems available for OS/2, Windows NT, or NetWare is about equal, with some systems able to run under all three. However, some only run under one OS. Unless the DBMS you choose is one of these single-OS versions, any of the three software platforms is acceptable for use on a dedicated database server, as platforms based on OS/2 or Windows NT can still be used on a NetWare LAN.

RISC and Other UNIX Workstations

Workstations based on Reduced Instruction Set Computing (RISC) processors are primarily used for scientific or engineering applications, since the RISC CPUs are generally faster and more powerful than the top-of-the-line Intel Pentium. A RISC CPU gets its enhanced performance by reducing the amount of microcode in the chip itself; less code means the CPU can perform its internal operations faster. There are numerous RISC chips available today, such as the Sun SPARC, DEC's Alpha, the MIPS line of third-party CPUs, and the Motorola 88000 series. Most RISC chips are proprietary to a single vendor's hardware, but all share similar performance capabilities. Since the usual operating system for a RISC workstation is UNIX, this platform has recently come into use as a database server.

The line between a high-powered RISC or other UNIX workstation and a full minicomputer can become very fuzzy. To make things simple, workstations include any desktop single-user UNIX-based multitasking system that can be used as a server through a network connection. In contrast, minicomputers are multiuser systems that support both network connections and directly connected terminals.

Hardware

Most workstations resemble and operate like PCs—they sit on the desktop or alongside the desk in a tower-type case, and have a directly attached keyboard, mouse, and screen (usually high-resolution color). Common entry-level workstations come with 8Mb of RAM and a hard disk of 100Mb to 300Mb. Workstations are commonly used for scientific or engineering applications.

This configuration may be fine for a user's system, but, similar to PCs, a database server should have more RAM. A good working minimum is 16Mb of RAM (depending on the DBMS software), including support for at least 32Mb for later expansion. Of course a larger hard disk is needed as well, as the UNIX operating system can easily take up close to 100Mb of disk space all by itself.

Most of the smaller hard-disk subsystems ("smaller" meaning below 300Mb in the UNIX world) are SCSI-based. For larger disk subsystems, the vendors use a proprietary disk interface for higher performance, which can add considerable cost to the workstation.

Having to rely solely on a single system vendor for most of your expansion equipment (RAM or disk drives) is the price you pay for getting the extra power of a RISC workstation. RISC systems aren't as widespread as PCs, so the large market for third-party add-ons doesn't yet exist. While entry-level workstations only cost a little more than a high-powered PC, expanding the system to server capabilities can increase the cost two to four times over an equivalent PC in the long run.

A number of well-known RISC vendors and systems are available today. The ones most commonly used for database servers are the Sun SPARCstation series, the IBM RS/6000 series, the workstations offered by Apollo (a subsidiary of Hewlett-Packard), and Digital Equipment Corporation's DEC-station.

The increasing interest in Client/Server computing has led some workstation vendors to create high-powered RISC systems designed explicitly as database servers. These approach the traditional minicomputers in capabilities and power. The best examples of this type of RISC system are Sun's 470 and IBM's RS/6000 Server.

Operating System Software

All the RISC workstations used for Client/Server DBMSs use a variant of UNIX as their operating system. While at first glance this may seem ideal, the truth of the situation is that each vendor's UNIX system software differs slightly from other vendors' software, so they're not 100 percent compatible. This prevents software vendors from selling one version of their application software that can run on any UNIX system, and it is the primary reason that UNIX workstations haven't become more common on the desktop. The software vendors must tailor their application's source code to each UNIX variant that they want to support.

The bottom line is that even though most of the top Client/Server DBMSs started out on UNIX, a particular C/S DBMS may not be available in a version that runs on every workstation. If you decide to use a workstation as a database server, first choose the DBMS you want to run, and then find out which UNIX versions it runs under. You can then explore the hardware options from that vendor, as well as the DBMS's performance on that particular system.

UNIX is a multitasking operating system, originally developed on a DEC minicomputer at AT&T's Bell Laboratories in the early 1970s. It is well suited for multiuser applications. It includes support for virtual memory, but generally doesn't support multithreading—the Mach variant of UNIX used by NeXT is the only multithreaded version to date, though other vendors have promised it in upcoming versions. Most UNIX systems are based on one of two variations: UNIX System V (the current version of the AT&T original) and Berkeley UNIX, a variant of AT&T's UNIX developed at UC's Berkeley campus.

Criticized as a "techie" operating system, UNIX can be difficult for many computer users to understand. This criticism is not without merit and should be factored into your decision process. In addition to the extra cost of the RISC workstation platform, it can also be difficult to find support personnel who are familiar with the operating system. Some of these objections have been met in recent years through the increased use of a graphical user interface (GUI) on UNIX systems. Two of the most common UNIX GUIs are Sun's Open Look (co-developed with AT&T), and the Open Systems Foundation's Motif (OSF is a consortium of UNIX vendors, most notably DEC, IBM, and HP/Apollo). These GUIs add a degree of user-friendliness to UNIX and make it somewhat easier to use and support. Sun includes Open Look in its Solaris operating system, and IBM and DEC include Motif in their UNIX variants (AIX and ULTRIX, respectively).

As I mentioned in the previous section, versions of Microsoft's Windows NT are available for RISC platforms. At the time of this writing, you can get NT for systems running the DEC Alpha and MIPS CPUs. Using NT on a RISC system gives you the advantage of the higher performance while using a familiar interface. However, the RISC versions of NT share the same disadvantage as the various versions of UNIX—the databases and applications have to be specially designed and compiled to run on the particular CPU.

Minicomputers

Minicomputers and mainframes are the traditional workhorses when it comes to database applications, and minicomputers are generally optimized for multiuser applications. In recent years, various methods of connecting a mini to a PC-based LAN have been developed, and it's now possible to use a minicomputer as both a File Server and a database server. Mini-based DBMSs that provide either Class 2 or Class 3 C/S services will be covered in Chapter 6.

Many businesses already have one or more minicomputers. A Client/ Server DBMS can enhance the mini's capabilities by extending data access to the many PCs and LANs in the company. A C/S system also reduces the workload on the minicomputer by moving part of the processing to the front-end system, which lets the mini support more users without expanding or enhancing the hardware. The initial costs involved in purchasing and setting up a C/S DBMS can often be more than offset by the savings in not having to purchase additional hardware.

Hardware

Minicomputers are usually based on proprietary CPUs that are generally more powerful than those in the previous systems and on proprietary expansion equipment. They range in size from small tower-type systems to boxes that resemble overgrown refrigerators. Minis usually have a number of serial ports for connecting dumb terminals and commonly include network cards. They support much more RAM (typically 128 to 256Mb) than is common on PCs or workstations, which makes them better suited for applications that allow hundreds of users simultaneous access.

The high-end minicomputers also support multiple CPUs in the same box, which adds both processing power and system redundancy in case of failure.

Minis also support high-speed hard disk systems that can range into the hundreds and thousands of gigabytes, which makes them well-suited for company-sized databases. The disk systems usually support fault tolerance—a method of controlling and correcting errors caused by hardware problems—as an option through disk mirroring and/or duplexing, which provide more data redundancy and integrity.

Most minicomputers can be *clustered*, which means that machines are linked together through high-speed connections, and all the machines in the cluster share the same disks. Clustering lets users expand the capabilities of the computer (that is, number of users supported) without having to purchase more disk drives or move data between different machines.

Minicomputers suffer from the same problem as RISC workstations, namely, the general lack of third-party expansion products. In most cases, purchasing a minicomputer locks you into buying all future equipment from the same vendor, at proportionally higher costs over third-party hardware.

The more common minicomputers are made by Digital Equipment Corporation (DEC), IBM, and Hewlett-Packard (HP). DEC's line ranges from the tower-sized MicroVAX that supports less than 100 users to the VAX 6000 that approaches mainframes in size and capabilities. IBM's primary minicomputer is the AS/400 line, which comes in a number of sizes and capabilities; all of them include hardware support for the database applications that the AS/400 is primarily designed for. HP's HP3000 series comes in both proprietary CPU and RISC CPU models.

An interesting variation on the minicomputer theme is the Teradata systems. Especially designed to be Relational database servers, these minicomputers contain much of the code that supports the DBMS in ROM for speed. They support from three to 1024 CPUs (80386 or higher), up to 8G of main memory, and come with fault tolerant disk systems as standard equipment.

Operating System Software

Just about all minicomputers use a proprietary operating system with UNIX as an optional OS. DEC systems are based on VAX/VMS, and IBM's systems on the AS/400 Operating System. HP has both the older MPE operating system, and the new MPE/XL OS, which is designed for RISC-based systems.

DEC's ULTRIX also runs on the entire VAX line, and IBM's AIX runs on all the AS/400s. HP's version of UNIX is HP-UX, a variation on AT&T's UNIX. The Teradata machines run either UNIX or MS-DOS. While C/S DBMSs are available for all these operating systems, running UNIX on a minicomputer has the advantage of giving you a wider choice in applications software and DBMSs, and generally a larger pool of support personnel to choose from. I recommend using UNIX if you're going to run your DBMS on a mini, unless you also need to run applications that are specific to the vendor's proprietary operating system.

Versions of NetWare are also available for VMS and UNIX systems, and Microsoft's LAN Manager/X is available for UNIX systems. Both let you use a minicomputer as a File Server on a PC-based LAN through a familiar network operating system (NOS) interface. However, the degree of integration between the LAN software and the native minicomputer system varies, and the LAN NOS may run only as an application on the minicomputer host without giving you access to other applications running on the same machine. Before you decide to use a mini as a LAN server, make sure that the particular minicomputer's operating system supports access to the applications you need through the NOS.

Some minicomputer operating systems still don't support Class 2 Client/ Server applications and require some type of gateway system to provide PC access to the DBMS running on the mini. The gateway can either be an additional hardware/software combination or can be a software application that runs on the mini and interfaces between the PC-based front-ends and the DBMS on the host. You should check to see which type of access your DBMS software supports, as a gateway system can add considerable hardware, software, and support costs, as well as additional complexity in the overall network. As C/S applications become more common, most mini-based DBMS vendors are adding direct Client/Server support to their software, so this is less of a complication than it once was.

Mainframes

The mainframe is the most powerful general-purpose computer available; it supports multiple high-speed processors, enormous amounts of hard disk space, and hundreds to thousands of simultaneous users. Mainframes offer the most security of any available systems, both in terms of data security and hardware redundancy.

Mainframes are also the most expensive computers available, in terms of hardware, software, support environments, and personnel. Unlike the smaller computer systems, a mainframe requires a controlled environment, including a constant temperature, raised floors, and even special cooling equipment (the larger mainframes are still water-cooled). Because of this, mainframes are usually found in company-owned data centers, which can be located in either a section of a company's office building or a completely separate building.

Today's mainframes can support hundreds and even thousands of users accessing multiple applications through terminals or network connections. While still used as the primary system for central database applications in many large companies—IBM calls mainframes the "data warehouses" for large businesses—the rapid spread of PCs and workstations has led to a slow evolution in the role of the mainframe as host for Client/Server DBMSs.

It was in the mainframe world that the term *mission critical* first came to be used, referring to database applications that are so critical to a business's operations that the business could collapse if the data wasn't available. For this reason, the mainframe is still looked upon as the most important system for central data storage for large corporations—even with moves toward downsizing corporate databases to minicomputers and PC-based LANs, mainframes will be around for years to come, fulfilling their role as "data warehouses" for businesses.

Hardware

Unlike most other computers, a mainframe is not contained in a single box—it usually consists of a number of different *subsystems* that handle different tasks, all linked together through high-speed copper wire and/or fiber-optic cables. Typical subsystems include the CPUs, RAM modules, communications systems, and disk and tape drives.

The computer is accessed through terminals or PCs with terminal emulators, which are connected to *terminal controllers* (specialized subsystems that handle the terminal's communications network connections). They are then connected to the mainframe. Dial-in access is accomplished through a *front-end processor* (FEP)—a hardware subsystem not to be confused with the front-end applications used to access a C/S database. This processor handles the communications between the remote terminals and the central host. Network connections are also accomplished through add-in controllers that go into the front-end processor.

The mainframe's processing power and speed comes from proprietary multiple CPUs, high-speed disk drives, and high-speed communications paths between all the different elements that make up the system. Fault tolerant disk subsystems and redundant processing systems and data paths are also typical features. Mainframes generally have over 256Mb of RAM; the top-end machines can support gigabytes of RAM. The disk drive subsystems are measured in the hundreds of gigabytes, and it's not uncommon for a mainframe to have disks that hold more than a *terabyte* (1 trillion bytes) of data.

The most common mainframes are those put out by IBM. They range in size from the 4381s, which are not much larger than some of the bigger minicomputers and support only a few hundred users, to the room-filling 390 series that can support thousands of users. IBM-compatible mainframes are also available, such as those from Ahmdal and Fujitsu.

The machines in DEC's top-of-the-line VAX 9000 series also qualify as mainframes, based on size and the number of users supported. They also have most of the same hardware support requirements as other mainframe systems.

IBM and DEC mainframes have existed long enough for the development of a stable third-party hardware industry that provides "plug-compatible" disk and tape drives, front-end processors, terminal controllers, and terminals that can be added to the system via common adapters. While most of the third-party hardware is cheaper than equivalent parts from IBM and DEC, the overall cost of mainframe equipment is usually measured in the hundreds of thousands to millions of dollars.

The top-end mainframes in speed and processing power (and cost) are the super computers, such as those by Cray and Control Data Corporation. These computers are usually used for specialized applications such as weather forecasting, where billions of calculations per second are necessary. Super computers, rarely used for database systems, are not a factor in the Client/ Server world at this time (or in the foreseeable future).

Operating System Software

Mainframe operating systems are very modularized, with different subsystems handling CPU assignments, communications with the disk and tape storage systems, and user interactions with the computer.

IBM mainframes were the host to the original developments in multitasking and multiuser operating system software, and today they run the most sophisticated operating systems available. IBM's mainframes run one of two proprietary multitasking, multiuser operating systems: VM (usually on the low to midrange systems) and various versions of MVS (such as MVS/ XA and MVS/ESA) on the midrange and high-end systems. IBM also provides a version of AIX that lets users run UNIX applications on the mainframe. The underlying IBM operating system software is only a part of the whole—all it provides are the system services. Other system-level software from IBM or third-party vendors provides the interface between the users and the applications on the mainframe. Specialized security software governs user access and data security.

DEC's mainframes primarily run on the same VAX/VMS operating system as their minicomputers and can be clustered with the minicomputers as a company's data processing needs grow. DEC's UNIX-variant ULTRIX is also an option on the 9000 series.

The interrelationships between the various system-level software applications and user applications add to the mainframe system an enormous cost in support personnel. It's not uncommon for a corporation with a mainframe to have an entire Information Systems (IS) or Management Information Services (MIS) department consisting of system programmers, communications network specialists, and system operators to keep the whole system up and running. Program analysts and applications programmers are also necessary to create the applications for the ultimate end-users of the mainframe, since most mainframe applications are custom-written.

It's these large personnel and maintenance costs that have led to the concept of and trend toward downsizing mainframe systems to minicomputers and PCs, as the smaller systems have increased in power and features. Client/ Server systems are approaching the power and capabilities of many mainframe applications while using more "off-the-shelf" software that doesn't require such large support staffs.

However, the smaller systems cannot yet completely replace mainframes as the systems of choice for large corporate-wide databases. Because of this, a number of Class 3 C/S hardware and/or software systems have become available; they provide Client/Server-type access to databases residing on an IBM mainframe. DEC mainframes have more native support for C/S applications, as DBMSs that run under the VAX/VMS OS run on the entire line of VAXes.

The trend today is toward integrating existing mainframes into new corporate-wide Client/Server systems rather than toward installing new mainframes, and it's in this light that I'll be discussing mainframe DBMSs later in this book.

■ Communications

A Client/Server Database System depends on splitting the processing between an intelligent front-end system (usually an IBM PC compatible, a Macintosh, or a RISC workstation) and the database server. Networks allow communication between these two parts of the overall system. While the topic of computer networks is beyond the scope of this book, this section covers some basic concepts necessary for understanding Client/Server communication. (Appendix C provides references for a more thorough understanding of networks.)

Network Hardware and Software

The client systems communicate with the server through a network that consists of a combination of hardware and software. The hardware which connects the PC to the network's wiring consists of a network interface card (NIC) that's added to the PC, workstation, and server (in some cases, the NIC is built right into the system).

A network of PCs, workstations, and servers is referred to as a local area network (LAN) if all the systems are in the same building. When a LAN extends across buildings (either in the same location or across the country), the entire network is referred to as a wide area network (WAN).

Three LAN topologies (cabling schemes) are in common use today: Ethernet, ARCnet, and Token Ring. Unless some type of bridging system is used, all the PCs and servers on the network have to have NICs that support the same topology. An Ethernet system commonly runs at 10 megabits/second (Mbps) and uses either coaxial cable in a bus (daisy-chain) configuration (see Figure 2.1) or twisted-pair (TP) cable in a hub-and-star configuration from one or more central concentrators (see Figure 2.2).

Token Ring, a token-passing network that uses twisted-pair wiring in a ring configuration, runs at 4 or 16Mbps (see Figure 2.3). Note that most Token Ring networks resemble star-and-hub Ethernet in real life, as the ring actually exists in the central wiring closet between the various multiple access units (MAUs).

ARCnet, a 2Mbps token-bus network, uses a series of active and passive hubs connected with coaxial cable (shown in Figure 2.4). Passive hubs connect to the PCs, and active hubs connect the passive hubs to other passive hubs and PCs. A 20Mbps version of ARCnet has been released, but is not in wide-spread use.

Figure 2.1

Ethernet bus network

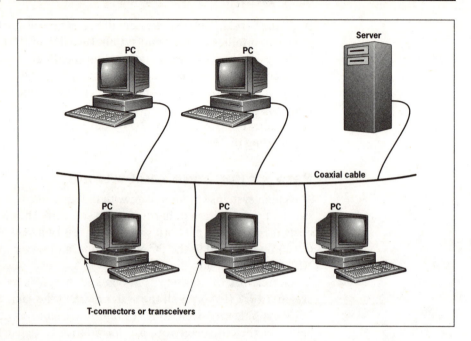

Figure 2.2

Twisted-pair Ethernet network

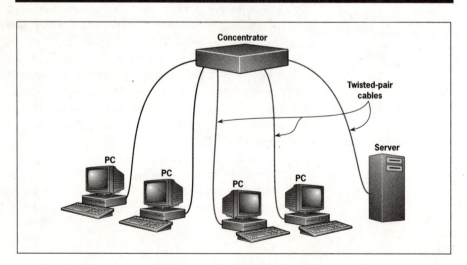

Figure 2.3

Token Ring network

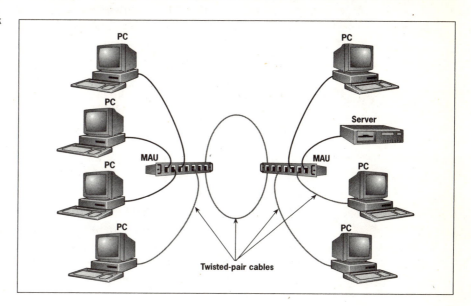

Figure 2.4

ARCnet network

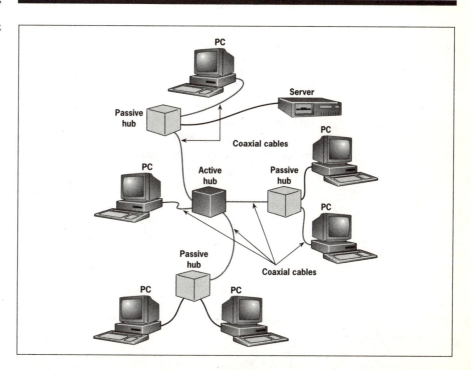

Due to the speed limitations of copper-based cable (20Mbps or less), high-speed fiber-optic (light-based) cabling schemes have increasingly come into use. Fiber-optic cabling is generally more expensive to install and support than copper cable, but is resistant to outside interference, so it's most commonly used for connecting LANs on different floors to a building-wide backbone or as a high-speed link between different LANs across a site. Widely scattered WANs can be linked through standard telephone lines via modems, though current technology limits these links to 38,400bps. Higher-speed (and higher-cost) WANs can be linked with special modem-like devices called Data Service Units (DSUs) through data-grade T-1 (1.54Mbps) phone lines provided by all the major telephone companies. Modems are also used for individual remote PCs to dial in and connect to the LAN to share data and services.

Once the PCs are connected to the network cabling, software drivers are installed to tell the PC how to communicate on the cable through the NIC. Other software drivers allow the PC's applications to access data and files on the LAN's File Server, send print jobs to shared printers on the server, or communicate with the database server.

Network Protocols

A protocol is a standard method of communicating between two computer systems across a network. Many proprietary network protocols exist today, but only a few are relevant to designing a Client/Server Database System.

NetWare LANs use the Novell IPX/SPX protocol to provide communications between workstations and server(s). Microsoft's Windows NT Advanced Server and IBM's LAN Server use variations of the NetBIOS protocol, and DEC-based LANs use the DECNet protocol. IBM mainframes primarily use System Network Architecture (SNA) to communicate with terminals and LAN Gateways, and IBM's LANs also support the Data Link Control (DLC) protocol for direct communications between the LAN PCs and the mainframe front-end processors.

The most common cross-platform protocol is the Transmission Control Protocol/Internet Protocol (TCP/IP). Originally developed as the UNIX networking protocol, TCP/IP is now available for almost every platform and operating system, and it is widely used for linking together PCs, workstations, minicomputers, and sometimes mainframes.

Though sufficient for basic LAN communications, these protocols generally don't provide sufficient capabilities for Client/Server applications, so a second protocol layer is required. One such C/S protocol, Named Pipes, is primarily used by database servers that run on OS/2 and Windows NT. Other

Client/Server DBMS vendors provide their own (usually proprietary) protocols for communications between the front-end applications and the database server. These protocols will be discussed in more detail in the descriptions of the particular database server software packages in Chapters 4 through 8.

- *Asking the Right Questions*
- *What Are the Next Steps?*

3

The Decision Tree

Choosing the right type of client/server system can be an intimidating process; there are a number of different ways to go, and a wrong choice early in the process can waste a lot of time and money over the long run.

No one Client/Server system is right for every situation. Your solution may be to replace existing systems with a single-vendor C/S DBMS, or you may need to keep the existing databases and integrate them with a new C/S system. Or, you may find you require multiple C/S databases on multiple platforms to fulfill different functions.

A fold-out Decision Tree is bound in the back cover of this book to guide you through the process of choosing the right Client/Server platform for your needs. This chapter explains how to use the Decision Tree, so you'll want to keep the tree handy while you're reading through it.

■ Asking the Right Questions

Before you take the first steps toward a Client/Server solution, you need a knowledgeable database expert to help you decide which system is right. This expert should also help design and install the system, and support it once it's up and running. If you don't have this expertise in-house, your best course of action is to hire a qualified consultant. Be careful, though, and check the consultant's credentials before hiring him—it's unfortunate but true that anyone with the slightest amount of computer knowledge can call themselves a consultant, and there's (as yet) no certification standard to rely on to prove any level of expertise. It's also a good idea to contact the consultant's previous clients and ask them if they were satisfied with his performance. A Client/Server Database System can be a long-term and expensive investment; you want to be quite certain that you've investigated your options fully before committing yourself and your company.

While the Decision Tree won't replace the services of an expert, it will help you to ask the right questions along the way. It will also make you aware of any issues you may have overlooked in your early investigations of Client/Server DBMSs.

Do You Need a Client/Server Database System?

First you should decide if you actually need a Client/Server system. Starting in the upper-left corner of the Decision Tree, you'll see that the first question addresses whether multiple users must have access to the database. If not, any of the stand-alone PC DBMSs would solve your problem without a Client/ Server system.

If you do need multiuser access, the next question is how many simultaneous users must you accommodate? If the answer is less than 20, follow the tree to the right, where the next question asks if you have an existing LAN. If you do have a LAN, a multiuser PC-based DBMS would more than suffice. If you don't have a LAN, you might want to consider one of the smaller multiuser operating systems (such as one based on a multiuser DOS, multi-user OS/2, or UNIX) running on a high-powered PC or RISC workstation/minicomputer. Your existing PCs can act as terminals to the multiuser host, and future expansion can be via PCs or dumb terminals, depending on the needs of your end-users.

If you expect to have more than 20 simultaneous users, you must determine what type of access the users are going to have to the database. If the bulk of the access is for data lookups, and only a few users will be modifying data (insertions, deletions, and updates), a traditional multiuser DBMS should provide acceptable performance for up to 32 to 40 users. However, if most or all of the DBMS users have data modification rights (for example, in a transaction-processing system such as an inventory and order-taking database), you'll need the multiuser power and data integrity of a Client/Server database. Twenty simultaneous users is an admittedly arbitrary figure, though testing in the PC Magazine Labs has shown that the performance of traditional PC-based DBMSs can vary widely above that number.

How Can You Design Your Own C/S System?

Congratulations! If you've gotten to this point, you're on the road to designing and installing a Client/Server Database System. From here on, your decisions will primarily address whether or how to integrate existing DBMSs into the new C/S system.

Following the tree, you'll see that if you have an existing PC-based single or multiuser database, you should first determine how to upgrade it. If your database relies heavily on existing dBASE-type code (sometimes referred to as "xBASE") and you don't want to completely rewrite it, you can reap some of the benefits of a Client/Server system by moving your data to the File Server and using a Class 4 DBMS to provide data access to the users. This method is the easiest way to move an existing system to the C/S architecture, though it does not provide as much data integrity control as a full Client/Server system.

If you're willing to rewrite existing applications or don't have them to begin with, the next question is whether you already have RISC workstations in your organization. If you do, you might want to consider a full C/S DBMS that runs under UNIX on the workstation. This provides a high-power solution, although it does add some complexity to communications and operating systems. If you don't already have RISC systems or decide that you don't want the added complexity of having to support a new type of hardware platform on the server side, your choice is clear: You want one of the many PC-based Client/Server DBMSs that are available. A PC-based system can be easily integrated into existing LANs and doesn't add the complexity of a different hardware platform (though you may have to learn and use a new operating system for the database server).

Returning to the "Existing multiuser PC-based DBMS?" question in the tree reveals another path to take. If you already have a DBMS on a mini-computer or mainframe, you can either replace the existing system or integrate it into your Client/Server system. If you don't have an existing large system, you should follow the tree along the RISC path described in the previous paragraphs.

Should You "Downsize" from Your Existing Platform?

When you already have minicomputers and/or mainframes, your biggest decision is whether to downsize those systems to a PC-based Client/Server DBMS or to integrate them into the total C/S architecture. If you decide that downsizing is right for you, your choice is easy: Design and install a PC-based Client/Server DBMS and move your existing data to it.

However, you may not want to downsize your systems right away. The amount of data may be more than a PC-based system can handle, or you may have a large investment in custom-written applications which would take a long time to rewrite. In such cases, you must consider the different methods of providing Client/Server functionality on the existing systems.

Many large system DBMS vendors provide a Client/Server option for their software (usually gateway-type software that runs on top of the DBMS). If your vendor is one of these, one final question needs to be answered: Does the vendor's C/S software use the same protocols that the proposed front-end platforms support? If so, you can just install the vendor's gateway software, and you're ready to go. If not, you'll need the extra complexity of a hardware and software gateway that translates both the C/S and network protocols into something the systems on the other side of the gateway understand.

If the DBMS vendor doesn't provide a Client/Server option, your only choice is one of the third-party C/S gateways. These gateways can be either software only or hardware/software combinations that do all the translations necessary for the front-end systems to access the data on the host. While these gateways give you the ability to link multiple systems together, they also add a high level of complexity to both the DBMS software and the network itself; they're also generally more costly to implement and support.

■ What Are the Next Steps?

Now that you've looked over the Decision Tree and have an idea of which direction to go to move to a Client/Server DBMS, it's time to examine the choices available. The next five chapters will cover the various C/S DBMSs currently available for the different platforms described earlier in Chapter 2. Each chapter will have comparison charts of the features of each DBMS, and Appendix A will summarize all the charts for all the products. You'll find suggestions for further reading on the topics covered so far in Appendix C.

Chapters 8 and 9 cover a broad representative sampling of the many different types of front-end software available and what DBMSs they support. Appendix B gives a listing of contact points for all the vendors discussed in this book. Finally, Chapter 11 considers the current and future trends in the DBMS world that may influence your long-term plans.

- *Evaluating Client/Server Databases for PC Platforms*
- *Microsoft SQL Server 4.21*
- *SYBASE SQL Server for NetWare 10.0*
- *Gupta SQLBase 5.2 and 6.0*
- *IBM DB2/2*
- *ORACLE7 Server*
- *Watcom SQL 4.0*

- *XDB-Enterprise Server*
- *Ingres Server for OS/2*
- *Class 3 C/S Databases for .DBF Files*

4

Client/Server Databases
for PC Platforms

I N THE SPRING OF 1992, A REPORT ON THE CURRENT STATE OF CLIENT/ server computing was released by the Business Research Group (BRG), an industry research firm and was reported on in the weekly computer newspapers. BRG's survey of existing users of C/S DBMSs found that an overwhelming 58 percent of the sites depended on 386- and 486-based PCs for their database servers. Mainframes came in a distant second, and minicomputers and RISC systems brought up the rear. Since that time, studies have shown that this trend is continuing. More recent reports have estimated the percentage of PC-based database servers running as high as 70 percent.

The choice of PCs as the prevalent platform-of-choice for Client/Server systems isn't as surprising as it may seem at first glance—C/S computing is the natural evolution of PC-based LANs beyond simply sharing files and printers. And the high-end PCs have become powerful enough to function as cost-effective database server alternatives to minicomputers and mainframes. As LANs become more and more widespread in businesses (and as PCs become more powerful), this trend will probably continue, and PCs will remain the dominant base for C/S systems.

■ Evaluating Client/Server Databases for PC Platforms

The Client/Server database field is rapidly evolving, with both enhancements to existing products and new products becoming available almost monthly. In fact, there are two entirely new products here, as well as new versions of most of the other products, that came out after the first edition of this book. The product information in this chapter, as well as the next four chapters, is at most a snapshot of what's available on the market in the late winter of 1995.

Before discussing the individual products, each chapter will cover the overall advantages and disadvantages of the particular platform. I'll also be pointing out any considerations or problems you should be aware of when considering this platform for your C/S system. Finally, I'll pass along advice and tips about C/S databases and particular platforms that I've learned through my own experience or in conversations with those who have successfully (or unsuccessfully) implemented their own C/S systems.

Each section describing the individual products is followed by a table listing the key features of the product. Pricing for the products has proven to be very volatile, so I've dropped this information from the tables for the second edition of the book. Your best bet is to contact the vendors or their sales representatives directly and get the current pricing.

Use the information in these introductory sections and the details about the individual products as the basis for your own evaluation of which product and platform is right for your organization.

Advantages and Disadvantages

The clear advantages of PCs are that they are well known and widely available. LAN support staffs will require minimal additional hardware training (if any) to add a PC to the network as a database server. Depending on which LAN OS is used, support staff may not even need training on the operating system that the DBMS runs under. Widespread availability also ensures that it's easy to find and purchase the support hardware needed to maintain the integrity of the server, hardware such as tape drives for backups and uninterruptible power supplies (UPSs) for protection against power outages.

There's also a wider choice of operating systems that can be used for the database server; unlike the larger systems, PC-based DBMSs aren't limited to running only on UNIX or on a proprietary OS. Client/Server databases can be run under NetWare 3.11 or higher, OS/2 1.3 or higher, Windows NT, or any of the various UNIX packages for 486 and higher systems. Any of the major LAN operating systems and protocols can be used for communications between the clients and the servers. The rise in other 32-bit operating systems, such as OS/2 2.x and higher, Microsoft's Windows NT, and the forthcoming Windows 95 (due for release in late 1995), will only serve to increase the number (and power) of C/S software choices.

The dominance of PCs as the platform for C/S databases also leads to a self-perpetuating cycle in DBMS software development. The early PC-based C/S DBMSs were mostly ported down from minicomputer systems, so the products were already mature and didn't usually suffer from the problems associated with new software. As the size of the market increases (driven by enhancements to the current offerings), new DBMS vendors enter it, offering more powerful and feature-filled server software packages. This increased power and sophistication then leads more users to install C/S databases, increasing the market's size, and so the cycle continues to expand.

Since most PC C/S DBMSs are based on existing large-system database packages, you'll be able to draw on a large pool of experienced support personnel and DBMS programmers, which reduces the need for (and cost of) training existing staff on the new systems. Minicomputer and mainframe programmers can usually adapt to the different platform.

The downside is the increased cost of purchasing new high-powered PCs for use as dedicated database servers. There's also the cost of equipment duplication (that is, UPSs or tape drives), or of replacing existing equipment with higher-capacity versions to support the additional servers.

Personnel costs can also increase dramatically, especially if the existing large system staff can't be moved to the new platform. While a small C/S system can usually be supported by existing LAN personnel, increased size and complexity eventually leads to the need for a support staff for the DBMS alone. The Client/Server DBMS market is also evolving rapidly, and it will probably become necessary to provide time and money for regularly scheduled training on the new features and capabilities of the software.

Existing databases may prove incompatible with the new system, making it difficult to integrate the new Client/Server system into the enterprise-wide data services. You may also have difficulties moving data from existing systems to the C/S DBMS designated as the replacement. Fortunately, the increased popularity of C/S systems since 1992 has made this less of a consideration, as more and more vendors work to ensure backwards-compatibility.

Finally, it's very easy to get caught up in the rush to Client/Server systems and to overestimate their current (and maybe even future) capabilities. Doing so can lead to major problems in both the MIS and financial areas; personnel costs can rise dramatically when your staff spends more time getting the systems to work than in actually using them. Losing access to mission-critical data while the problems are being resolved can have a ripple effect across the entire business organization, leading to major financial losses. A *mission-critical* application is one that is so important to the functioning of a business that, should the application fail, the business would suffer a serious disruption in its operations.

C/S systems still aren't the be-all and end-all solution to data-management problems, and the decision to move to one should be based on extensive research and careful planning. There's no room for impulse buying or cost-cutting without careful study when designing a Client/Server DBMS system for business use.

Special Considerations

There are some important points to keep in mind when you're deciding whether or not to base your Client/Server database system on a PC server. Use the information in this section as the starting point for questions to ask the different DBMS vendors before making your purchase:

- **Hardware**: Is the server hardware already in place, or will it be purchased as part of the total system? Either way, make sure the hardware is compatible with the operating system the DBMS runs under. Client/Server vendors are usually happy to provide a list of PCs that have been tested for compatibility. It's a good idea to get a copy of the list before purchasing the hardware. The data that resides on the database server is too critical to your business to trust it to an off-brand, knocked-together PC.

  Find out if any other hardware is needed, such as tape drives for backups. Some DBMSs support backups to any tape drive on the network; others require that the tape drive be connected directly to the database server to get the full functionality of the built-in backup capabilities.

- **Compatibility with existing networks:** It may be easier in the long run to get a DBMS that runs under the operating system that your support staff already knows. Balance the features of the different DBMSs against the costs and complexities of having to learn (and support) a new operating system.

- **Support:** Support from the vendor is critical to successfully designing, developing, and running a Client/Server system. What kind of support plans does the vendor offer? Do they cover bug fixes and minor updates to the DBMS software or is that an extra-cost option? Does the vendor provide on-site support or only telephone support? Or is support only provided through the dealer or VAR (value-added reseller) that you bought the software from? And what are the support hours? Does the vendor provide support 24 hours a day, seven days a week? Or is it limited to the vendor's business hours (which may not be the same as yours, due to time zone differences)? Depending on the size and complexity of your system, it can be very helpful to have a technical representative in your offices while the system is being set up and programmed.

If the vendor provides telephone support only, will a support technician be assigned to your account or will support be provided by whoever answers the phone? Having an assigned technician saves time and money in the long run. If you're dealing with someone familiar with your system, you won't have to describe it every time you call for support.

If support is only provided through the dealer or VAR, find out how the support staff is trained. It's also important to find out what kind of fallback support is available if the dealer is unable to fix any problems you're having—or worse, if the dealer goes out of business in your area.

Finally, it would be a good idea to contact other customers of the vendor or dealer to find out about their experiences with the support provided. The best product in the world doesn't do you any good if you can't get proper support when you need it the most.

- **Training:** What type of training does the vendor provide for your in-house staff? Will they send a trainer to your site, or do you have to send your staff out to a training center? If you have to send the staff to a center, find out if the vendor has one near you; the costs for training obviously increase the farther away the training center is, due to transportation and housing needs.

- **Performance monitoring:** Does the DBMS have built-in performance monitoring functions? Or are third-party monitors available? A database monitor is the only way to detect whether a delay in response is due to a temporary increase in data requests or a permanent degradation in performance. Also make sure that the monitor provides some type of historical records so you can check database performance over a period of days, weeks, or months.

- **Front-end software:** Client/Server DBMS vendors will also provide an up-to-date list of the front-ends that support their server. Get a copy of the list, and make sure the software you want to use for your application development is on it.

Advice and Tips

Every Client/Server system is unique; each has its own requirements, quirks, and special performance features. However, a few tricks, applicable to all of them, can make it easier to get and keep a Client/Server database up and running.

First, buy the fastest machine you can for the database server. It doesn't take long for the database to get large enough to start bogging down on a slower system. The disks can be the cause of the most serious performance bottleneck, so make sure the system's disks are high-performance. I'd recommend at least a 66 MHz 80486 with fast-access (under 120ms) hard disks.

Next, get as much memory as the server system supports. Every user on the DBMS requires an area of memory on the server, so it makes sense from a performance standpoint to load up the server with as much memory as possible. When first starting out, add at least 4Mb to 8Mb of RAM beyond the minimum recommended by the vendor for best performance and make sure you have room for future memory expansion.

Also make sure the hard-disk subsystem on the PC is expandable. SCSI drives are a good choice, as one SCSI card can support up to seven devices. Disk array systems, also expandable, are good alternatives. Disk throughput is also a factor; 32-bit disk controllers provide better data transfer-per-second rates than 16-bit controllers. Use a system that supports 32-bit disk controller cards or provides a 32-bit disk controller as part of the motherboard whenever possible.

A Client/Server database is best run on its own dedicated system. While you can run just about all the PC-based DBMSs on the same system as the LAN file server, I recommend doing this only in the early design and development stages. As noted previously, it doesn't take long for a database to get large, and the contention between the database services and the file and print services can ultimately have a severe impact on performance. Data integrity may be jeopardized if you run a DBMS on the same server as other network services, because an errant application can bring down the server, possibly damaging the database. Running the DBMS on a dedicated server reduces the risk of this happening.

One final bit of advice—whenever you can, run the C/S DBMS under a LAN operating system that the DBMS has native support for. For example, while you can use an OS/2 or Windows NT-based DBMS on a NetWare LAN, slight incompatibilities and/or differences are likely to arise in the functions if you run it on a Windows NT Advanced Server or LAN Server network. I'll be pointing out these differences wherever necessary in the descriptions of the Client/Server DBMSs that follow.

■ Microsoft SQL Server 4.21

Shortly after their announcement of OS/2 in April 1987, Microsoft announced that they were working with SYBASE (a UNIX and VAX-based RDBMS vendor) to port the SYBASE SQL Server to the new operating system. The 1.x versions of the Microsoft/SYBASE SQL Server were actually subsets of the SYBASE product, which contained most of the features of the UNIX version. However, the OS/2-based DBMS had a major impact on the PC community, as it was the first product from a major PC vendor to bring the concept of Client/Server databases to PC-based LANs. It soon became the top-selling C/S DBMS for PC LANs; to date it has the widest support among third-party, front-end vendors.

In early 1992, Microsoft released SQL Server Version 4.2, which brought the DBMS up to full compatibility with the then-current SYBASE product. The significant enhancements over the 1.x versions raised 4.2 to the level of an entirely new product. In late 1993, Microsoft released Version 4.21 for Windows NT, a major rewrite of the basic SYBASE product. The OS/2 version remains at 4.2. I'll be pointing out differences between the two versions as the discussion progresses.

In mid-1992, SYBASE released a NetWare 3.11 NLM (NetWare Loadable Module) version of SQL Server 4.2, which was functionally compatible with the Microsoft version. However, in early 1994 Microsoft and SYBASE announced that they were going their separate ways and that they would no longer jointly develop SQL Server. Microsoft has a new version under development at the time of this writing, but few details are available. SYBASE has moved on to an entirely new version, which is covered in the next section.

Significant Features

Microsoft SQL Server is a Class 2 DBMS whose traditional claim to fame has been its support for stored procedures on the database server. Stored procedures are SQL routines that are stored as part of the database itself; they are executed entirely on the server when called from a client. Because they move more of the processing to the server, stored procedures can have a significant, positive impact on database performance. Access to them is controlled through the DBMS's security features, adding a measure of additional data integrity by preventing unauthorized users from inadvertently changing the database. A number of stored procedures are included in the package to provide functions such as administering users, monitoring the server, and assisting in creating new databases.

Version 4.2 added support for remote stored procedures, which provide a form of distributed processing by letting a procedure on one database server call and execute stored procedures on another database server running any version of SQL Server. Version 4.21 adds extended stored procedures, which are special hooks into the Windows NT operating system. Extended stored procedures can be used to trigger external events, such as sending an e-mail message to the DBA when certain values in the database reach a critical point.

SQL Server also supports a special type of stored procedure called a trigger, which is a procedure that is automatically executed when certain events (such as an INSERT, UPDATE, or DELETE) take place on the server. Triggers are particularly useful in creating and enforcing data and referential integrity rules (SQL statements which preserve the data and referential integrity requirements of the Relational model); because they're automatically activated, they can be used for a number of database checks and alerts. For example, a trigger can be set for a DELETE command on a particular table, which then automatically checks to make sure that the data being deleted is not linked to dependent data in another table. Or, one can be set to calculate the value of a column on an update and alert the user when the value reaches a certain threshold. And as mentioned above, triggers can be used with extended stored procedures to execute external events.

SQL Server supports groups of users for security and database access. Groups make database privilege administration easy, as privileges can be assigned on both a group and an individual level.

Version 4.2 has built-in, fault-tolerance features, such as real-time backups and disk mirroring, which increase the reliability of the database server. Real-time, on-line backups to tape are performed using the included OS/2 Systron Systos Plus tape backup software, which supports a number of different tape drives. The Windows NT version uses NT's built-in backup services. Backups can be run while users are accessing the database server and can be scheduled to run automatically throughout the day.

Database disk devices, which contain either the data itself or the transaction recovery logs (log files maintained by the DBMS that keep track of all database transactions), can optionally be automatically mirrored. Mirroring constantly creates an exact duplicate of the primary files on a backup disk, and the DBMS will automatically switch to the mirrored drive if an error occurs on the primary one. Mirroring slows down performance somewhat; however, the increased data integrity and security may be worth the penalty in system overhead.

The maximum number of database devices per server is 256, and, for additional performance, you can store the transaction logs on a device other than the one where the actual databases are stored. A database can span multiple disks, so databases can store up to the maximum disk size supported by the underlying operating system.

Microsoft provides a service known as Open Database Connectivity (ODBC), an API and programming library that lets SQL Server clients connect to any other SQL Server, regardless of platform. Their Open Database Services (ODS) option provides vendors with the ability to create gateways between SQL Server clients and other non-Microsoft database servers. ODBC is covered in greater detail in Chapter 9.

Hardware and Software Requirements

The OS/2 version of Microsoft SQL Server requires at least an 80286-based system running OS/2 1.3 or higher, though an 80386 or better is strongly recommended. The minimum memory needed is 8Mb, though again at least 12Mb is recommended; minimum disk space needed is 20Mb. SQL Server ships with a server-adapted version of OS/2 1.3 that is certified for well over 100 different PC systems.

Version 4.21 runs on Windows NT 3.1 or higher (Version 3.5 is recommended) on an 80386 or better with 16Mb RAM. It needs at least 25Mb hard-disk space.

Microsoft's SQL Server uses Named Pipes as its communication protocol, so it works with any NOS that supports Named Pipes, such as LAN Manager, Windows NT Advanced Server, Novell's NetWare, or IBM's LAN Server. Version 4.21 also uses the native NetWare IPX/SPX protocol, NETBEUI (Microsoft's implementation of NetBIOS), and TCP/IP.

Native SQL Language

TRANSACT-SQL, the native language used by SQL Server, provides complete ANSI SQL level 1 (1986) compatibility, with some elements of the level 2 (1989) standard. The enhancements provided by TRANSACT-SQL over the standard SQL language are particularly aimed at programming and using stored procedures and triggers. A number of math, financial, and statistical functions are also provided for use in data analysis.

Version 4.2 supports the concept of scrollable cursors, an SQL construct that treats the result of a query as a set that the client application can scroll through backward and forward; however, it implements them on the client end through the use of a data buffer with pointers. (Scrollable cursors are discussed in further detail in "Gupta SQLBase 6.0," later in this chapter.) While this method is better than not having scrollable cursors at all, it doesn't provide the data manipulation benefits of implementing them on the server itself.

TRANSACT-SQL statements are optimized using cost-based algorithms; a cost-based optimizer determines the best and fastest way to execute the SQL statements based on the structure, size, and indexing of the tables in the database, in order to reduce the transaction's "cost" in time and CPU cycles.

TRANSACT-SQL has no statements that provide database and referential integrity. Referential integrity, one of the key aspects of the Relational model that deals with overall database integrity, ensures consistency between tables when the values in one table are dependent on parent values in another table. DI and RI are provided through the use of programmed stored procedures and triggers to ensure that the database tables are consistent. While this is again better than not providing RI at all, the preferred method is to include it as part of the DBMS.

Front-ends Provided

Microsoft's SQL Server includes a Windows 3.x-based SQL Administrator tool that lets the database administrator (DBA) easily administer one or more SQL Servers through Windows's usual icons, drop-down menus, pick lists, and dialog boxes. The SQL Administrator program also provides the DBA with a real-time monitor of server performance, as well as a way to preserve a history log of performance for analysis and comparison when tuning the server. Figure 4.1 shows an SQL Query Window used for performance monitoring.

Figure 4.1

Microsoft's Windows-based SQL Administrator provides real-time database performance monitoring.

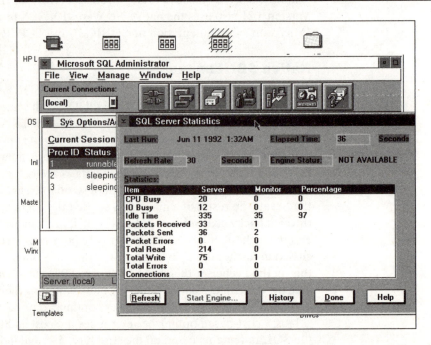

Microsoft also provides two character-mode utilities that provide administration and interactive SQL query capabilities. ISQL (Interactive SQL) is a command line tool that lets the user access or administer the databases through directly entered TRANSACT-SQL statements. System

Administration Facility (SAF) is a character-based graphics mode interface that provides fairly easy menu access to administrative facilities, as well as a method of scrolling back and forth through the query results. Figure 4.2 shows some of the on-line help available from SAF.

Figure 4.2

The character-based Microsoft/Sybase System Administrator Facility (SAF) runs on a number of client platforms.

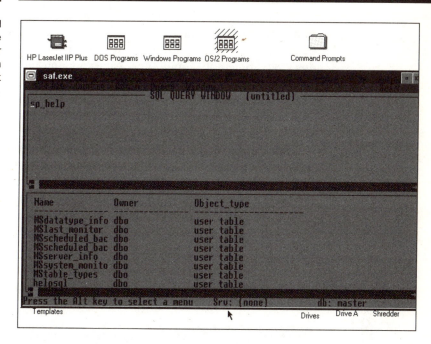

Microsoft also offers a line of programmer's toolkits that can be used to create custom client applications for SQL Server. Versions are available for Visual BASIC, C, and COBOL. A single-user SQL Server Developer's System is available for those who want to create SQL Server clients without the expense of a full system.

Advantages and Disadvantages

The most significant advantage of the Microsoft Server DBMS is the wide variety of third-party client support available. Every type of front-end software is available, from those designed strictly for application development to add-in SQL Server access modules for standard PC-based DBMSs such as Paradox and dBASE. There are even access modules that let the users query the database from the leading spreadsheet programs (such as Lotus 1-2-3 and Microsoft Excel).

For all intents and purposes, the OS/2 version of Microsoft SQL Server is an orphaned product. Microsoft continues to sell it, but has no plans to update it. All future updates will be on the Windows NT version, and Microsoft is encouraging its customers to move to this platform. The OS/2 version is still based on 16-bit code, while the Windows NT version is a full 32-bit application.

Running on Windows NT is an advantage, but it's also in part a serious disadvantage. On the plus side, a Windows NT database server is network independent and can be used with any of the popular NOSs. In addition, Windows NT's preemptive multiprocessing and built-in multithreading make it an ideal platform for mission-critical databases. Windows NT also supports symmetrical multiprocessing (SMP) systems, which gives SQL Server the ability to split tasks among different processors. (See Chapter 5 for more details on multiprocessor platforms.)

On the down side, Windows NT Advanced Server isn't as popular as other NOSs, especially NetWare. Adding a Windows NT server to another NOS can be done, but it does increase the level of complexity in the overall system. At the very least, it requires running additional protocols on the clients to take full advantage of SQL Server's advanced security features.

Microsoft SQL Server has a proven track record and wide support. Only time will tell if future versions maintain its reputation as they move away from the joint Microsoft/SYBASE code.

Table 4.1

Microsoft SQL Server
Quick Summary

PRODUCT INFORMATION	
Name	Microsoft SQL Server 4.2 (OS/2); Microsoft SQL Server 4.21 (NT)
Vendor	Microsoft Corporation
OPERATING SYSTEMS	
On Database Server	OS/2 1.2 or higher; Windows NT 3.1 or higher
On LAN server	MS LAN Manager, Windows NT Advanced Server, Windows for Workgroups; IBM LAN Server; Novell NetWare; or any other network that supports Named Pipes or NETBEUI
On Workstations	DOS 3.0 or higher; Windows 3.0 or higher; Windows NT 3.1 or higher; OS/2 1.2 or higher
MINIMUM REQUIREMENTS	
RAM on Server	8Mb OS/2; 16Mb Windows NT

**Table 4.1
(Continued)**

Microsoft SQL Server
Quick Summary

MINIMUM REQUIREMENTS	
RAM on Workstation	640k DOS; 4Mb Windows; 6Mb OS/2; 12Mb Windows NT
Disk Space on Server	20Mb OS/2; 25Mb Windows NT
UTILITIES PROVIDED	
Administration Utility	Yes
Interactive User Utility	Yes
Operating Systems/Environments Supported	DOS 3.0 or higher; Windows 3.0 or higher; Windows NT 3.1 or higher; OS/2 1.2 or higher
NATIVE LANGUAGES	
ANSI SQL	Level 1 with some Level 2 elements
DB2 SQL Extensions	No
Other SQL Extensions	Yes
Non-SQL Language	No
MAXIMUMS	
Database Size	Maximum supported by operating system
Column Size	Normally 1,962 bytes; "image" and "text" data types store 2G through pointers to external data
Row Size	1,962 bytes
# of Columns in Row	255 columns
# of Rows in Table	Limited by disk
# of Rows per Database	Limited by disk
# of Tables per Database	2 billion
# of Views per Database	Unlimited
# of Tables per View	Unlimited tables, but only 250 columns per view

■ SYBASE SQL Server for NetWare 10.0

SYBASE, Inc. was founded in late 1984, but it wasn't until mid-1987 that it began shipping the SYBASE System. SYBASE System was the first

RDBMS especially designed for on-line transaction processing, as the founders of the company recognized early on the impact microcomputer-based networks would have on the evolution of corporate databases. They based their new database system on the *host/server* architecture the company invented.

Host/server? Well, that was the first name SYBASE gave to the concept of splitting the database processing between a workstation and a database server. The company founders weren't quite comfortable with that term, though, so when the initial SYBASE System finally shipped, SYBASE referred to it as a "requestor/server" database.

This book would probably be called *Guide to Requestor/Server Computing* if it weren't for a report released by Forrester Research, Inc., one of the many companies that specializes in analyzing trends in the computer industry. The title of the report was *The New Client/Server Paradigm*, and it came out just as SYBASE and Microsoft were preparing to announce that the latter was licensing SQL Server for its new OS/2 operating system. SYBASE's marketing department liked the term Client/Server much better than requestor/server, and decided to use it instead. The rest, as they say, is history.

In spite of other companies' claims, SYBASE was really the first to develop a RDBMS that was designed from the ground up to share the processing between a front-end application running on a workstation and the database engine running on a server. SQL Server both introduced the C/S architecture and set the standard for other RDBMS companies to match or beat. The combination of SYBASE's technology and Microsoft's respected name and marketing abilities proved to be the spark that got the whole C/S industry off the ground.

SYBASE SQL Server 4.9 is the version that's compatible with Microsoft SQL Server 4.2. In 1992, the company announced a major upgrade to their flagship product as well as specialized products and database servers designed to make it easier to create enterprise-wide C/S systems. SYBASE System 10 is the name the company chose to refer to all these updated and new products. SQL Server 10.0, the cornerstone of System 10, started shipping for a limited number of platforms in mid-1993 and for other platforms during 1994. This section will cover the NetWare version of SQL Server 10.0; the UNIX and versions will be covered in the next chapter.

Significant Features

SYBASE SQL Server for NetWare 4.9 was essentially the same product as Microsoft SQL Server 4.2. It also supported stored procedures and triggers and used them to create and enforce RI. However, extended stored procedures aren't supported in any version of SYBASE SQL Server at this time.

SQL Server 10.0 is the heart of the System 10 family of products, and it adds quite a few new features and capabilities over Version 4.9. Chief among them is the updating of TRANSACT-SQL (covered in the Native SQL Language section), the expansion in the number of stored procedures allowed, and increased system security.

SQL Server 10.0 increases the storage space available for stored procedures to 16Mb. In Version 4.9, the system-wide stored procedures were kept as part of the master database. Because of the increase in storage Version 10.0 provides, the system-wide stored procedures have been moved out of the master database and into their own database, called sybsystemprocs. SQL Server 10.0 will automatically place any stored procedure that starts with "sp_" in the new database. It will also automatically search this database when an application executes a procedure that starts with "sp_". Over 25 new system procedures have been added to manage the new features and capabilities.

Version 10.0 also has a new feature called the threshold manager. The threshold manager monitors how much free space exists on a particular database device segment; when the amount falls below a user-defined threshold, the manager automatically executes an associated stored procedure. These associated stored procedures can take such actions as automatically dumping the transaction log, or sending an alert to the DBA when a database is running out of storage space.

Triggers have also been enhanced. TRANSACT-SQL has a new command called ROLLBACK TRIGGER. When this command is issued, it rolls back a transaction up to the point where a trigger was fired, instead of rolling back the whole transaction. Triggers can also be self-recursive; in other words, a trigger can fire again when it changes data in a column the trigger is associated with. This capability is optional and is turned off by default, as it could have various negative effects on a database if it isn't used properly.

Two new data types have been added in Version 10.0, and the behavior of others has changed. Also new to Version 10.0 is the IDENTITY column. An IDENTITY column has the numeric data type and automatically generates and stores sequential serial numbers. A table can only have one IDENTITY column. Users can only read the values in IDENTITY columns; they can't be updated or inserted by an application. The DBA, database owner, or table owner can explicitly insert initial values in IDENTITY columns after setting a system variable on for the particular table.

Optimization has also been improved. Version 10.0 will automatically update the server statistics used by the optimizer when one or more indices are added, deleted, or changed. The new UPDATE STATISTICS command replaces the stored procedure that handled this function in Version 4.9.

Security has been enhanced in the new version in a number of ways. The most important is the expansion of system administrator capabilities to other users. In 4.9, only the SA user could administrate the database. Version 10.0 adds three new security roles (System 10's name for user groups): System Administrator, System Security Officer, and Operator. A System Administrator can monitor and modify disk and memory usage, grant and revoke CREATE DATABASE rights, run diagnostic and repair functions, grant and revoke the System Administrator role to other users, and modify, drop, or lock user login accounts. System Security Officers can add login accounts, change passwords, grant and revoke role/group rights, and manage the audit system. Finally, the Operator can backup and restore databases.

Any user can have one or more of these new roles assigned. The SA account is still created when the software is installed, and has all three roles assigned to it. The DBA can use these new roles to create other administrators responsible for maintaining various parts of the database server without having access to the entire security system.

User passwords can be encrypted on the database server and also on the client side. Server encryption prevents anyone from seeing the user's password on the server; the only thing an administrator can do is delete the existing password and assign a new one. Client-side encryption encrypts the password between the client and the server, preventing anyone using a network analyzer from capturing the data packets and reading the passwords from them.

SYBASE has made numerous other changes to SQL Server 10.0; so many that it would take an entire book to discuss all of them. Fortunately, that book exists—each copy of Version 10.0 comes with a 78-page manual called *What's New in SYBASE SQL Server Release 10.0*. This manual details all of the changes, how they affect existing applications, and any special requirements you need to be aware of before upgrading from a Version 4.9 server.

In addition to SQL Server 10.0, the System 10 family consists of two related database engines, a number of gateways, and management and control applications. Of special interest are the two database engines: the SYBASE Replication Server, and the SYBASE Navigation Server. I'll be covering these products in the SQL Server section in Chapter 5.

Hardware and Software Requirements

SYBASE SQL Server 4.9 runs on NetWare 3.11 or higher. It requires 12Mb RAM and at least 20Mb disk space on the server. SQL Server 10.0 requires 32Mb RAM, 30Mb hard-disk space, and NetWare 3.12 or higher. Both require an 80386 or better.

Both versions use NetWare's IPX/SPX protocol to communicate between the clients and the server. The SYBASE Open Server and Open Client APIs give developers and front-end vendors the ability to write applications that use other networking protocols. So, a third-party vendor could create a front-end that uses IBM's SNA protocol to communicate between a SQL Server client and an IBM mainframe. Or, a vendor could create a TCP/IP interface between the front-end and a VAX/VMS server or NetWare server.

Native SQL Language

SYBASE SQL Server 10.0's TRANSACT-SQL has been brought up to full compliance with the ANSI-89 SQL standard, including the integrity addendum. This means that in addition to using triggers to support RI, SQL Server now has built-in RI support for handling cascading deletes. It also fully supports integrity constraints instituted by primary and foreign database keys.

SYBASE has also added support for the ANSI-92 Entry Level standard. In particular, TRANSACT-SQL now has keywords for cursor control, including DECLARE CURSOR, FETCH, OPEN, CLOSE, DEALLOCATE. SQL cursors let applications retrieve data on a row-by-row basis and provide support for scrollable cursors.

Front-ends Provided

The primary administration tool that ships with every version of SQL Server is ISQL. ISQL is a character mode command line utility that lets you enter TRANSACT-SQL commands directly or as part of a text file of commands. Because it doesn't use any special system-specific graphics, ISQL is capable of running on any platform that SQL Server runs on. All versions of SQL Server come with a version of ISQL that runs on the same operating system that the RDBMS runs on. The NetWare version of SQL Server also comes with a DOS version of ISQL.

As part of its System 10 development efforts, SYBASE has written an enhanced and easy-to-use administration tool called SA Companion. SA Companion comes in both character and graphic versions, and works with both the 4.9 and 10.0 versions of SQL Server. It's only available for a number of UNIX platforms at the time of this writing; a Windows 3.x version is under development.

Advantages and Disadvantages

SQL Server 10.0's biggest advantage is its support for SYBASE's replication and navigation services, covered in the next chapter. Its biggest disadvantage is that it's only available for NetWare on PC platforms—if you run another NOS, you'll have to use one of the UNIX versions. It's rumored that SYBASE is working on either an OS/2 2.x and higher or Windows NT 3.x version (or both) of SQL Server 10.0 now that they're no longer associated with Microsoft's development efforts.

The other disadvantage is that the SYBASE versions of SQL Server don't have nearly as much third-party front-end support as Microsoft's version, though this is gradually changing. Front-ends written for Microsoft SQL Server sometimes work with the SYBASE version, but this isn't always dependable. Your best bet would be to check with your particular front-end vendor to see if its products support the SYBASE versions.

Table 4.2

SYBASE SQL Server
Quick Summary

PRODUCT INFORMATION	
Name	SYBASE SQL Server 10.0 (NT)
Vendor	SYBASE, Inc.
OPERATING SYSTEMS	
On Database Server	NetWare 3.12 or higher
On LAN server	Novell NetWare 3.12 or higher
On Workstations	DOS 3.0 or higher; Windows 3.0 or higher; Windows NT 3.1 or higher; OS/2 1.2 or higher.
MINIMUM REQUIREMENTS	
RAM on Server	32Mb
RAM on Workstation	640k DOS; 4Mb Windows; 6Mb OS/2; 12Mb Windows NT
Disk Space on Server	30Mb
UTILITIES PROVIDED	
Administration Utility	Yes
Interactive User Utility	Yes
Operating Systems/Environ-ments Supported	DOS 3.0 or higher
NATIVE LANGUAGES	
ANSI SQL	Level 2 with Integrity Addendum
DB2 SQL Extensions	No
Other SQL Extensions	Yes
Non-SQL Language	No

MAXIMUMS	
Database Size	Maximum supported by operating system
Column Size	Normally 1,962 bytes; "image" and "text" data types store 2G through pointers to external data
Row Size	1,962 bytes
# of Columns in Row	255 columns
# of Rows in Table	Limited by disk
# of Rows per Database	Limited by disk
# of Tables per Database	2 billion
# of Views per Database	Unlimited
# of Tables per View	Unlimited tables, but only 250 columns per view

■ Gupta SQLBase 5.2 and 6.0

Even though it's third in market share behind Microsoft and Oracle, Gupta's SQLBase is unique among the different PC-based C/S DBMS in that it wasn't ported down from a large system. The initial version of SQLBase that shipped in 1986 was developed for and ran under PC/MS-DOS. Since then, versions have been released for OS/2 and NetWare 3.11. Gupta has also developed a variety of front-ends and connections to other DBMSs; their goal is to be a "one stop" source for Client/Server computing.

Gupta released SQLBase 6.0 for NetWare as this book was being written. The rest of this section will cover the features of both versions.

Significant Features

Gupta's Class 2 SQLBase Version 5.2 comes in versions for DOS, Windows 3.x, Windows NT, OS/2, and NetWare. A version that runs on Sun's version of UNIX is also available and will be discussed in Chapter 5.

SQLBase was one of the first RDBMS to include full support for the ANSI Level 2 SQL standard with the Integrity Addendum. This means that SQLBase supports declarative referential integrity (RI), the preferred implementation. In SQLBase, RI is declared as part of the database definition, instead of being left up to stored procedures and triggers (as Microsoft implements it) or entirely up to the front-end application programmer. SQLBase implements RI as part of the table definition through primary and foreign keys, and through SQL keywords that tell the DBMS what actions to take when a parent row is deleted. The full implications of implementing referential integrity is beyond the scope of this book; for more information, check both the current ANSI standard papers and the reference books listed in Appendix C.

Databases can be partitioned so that portions can reside on multiple disks or disk volumes. Depending on the platform, a SQLBase database can range up to 500G in size. For additional performance, the transaction logs can be stored on a different drive than the database files. SQLBase also supports on-line (real-time) backups using the tape backup system appropriate to the platform.

SQLBase supports hashed clustered indices, which change the physical location of the data to reduce the amount of disk I/O when multiple rows of data are retrieved and increase performance. It also supports data compression, a built-in option in which the server compresses the query responses prior to sending them back to the client, further reducing the traffic over the network cable.

SQLBase also supports precompiled (another way of saying preoptimized) SQL procedures that are stored on the server for faster execution. While not as integral to the database as the stored procedures used by SQL Server and thus not as high performance, precompiled SQL speeds up database operations by performing the optimization of the SQL statement once, instead of each time the statement is executed. Because they're stored alongside the database on the server, precompiled SQL also adds a measure of data consistency by letting different front-end applications use the exact same statements to access the database—an advantage shared with DBMSs that implement stored procedures.

Gupta's SQLBase also supports true scrollable cursors. Standard SQL queries return the results one row at a time, and it's up to the front-end application to devise a buffer to store the results so that the user can scroll (browse) forward through the query results. A scrollable cursor is an SQL construct that lets the DBMS return, simultaneously, multiple rows of data that can be scrolled in either direction. RDBMSs such as the Microsoft SQL Server implement it through an automatic buffer (or pseudocursor) on the front-end that uses a pointer to track where the user is in the results set. If the user wants to scroll backward, the SQL request is first reexecuted on the server, and the response is restricted to the previously viewed rows. Gupta implements scrollable cursors on the server through the use of a temporary results table that the client application then views in either direction. Because the cursor is implemented on the server, the user can also manipulate the data to have the changes written back to the original database. However, implementing scrollable cursors this way adds a significant amount of over-head to server processing, so SQLBase makes them an option that can be turned on and off by the client application as needed.

In line with their stated goal of being a one-stop source for C/S solutions, Gupta provides an IBM DB2-compatible SQL syntax, so front-end applications can be created for SQLBase servers that can also directly access DB2 databases through a gateway system. This capability is aimed primarily at easing the transition for those looking to downsize their DB2 applications to a PC-based C/S platform. Gupta also markets a number of gateways/routers that let SQLBase users and developers access data on other DBMSs such as Oracle, SQL Server, and DB2 using SQLBase's standard SQL syntax. (A router is a hardware/software combination that links together different networks that use the same protocol.)

SQLBase 6.0 is only available for NetWare at this time. It adds support for stored procedures and triggers. It also supports timed events that can be triggered at prescheduled times. Finally, SQLBase 6.0 adds two-phase commit support for distributed databases.

Hardware and Software Requirements

The DOS version of SQLBase requires at least a 286 with 2Mb of RAM, 10Mb of disk space, and PC/MS-DOS 3.1 or higher. The OS/2 version is still 16-bit and also requires at least a 286 running OS/2 1.3 or higher with at least 4Mb of RAM and 10Mb of hard-disk space. The NLM version requires a 386 or higher running NetWare 3.12 with 8Mb of RAM and 10Mb of disk space. The requirements for SQLBase 6.0 for NetWare are the same as the 5.0 NLM version.

Gupta's SQLBase supports numerous network protocols, including IBM's Advanced Peer-to-Peer Communications (APPC), Named Pipes, NetBIOS, TCP/IP, and IPX/SPX. However, its own communication driver has one major problem—the amount of RAM it needs on top of the network protocols on the client workstation. While all the other C/S DBMSs keep their communications protocols under (in some cases, well under) 100k in size, SQLBase's takes a whopping 200k of RAM on the client.

Native SQL Language

As stated previously, SQLBase's native SQLTalk language is fully compatible with the ANSI Level 2 with Integrity Enhancements standard. It also has a number of optional extensions that make it fully DB2 compatible. Stored procedures and triggers are written in the SQLWindows Application Language.

Gupta has implemented a cost-based optimizer in SQLBase 5.2 that is particularly designed for speeding up database queries when using precompiled

SQL code. However, it's advisable to periodically recompile the stored code so that the optimizer can adjust the SQL statements to properly reflect the current state of the database.

Front-end Processors Provided

Gupta includes two front-end database administration utilities with SQL-Base 5.2: a character mode utility and a Windows 3.x-based utility. SQLTalk/Character is the command line interface that lets the DBA directly enter SQL statements at a command prompt. The rather primitive interface is similar to Microsoft's ISQL. Gupta doesn't provide a character graphics-based administration tool. Due to the high RAM requirement of SQLBase's client-side communications drivers, there isn't always enough RAM to run SQLTalk/Character, so Gupta also provides a version that includes the appropriate drivers as part of the program to get around the limitation.

The preferred interface is SQLTalk/Windows, a Windows 3.x-based administration utility that uses Windows's memory management capabilities to circumvent the RAM limitations of the SQLBase communications drivers. While not as sophisticated as Microsoft's SQL Administrator, SQLTalk/Windows makes it much easier to administrate and query the database than the character version. SQLTalk/Windows provides different windows for entering queries and viewing the results and also has a number of pull-down menus with predefined choices for creating users, setting security levels, and switching between databases.

SQLBase 6.0 includes a new utility called SQLConsole. It's a Windows 3.x management utility that makes it easier to manage, tune, and monitor multiple SQLBase servers.

A C/API library is included in the standard SQLBase package for creating custom client applications in C. A COBOL API library is also available from Gupta.

Advantages and Disadvantages

SQLBase has a significant advantage: scalability, particularly on PC platforms.

SQLBase's scalability is an important factor for those starting out with a small Client/Server system, because front-end applications designed for one server version are completely compatible with all the other versions. For example, your initial database design and development can take place with the DOS-based version, and the database can be moved up to the OS/2, Windows NT, or NLM version as needed.

SQLBase's compatibility with the DB2 SQL syntax and Gupta's various gateways/routers to other C/S RDBMSs make SQLBase capable of being a part of existing corporate-wide databases, either for integrating PC-based databases into the whole system or for gradually downsizing existing large databases to the smaller platforms.

The most notable disadvantage of SQLBase is its relative lack of support from third-party front-end applications, which is most likely attributable to the communication driver's high RAM requirements on the client side. However, Gupta markets a couple of Windows-based front-ends that are well designed and can access other DBMSs besides SQLBase. These products are discussed in Chapters 9 and 10.

I expressed reservations about Gupta's technical support in the first edition of this book. I'm happy to report that their support has somewhat improved over the last few years.

Table 4.3

Gupta SQLBase Quick Summary

PRODUCT INFORMATION	
Name	SQLBase 5.2; SQLBase 6.0
Vendor	Gupta Corp.
OPERATING SYSTEMS	
On Database Server	DOS 3.1 or higher, OS/2 1.3 or higher, Windows 3.1 or higher, Windows NT 3.1 or higher, NetWare 3.11 or higher (5.2); NetWare 3.12 or higher (6.0)
On LAN server	MS LAN Manager, Windows NT Advanced Server, Windows for Workgroups; IBM LAN Server; Novell NetWare 3.11 or higher; Banyan VINES
On Workstations	DOS 3.1 or higher; Windows 3.0 or higher
MINIMUM REQUIREMENTS	
RAM on Server	1Mb Windows, 2Mb DOS, 4Mb OS/2, 8Mb Windows NT and NetWare
RAM on Workstation	640k DOS; 4Mb Windows; 6Mb OS/2; 12Mb Windows NT
Disk Space on Server	10Mb
UTILITIES PROVIDED	
Administration Utility	Yes
Interactive User Utility	Yes
Operating Systems/Environments Supported	DOS 3.1 or higher; Windows 3.0 or higher

Table 4.3
(Continued)

Gupta SQLBase Quick
Summary

NATIVE LANGUAGES	
ANSI SQL	Level 2 with Integrity Enhancement
DB2 SQL Extensions	Yes
Other SQL Extensions	Yes
Non-SQL Language	Yes (6.0)
MAXIMUMS	
Database Size	500G
Column Size	Limited by disk space (LONG VARCHAR data type)
Row Size	Limited by disk space
# of Columns in Row	250 columns
# of Rows in Table	Limited by disk space
# of Rows per Database	Limited by disk space
# of Tables per Database	Limited by disk space
# of Views per Database	Unlimited
# of Tables per View	Unlimited

■ IBM DB2/2

IBM's first OS/2-based database server, called DB2/2, was released as a part of the OS/2 1.1 Extended Edition (EE) version. It was primarily designed as a local DB2/2; C/S capabilities weren't added until the release of Version 1.3. With the release of OS/2 2.0, IBM unbundled the Extended Edition services from the base operating system and marketed the DB2/2 as part of the OS/2 Extended Services 2.0 package.

In 1993, IBM released DB2/2 1.0, a somewhat compatible OS/2 2.x version of its DB2 mainframe-based database. DB2/2 is the successor to DB2/2; the current version is 1.2, with Version 2.0 in beta testing and due to be released sometime during 1995. This section will cover Version 1.2, with some brief details on the new features in 2.0.

Significant Features

IBM's DB2/2 is a Class 2 system that runs on OS/2 2.x or better—its essentially a 32-bit version of the DB2/2. Its most significant feature is its fairly close SQL compatibility with the mainframe-based DB2 and its ability to transparently connect and share data with a DB2 database through the additional Distributed Database Connection Services/2 (DDCS/2) package. DB2/2's DB2 compatibility is also its greatest strength; DB2 is IBM's premier RDBMS and any features implemented in it soon filter down to the OS/2-based product.

DB2/2 also includes support for declarative referential integrity; like SQLBase, RI is implemented through primary and foreign keys and includes SQL statements that govern how deletions of parent data are handled when dependent data exists in other tables.

DB2/2 supports IBM's Database Application Remote Interface (DARI), a method of moving large portions of the SQL statements to the server to be executed there. The SQL procedures are compiled into a Dynamic Link Library (DLL), an OS/2 and Windows feature that stores portions of an application in libraries that are linked to the application and used only when needed. IBM calls these programmer-created DLLs "stored procedures," but they're more like the precompiled SQL statements in SQLBase than the stored procedures implemented by the SYBASE SQL Server. The DLLs can be created using C, FORTRAN, or COBOL; once they're on the server, the routines in the library can be called by any front-end application. The routines are then executed on the server, reducing network traffic and boosting performance.

Unfortunately, DB2/2 limits you to storing a database on a single hard-disk volume. You can put the transaction log on a different volume, but your database is limited to the size of a single hard disk.

DB2/2 Version 2.0's new features will include an enhanced query optimizer, the ability to span multiple disks with a single database, and two-phase commit. Other enhancements include triggers, BLOB support, and support for user-defined functions.

Hardware and Software Requirements

OS/2 DB2/2 1.2 runs under OS/2 2.0 or higher. It needs at least a 386 with 12Mb of RAM and 15Mb hard-disk space. DB2/2 2.0 will be available for both OS/2 2.x and higher and Windows NT 3.5 or higher.

DB2/2 uses NetBIOS for communications between the client and server and will work with any network that supports it. Client communications are provided through IBM's Remote Data Services protocol. In addition to NetBIOS, Remote Data Services lets clients communicate with the server over such wide-area protocols as X.25 and IBM's SDLC and 3174 Peer Communications. The latter two provide access to DB2/2 from terminals connected to an IBM host network.

DB2/2 will add support for Named Pipes, TCP/IP, and possibly NetWare's IPX/SPX.

Native SQL Language

DB2/2's SQL is compatible with the ANSI Level 2 with Integrity Enhancement standard—not surprising, since SQL was originally created by IBM, and IBM is one of the major players on the ANSI SQL Standards Committee. Virtually all of the DB2 extensions are included as well, providing DB2/2 applications a large measure of source-code compatibility with DB2 databases.

Front-end Processors Provided

DB2/2 includes three OS/2-based front-ends, including the Command Line Interface (CLI), a Database Tools module, and the Query Manager. The CLI is a simple interactive SQL program that lets the DBA enter and execute SQL statements on a command line.

The Database Tools are a set of utilities specifically designed to assist the DBA in configuring and maintaining both the DB2/2 and individual databases. The Configuration tool makes it easy to configure and tune the server, and the Recovery tool provides database recovery services for backing up and restoring a database. The Directory tool is used to create and catalog databases.

The Query Manager is an interactive SQL utility that provides character-based menus and panels to speed the process of creating and administrating databases. It's the primary administration utility for DB2/2.

An SQL precompiler is included to allow application programmers to embed SQL statements in programs written in C, COBOL, and FORTRAN. Dynamic SQL statements can also be embedded in programs created in IBM's REXX, a powerful batch language that runs on every IBM system from PCs based on OS/2 to the largest mainframes.

Advantages and Disadvantages

DB2/2's most significant advantage is its DB2 compatibility, especially when the DDCS/2 package is added to provide transparent access to IBM's DB2, SQL/DS, and SQL/400 databases. This compatibility makes DB2/2 ideal for use in what are traditionally known as "IBM shops"—customers whose primary computer platform is an IBM mainframe. DB2/2 can be used as a platform for either downsizing existing DB2 databases or as a way of enhancing existing systems by providing distributed database capabilities. Unfortunately,

DDCS/2 only supports access to the large system databases through the DB2/2 CLI or programmed applications.

Its biggest disadvantages are its inability to have databases span more than one hard-disk volume, and its support for IBM's own version of NetBIOS only. Fortunately, these limitations will be removed in DB2/2 Version 2.0.

IBM has not entirely moved away from its former position of supporting only its own software products on IBM systems, so setting up and using DB2/2 on LANs with NOSs other than IBM's LAN Server can be a difficult process. Also, DB2/2 doesn't yet have wide support among third-party, front-end application vendors. IBM is very committed to seeing OS/2 become a success, though, and I expect that IBM will continue to pursue wider support for DB2/2, both on non-IBM networks and among the front-end vendors.

Table 4.4

IBM DB2/2 Quick Summary

PRODUCT INFORMATION	
Name	IBM DB2/2
Vendor	IBM, Inc.
OPERATING SYSTEMS	
On Database Server	OS/2 2.0 or higher
On LAN server	MS LAN Manager and Windows NT Advanced Server; IBM LAN Server; Novell NetWare 3.11 or higher; or any network that supports IBM's version of NetBIOS
On Workstations	DOS 3.1 or higher, Windows 3.0 or higher, OS/2 1.3 or higher
MINIMUM REQUIREMENTS	
RAM on Server	12Mb
RAM on Workstation	640k DOS, 6Mb OS/2
Disk Space on Server	15Mb
UTILITIES PROVIDED	
Administration Utility	Yes
Interactive User Utility	Yes
Operating Systems/Environments Supported	DOS 3.1 or higher; OS/2 2.1 or higher

NATIVE LANGUAGES	
ANSI SQL	Level 2 with Integrity Enhancements
DB2 SQL Extensions	Yes
Other SQL Extensions	No
Non-SQL Language	No
MAXIMUMS	
Database Size	Limited by disk space
Column Size	4,000 bytes, or 32,700 characters in a LONG VARCHAR data type
Row Size	4,005 bytes
# of Columns in Row	255 columns
# of Rows in Table	Limited by disk space
# of Rows per Database	Limited by disk space
# of Tables per Database	Limited by disk space
# of Views per Database	Limited by disk space
# of Tables per View	15

■ ORACLE7 Server

Oracle has the distinction of being the first company to create and sell a commercial RDBMS that used SQL, beating out even IBM by a few years. The early versions were developed on VAX/VMS systems, and VMS remains Oracle's primary platform; all new versions come out for VMS first.

Since the early 1980s, Oracle has committed itself to supporting a wide variety of platforms, and it was one of the first vendors to produce a DOS-based RDBMS. Oracle continues its string of firsts to this day, as it was the first vendor to release a full 32-bit OS/2 2.0 and Windows NT version of its DBMS. ORACLE's support for a variety of systems has made it the top-selling RDBMS in the world.

ORACLE7 Version 7.0, released in 1993, was the first major upgrade to Oracle's flagship product in almost four years. It added a number of new features that brought ORACLE's technology in line with other C/S databases. Version 7.1 is under development at this time, with various platform versions scheduled for release during 1995.

Significant Features

ORACLE7's most powerful feature is its portability and scalability. Versions are available for virtually every major hardware and software platform in existence, including PCs, Macintoshes, mainframes, and most UNIX variants. Code written for one platform can easily be ported to another, due to Oracle's SQL precompiler. PC-based versions of ORACLE7 are available for OS/2 2.x and higher, NetWare 3.11 or better, and Windows NT 3.1 or higher.

ORACLE7 provides the strongest distributed processing support of any of the C/S databases available at this time. The key to this database distribution is Oracle's SQL*Net communication protocol, which is available for a number of connection protocols, including NetBIOS, IPX/SPX, Named Pipes, IBM's APPC and 3270, DECNet, and TCP/IP; there's even a version that supports asynchronous connections over a modem. Since multiple versions of SQL*Net can be run at the same time on an ORACLE7 server, it can handle links to remote databases without user intervention.

ORACLE7 databases can be split among different disks or volumes, so the only limit is total available disk space. An ORACLE7 server can also connect to other ORACLE servers, which allows the DBA to create "virtual databases" many times larger than the size limitations imposed by a single server.

ORACLE7 supports two-phase commits and Remote Procedure Calls (RPCs) for distributing databases. ORACLE7 also added stored procedures, triggers, declarative referential integrity, and cost-based optimization.

Hardware and Software Requirements

All versions of ORACLE7 require a minimum of 12Mb of RAM, although at least 16Mb is required to support the maximum number of users. The software itself takes up about 30Mb of hard-disk space.

Oracle's SQL*Net communications drivers support every major network protocol, which allows ORACLE7 access to the widest available variety of client platforms. ORACLE7 is the only C/S database to support access from Macintosh clients; when used with TCP/IP, even UNIX-based clients can access PC-based ORACLE7 servers. The SQL*Net drivers take up a moderate amount of RAM, so it's possible to run at least two different versions on the same DOS client. For example, a user can access a NLM database using SPX while simultaneously accessing an OS/2 version using Named Pipes.

Native SQL Language

Oracle's SQL is compatible with the ANSI Level 2 standard with Integrity Enhancements.

Oracle also provides its own extensions to SQL through its Procedural Language/SQL (PL/SQL). Developed as a response to SYBASE's TRANSACT-SQL, PL/SQL includes logic and branching commands, support for variables and arrays, and a variety of string and math functions that can be used with the base SQL statements to create complete applications without an external language.

Front-end Processors Provided

The only front-end provided with ORACLE7 is SQL*DBA, a character-mode, command line interface that's used both to administrate and to query databases. In addition to executing directly entered SQL statements, SQL*DBA can execute a series of PL/SQL statements stored in a text file.

SQL*DBA has some built-in administration functions, including a real-time database monitor which lets the administrator examine current and historical database access, existing database locks, current user activity, and server performance statistics, as shown in Figure 4.3. SQL*DBA is available in DOS and OS/2 versions.

Figure 4.3

Oracle's SQL*DBA command line interface provides the DBA with a comprehensive system monitor.

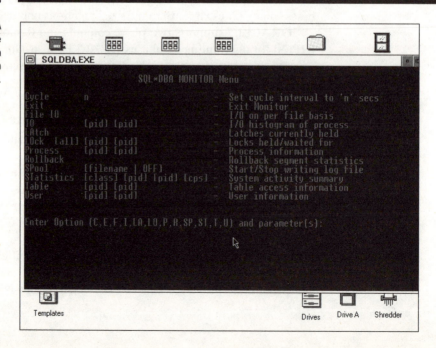

The base version of the server software comes with interface libraries for customizing applications in C using the Oracle Call Interface (OCI). In addition, a PL/SQL precompiler can convert the embedded SQL statements into C code, which can then be compiled with any C compiler into executable client applications. Libraries and precompilers are also available for COBOL, FORTRAN, Pascal, PL/I, and Ada.

Oracle sells a complete application development kit called Oracle Tools, which includes a menu generator, forms generator, report writer, and full-screen, interactive PL/SQL query utility.

Advantages and Disadvantages

Due to its widespread availability, ORACLE7 has the second-largest number of third-party, front-end support products. Only Microsoft SQL Server has slightly more support.

Oracle's database servers are the overall market leader for one simple reason—their scalability across a wide range of platforms. Corporations looking to create a complete Client/Server system including everything from PC LANs to mainframes can use ORACLE7 as the common RDBMS for all of their platforms, which reduces the need (and cost) of training programmers, developers, and support personnel in multiple database systems. In addition, ORACLE7 users can draw on a large pool of applications developers already familiar with the software when hiring new personnel.

Another advantage is ORACLE7's support for almost all of the major procedural programming languages (only BASIC is missing). It's a relatively simple matter for an experienced programmer to learn PL/SQL and start creating ORACLE7 applications right away. ORACLE7's support for Ada is unique among the PC-based C/S databases; Ada was designed by the U.S. government as a replacement for COBOL, and at some point in the future, all new applications designed for the U.S. government will have to be developed in it. ORACLE is the top RDBMS used by the federal government.

ORACLE7 has no real drawbacks—the current version addressed all the problems and limitations of ORACLE Version 6.0 and is at the forefront of technology. If you have the computing and financial resources, you'll find ORACLE7 to be about the best platform for company-wide Client/Server databases available today. I recommend it without hesitation.

I can't finish this discussion without crediting the folks who wrote ORACLE's manuals. Not only do they cover every aspect of setting up, running, using, and programming for ORACLE, but they do it in a clear and concise manner. The manuals are so well written that they can serve as an introductory text to many of the concepts covered in this book, such as SQL, the Relational model, and the Client/Server database architecture. As I was reading them, I was tempted to include them in Appendix C as a reference for further reading—they're that good. Unfortunately, the only way to get the manuals is to buy the product.

Table 4.5

ORACLE7 Server Quick Summary

PRODUCT INFORMATION	
Name	ORACLE7 Server 7.0
Vendor	Oracle Corp.
OPERATING SYSTEMS	
On Database Server	OS/2 2.0 or higher, Windows NT 3.1 or higher, NetWare 3.11 or higher
On LAN server	MS LAN Manager and Windows NT Advanced Server; IBM LAN Server; Novell NetWare 3.11 or higher; or any network supporting NetBIOS, Named Pipes, DECNet, or TCP/IP
On Workstations	DOS 3.1 or higher, OS/2 2.0 or higher, Windows NT 3.1 or higher
MINIMUM REQUIREMENTS	
RAM on Server	12Mb
RAM on Workstation	640k DOS; 6Mb OS/2; 12Mb Windows NT
Disk Space on Server	30Mb
UTILITIES PROVIDED	
Administration Utility	Yes
Interactive User Utility	Yes
Operating Systems/Environments Supported	DOS 3.1 or higher, Windows NT 3.1 or higher, OS/2 2.0 or higher
NATIVE LANGUAGES	
ANSI SQL	Level 2 with Integrity Enhancement
DB2 SQL Extensions	Yes
Other SQL Extensions	Yes
Non-SQL Language	No
MAXIMUMS	
Database Size	Limited by disk space
Column Size	2G

MAXIMUMS	
Row Size	2G
# of Columns in Row	254 columns
# of Rows in Table	Limited by disk space
# of Rows per Database	Limited by disk space
# of Tables per Database	Limited by disk space
# of Views per Database	Unlimited
# of Tables per View	Unlimited, with maximum 254 columns per view

■ Watcom SQL 4.0

Watcom SQL is a relative newcomer to the C/S database field—the industry first heard of it in 1993 when Powersoft began bundling a single-user copy of Watcom SQL 3.0 with every copy of PowerBuilder. Watcom SQL is a moderately priced, low- to mid-range DBMS, with versions that run on DOS, Windows, Windows NT, OS/2, and NetWare. In early 1994, Watcom International Corp. was acquired by Powersoft (which has since merged with SYBASE), though it remains a separate division.

Version 4.0 was released in late 1994, concurrent with PowerBuilder 4.0. It added a number of features previously only seen in the high-end RDBMSs.

Significant Features

Probably the most significant feature of the Class 2 Watcom SQL is its support for multiple platforms. 16-bit versions are available for DOS and Windows 3.0 or higher, and 32-bit versions are available for OS/2 2.0 or higher, NetWare 3.11 or higher, and Windows NT 3.1 or higher. Every version is compatible with the others—databases created in one can be easily moved to another, and a front-end application for one can access any of the others. This makes Watcom SQL a fully scalable PC-based database server.

Watcom SQL 4.0 includes support for stored procedures, triggers, and built-in RI. It also has bi-directional scrollable cursors (similar to those in SQLBase), full transaction processing, and a cost-based query optimizer. Both the scrollable cursors and views are updatable, which is still a rare feature in RDBMSs.

Watcom SQL uses ODBC drivers to access the server, which makes it compatible with any ODBC-capable front-end application. It supports on-line backups, but to disk files instead of directly to tape. The disk files can be copied to tape after they're created.

Hardware and Software Requirements

Watcom SQL runs under DOS 3.1 or higher, Windows 3.1 or higher, OS/2 2.0 or higher, Windows NT 3.1 or higher, and NetWare 3.11 or higher. Its system requirements are minimal, needing only 3Mb RAM for all versions, and approximately 5Mb disk space.

Watcom SQL uses its own network protocol, which runs on top of whatever native protocols the NOS supports, though NetBIOS is preferred. It uses ODBC as its programming interface.

Native SQL Language

Watcom SQL's native language is compliant with ANSI SQL Level 2 with Integrity Enhancements. It also supports some of the ANSI 92 SQL referential integrity features, including cascading and null deletes.

Front-ends Provided

Watcom SQL 4.0 comes with its own administration and direct access utility, also called ISQL. Both DOS and Windows versions are included in the package. The Windows version of ISQL is shown in Figure 4.4; SQL statements are entered in the bottom window, and the results appear in the top. The center window lets you monitor how the database optimized the query, which lets you further tune the SQL statements for best performance.

Figure 4.4

Watcom SQL 4.0's administration and access utility is also called ISQL.

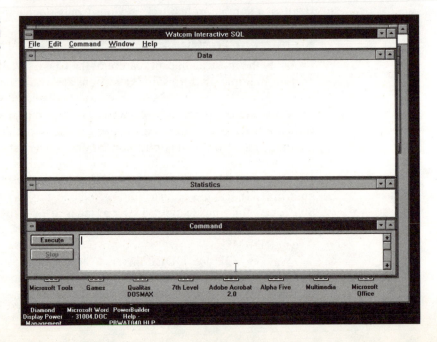

The package also includes a character-mode front-end builder called ACME, for Application Creation Made Easy. ACME isn't designed for more than creating simple front-ends. Watcom SQL's real, high-end front-end builder is PowerBuilder, covered in Chapter 10.

Advantages and Disadvantages

Watcom SQL has a simple goal—bringing the power of Client/Server databases to the masses. It fulfills this goal quite well by being a moderately priced database server that provides advanced RDBMS features and capabilities. Its support for the ANSI SQL standards and availability on all of the standard PC-based operating systems makes it an excellent product for building small to mid-sized C/S systems that can grow as your needs change. You can start small with a Windows-based server and easily move up to OS/2, Windows NT, or NetWare as your databases get larger and more demanding of system resources.

It's scalable, but also limited in how far you can go. Watcom SQL is built for features, not speed, and its performance begins to suffer when more than about 25 users access the database, regardless of the platform. It has no connectivity options to other databases, and you can't use it to move beyond a PC-based platform. Watcom does provide tools to dump the entire database, including the schema and the data, to a file; the file is constructed as ANSI SQL statements, so it can be used to recreate the database on a different platform. While this works, it isn't straightforward or simple.

However, I must say that I personally like Watcom SQL 4.0 a lot and wouldn't hesitate to recommend it for small C/S systems. Its moderate cost and advanced features make it a great product for beginners to learn the ins and outs of C/S programming.

Table 4.6

Watcom SQL Quick Summary

PRODUCT INFORMATION	
Name	Watcom SQL 4.0
Vendor	Watcom International Corp. (a subsidiary of Powersoft Corp.)
OPERATING SYSTEMS	
On Database Server	DOS 3.1 or higher, Windows 3.1 or higher, OS/2 2.0 or higher, Windows NT 3.1 or higher, NetWare 3.11 or higher
On LAN server	MS LAN Manager, Windows for Workgroups, Windows NT Advanced Server; IBM LAN Server; Novell NetWare 3.12 or higher; or any network supporting NetBIOS

**Table 4.6
(Continued)**

Watcom SQL Quick
Summary

OPERATING SYSTEMS	
On Workstations	DOS 3.1 or higher, Windows 3.1 or higher
MINIMUM REQUIREMENTS	
RAM on Server	3Mb
RAM on Workstation	640k DOS; 4Mb Windows
Disk Space on Server	5Mb
Administration Utility	Yes
Interactive User Utility	Yes
Operating Systems/Environments Supported	DOS 3.1 or higher, Windows 3.1 or higher
NATIVE LANGUAGES	
ANSI SQL	Level 2 with Integrity Enhancement
DB2 SQL Extensions	No
Other SQL Extensions	Yes
Non-SQL Language	No
MAXIMUMS	
Database Size	2G per file, 12 files per database
Column Size	No limit for individual columns; tables limited to 2G in a single file
Row Size	Limited by table size
# of Columns in Row	999 columns
# of Rows in Table	Limited by table size
# of Rows per Database	Limited by disk space
# of Tables per Database	32,767 tables
# of Views per Database	Unlimited
# of Tables per View	Unlimited

■ XDB-Enterprise Server

XDB System's claim to fame has always been products and toolkits that let developers create on a PC DB2 applications that can easily be ported to the mainframe once they're completely designed and debugged. What many potential users may not know is that XDB also sells a PC-based database server that's 100 percent compatible with DB2; it can be used either to share data with DB2 databases or as a platform for downsizing them.

Significant Features

Ironically, XDB-Enterprise Server Version 4 is more compatible with DB2 than IBM's DB2/2. This Class 2 RDBMS is 100 percent DB2 compatible in both SQL syntax and database structures. XDB-Server includes DB2's declarative referential integrity and domain integrity, and user-created rules can be added to the database to provide further data integrity.

XDB-Enterprise Server is available in OS/2 2.x and Windows NT 3.x versions; an NLM version is under development for release sometime in 1995. Stand-alone DOS and Windows 3.x versions are available for creating DB2 applications on a PC. The XDB-LINK package provides the capability of accessing DB2 databases from PC workstations running the stand-alone engine, or workstations using any of XDB's DB2 development tools.

XDB-Enterprise Server supports a maximum of 256 total users per server. It also implements DB2's database location independence, which lets users transparently access multiple XDB-Enterprise Servers at the same time. The server software's main screen includes a real-time monitor that lets the DBA examine the database's current workload so that it can be tuned as needed, as shown in Figure 4.5.

Hardware and Software Requirements

The DOS stand-alone version of XDB-Enterprise Server requires an 80386 or better running DOS 3.1 or higher and at least 1.5Mb of RAM; the Windows stand-alone version runs under 3.1 or better, with 4Mb RAM. The OS/2 and Windows NT versions need at least an 80486 with 16Mb of RAM; the NLM version will also require at least 16Mb of RAM on an 80486 running NetWare 3.12 or better. All versions take approximately 10Mb of disk space.

The OS/2 and Windows NT versions use either Named Pipes or NetBIOS as their network protocol, though XDB recommends using NetBIOS when accessing an XDB-Enterprise Server across a NetWare LAN. The other versions use NetBIOS as their communication protocol.

Native SQL Language

Almost everything I said previously about DB2/2's SQL applies to XDB-Enterprise Server, the major difference being that XDB is 100 percent DB2 compatible. In addition, XDB offers the developer the option to switch the SQL syntax to SQL/DS or ANSI Level 2 compatibility modes, letting her use the XDB tools to create applications for other back-ends.

Figure 4.5

XDB-Enterprise Server's
real-time monitor screen
lets the DBA keep an eye
on the server's
performance.

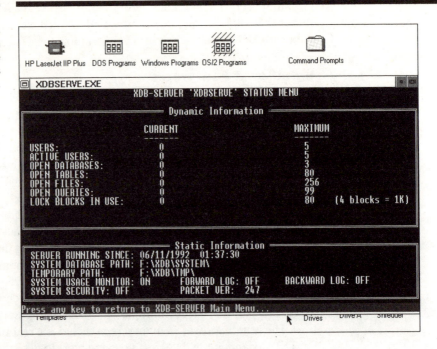

Front-end Processors Provided

XDB-Enterprise Server includes a character-based, full-screen interactive SQL query utility that can be used to create and access databases on the server. No other front-end processors are provided in the base package.

XDB does sell a number of other packages that can be used to create DB2 or XDB-Enterprise Server applications. XDB-SQL Plus provides a report writer, menu generator, forms manager, and additional 4GL for creating XDB-Enterprise Server applications. XDB-Workbench for DB2 lets developers create COBOL applications on a PC that access (or can be ported to) the mainframe. XDB-Tools is a prototyping toolkit that offers the same services as XDB-SQL Plus to DB2 programmers.

The XDB-C and XDB-Windows SDK give C programmers the ability to write DOS or Windows 3.x-based applications that can access the XDB-Enterprise Server.

Advantages and Disadvantages

XDB-Enterprise Server's greatest advantage is its 100 percent DB2 compatibility, which makes it an even better choice for IBM shops than IBM's own product, despite its extra cost. XDB-Enterprise Server is ideal for use as a cost-efficient base for creating applications that access DB2 databases, and it can also be used as a downsizing platform. Unfortunately, it doesn't yet have all the distributed processing capabilities present in IBM's products.

XDB-Enterprise Server also suffers from a lack of third-party, front-end support; there are very few client applications outside of XDB's own. This can probably be attributed to XDB's emphasis on supporting DB2 applications development. In this light, XDB is a better choice for companies looking to integrate or downsize DB2 databases than for those seeking an overall Client/Server solution.

Table 4.7

XDB-Enterprise Server
Quick Summary

PRODUCT INFORMATION	
Name	XDB-Enterprise Server 4.0
Vendor	XDB Systems, Inc.
OPERATING SYSTEMS	
On Database Server	OS/2 2.0 or higher, Windows NT 3.1 or higher
On LAN server	MS LAN Manager and Windows NT Advanced Server; IBM LAN Server; Novell NetWare 3.11 or higher; or any network supporting NetBIOS
On Workstations	DOS 3.1 or higher, OS/2 2.0 or higher, Windows NT 3.1 or higher
MINIMUM REQUIREMENTS	
RAM on Server	16Mb
RAM on Workstation	640k DOS; 6Mb OS/2; 12Mb Windows NT
Disk Space on Server	10Mb
UTILITIES PROVIDED	
Administration Utility	Yes
Interactive User Utility	Yes
Operating Systems/Environments Supported	DOS 3.1 or higher, Windows NT 3.1 or higher, OS/2 2.0 or higher
NATIVE LANGUAGES	
ANSI SQL	Level 2 with Integrity Enhancement
DB2 SQL Extensions	Yes
Other SQL Extensions	Yes

**Table 4.7
(Continued)**

XDB-Enterprise Server
Quick Summary

NATIVE LANGUAGES	
Non-SQL Language	No
MAXIMUMS	
Database Size	Limited by disk space
Column Size	4,056 bytes
Row Size	32,767 bytes
# of Columns in Row	400 columns
# of Rows in Table	Limited by disk space
# of Rows per Database	Limited by disk space
# of Tables per Database	Unlimited
# of Views per Database	Unlimited
# of Tables per View	Unlimited, with maximum 400 columns per view

■ Ingres Server for OS/2

Ingres has always been one of Oracle's biggest competitors in the VAX and UNIX RDBMS markets, and its QUEL language was one of the strongest competitors to SQL as the standard relational language during the early 1980s. Even though Dr. Codd (the developer of the Relational model) considers QUEL to be the better relational language to this day, for better or worse, SQL has become the industry standard. Ingres has since added SQL to its products, and the company now concentrates on creating both technically proficient database servers and advanced client application tools.

Unfortunately, Ingres has had a somewhat checkered history since the first edition of this book. In 1993, it was purchased by The ASK Group, who updated it to Version 6.4. Then in 1994, The ASK Group was purchased by Computer Associates International (CA). One of CA's first actions was to pull all of the PC-based Ingres products from the market due to serious bugs. At the time of this writing, CA has not yet announced when they'll be re-releasing Ingres Server. The information in this section is based on the last release of Version 6.4.

Significant Features

Ingres was the original developer of cost-based optimization in a RDBMS, a feature that has since become a standard throughout the industry. Their optimizer is still considered the industry's best, because it translates the SQL queries into a syntax-independent, set-based algebra that ensures the query will be performed as fast as possible, regardless of how it's constructed.

Ingres's Class 2 DBMS also supports the creation of user data-types and user-defined functions, and it has the strongest domain integrity features of any RDBMS. It supports stored procedures, which Ingres calls "rules;" Version 6.4 added the ability to access rules interactively. 6.4 also added support for triggers and full referential integrity.

INGRES is unique in that it supports four different types of data-storage methods. These are determined by the DBA when a table is created and can be changed at any time as the table grows or changes. Heap storage is designed for tables that will usually be accessed sequentially, and hashed storage is for fast random access with no keys or indices. ISAM storage is based on a key field in which the index is static, such as a table primarily used for data lookups, and BTree storage is designed for random access on indexed tables that are constantly being modified or updated.

It also supports event alerters, which let the DBA set triggers that automatically generate an external event. This is similar to the extended procedures found in the Windows NT version of Microsoft SQL Server, though Ingres pioneered the concept.

Users of the OS/2 version can access non-OS/2 INGRES databases through the INGRES/Star server, a UNIX-based distributed database server. Version 6.4 removed the 32-client limitation found in earlier OS/2 versions.

Hardware and Software Requirements

INGRES Server for OS/2 requires OS/2 2.0 or higher, running on a 386 with at least 16Mb of RAM. The database requires 100Mb of disk space. An NLM version is under development.

The requirements for DOS clients are also high; the INGRES/NET software that's needed for client communications requires at least an 80286 system with 2Mb of RAM, and take up an incredible 6.3Mb of hard-disk space. The INGRES/NET drivers work with NetBIOS, NetWare's IPX/SPX, and TCP/IP.

Native SQL Language

Ingres provides two versions of SQL; INGRES/SQL, which is ANSI Level 2 with Integrity Enhancements compatible, and Open SQL, a subset that can be used with the INGRES/Gateway product to query non-INGRES RDBMSs.

For backwards compatibility (and for those who still prefer it), Ingres continues to support QUEL across its entire line of products. Additional support is available for EQUEL, an enhanced version of QUEL that almost doubles the number of commands.

Front-end Processors Provided

INGRES comes with a rather limited OS/2 character-based, front-end administration tool that shows its VAX/VMS roots; the interface feels like it belongs on a dumb terminal not on a PC. Doing even the simplest task, such as adding users to the database, requires a number of steps that don't seem to have any logical flow.

A command line SQL query tool is also included, to provide administrators and users with a simple way of executing SQL statements. It also shows its terminal-based roots by its command syntax, which is neither intuitive nor well documented. Ingres has a number of DOS and Windows 3.x-based tool-kits that are much easier to use than the provided utilities. However, they cost extra and are very resource intensive on the client side.

DOS versions of these utilities are included in the INGRES/Net client-side package. Custom access for creating client programs in C is provided by the INGRES/Embedded Language toolkit, which is also available separately.

Advantages and Disadvantages

Ingres Server for OS/2 is as technically advanced as its UNIX siblings—in fact, it's still one of the very few RDBMSs that provides strict adherence to the Relational model. Unfortunately, it has one big disadvantage at this time—you can't buy it.

It does have the potential to become a serious competitor to SQL Server and ORACLE7 when it's re-released by CA. Only time will tell for sure.

Table 4.8

Ingres Server for OS/2
Quick Summary

PRODUCT INFORMATION	
Name	Ingres Server for OS/2 6.4
Vendor	Computer Associates International
OPERATING SYSTEMS	
On Database Server	OS/2 2.0 or higher
On LAN server	MS LAN Manager and Windows NT Advanced Server; IBM LAN Server; Novell NetWare 3.11 or higher; or any network supporting NetBIOS

**Table 4.8
(Continued)**

Ingres Server for OS/2
Quick Summary

OPERATING SYSTEMS	
On Workstations	DOS 3.1 or higher, OS/2 2.0 or higher, Windows 3.1 or higher
MINIMUM REQUIREMENTS	
RAM on Server	16Mb
RAM on Workstation	2Mb DOS; 6Mb OS/2; 12Mb Windows NT
Disk Space on Server	100Mb
UTILITIES PROVIDED	
Administration Utility	Yes
Interactive User Utility	Yes
Operating Systems/Environments Supported	OS/2 2.0 or higher; DOS versions available as part of the client-side package
NATIVE LANGUAGES	
ANSI SQL	Level 2 with Integrity Enhancement
DB2 SQL Extensions	Subset
Other SQL Extensions	Yes
Non-SQL Language	Yes, QUEL
MAXIMUMS	
Database Size	Limited by disk space
Column Size	2,000 bytes
Row Size	2,008 bytes
# of Columns in Row	127 columns
# of Rows in Table	Limited by disk space
# of Rows per Database	Limited by disk space
# of Tables per Database	Limited by disk space
# of Views per Database	Limited by disk space
# of Tables per View	Unlimited, with maximum 127 columns per view

■ Class 3 C/S Databases for .DBF Files

Interest in expanding to the Client/Server architecture has extended into the dBASE-compatible world. There's a tremendous amount of PC-based data in the .DBF format, and companies whose primary databases reside in that format want to benefit from C/S computing without having to replace or re-program all their existing applications. Three vendors have announced and released server databases that provide Class 3 C/S functions for .DBF files. These database servers don't provide all of the benefits of the Client/Server architecture, and they also don't add much more than a limited amount of data integrity services to dBASE-compatible applications. However, they're perfectly acceptable for situations in which the power of a full C/S database is unnecessary. They're also good options for companies without the hardware or manpower resources to move existing databases and applications to a new platform.

ExtendBase for NetWare 386

ExtendBase for NetWare 386 from Extended Systems was the first dBASE-compatible database server to reach the market. It runs as an NLM under NetWare 3.11 or higher, requiring a mere 200k of RAM on the server. Extend-Base uses dBASE-compatible programming commands to index, query, and report on dBASE and Clipper .DBF files residing on the server.

Four different access interfaces are included in the package. ExtendBase USE emulates the dBASE dot prompt, allowing experienced dBASE users to access the data on the server by entering direct commands as though the data resided in a local database. The ExtendBase Query Processor provides a menu-driven query interface for users unfamiliar with dBASE-compatible syntax. Extended Systems also provides a Lotus 1-2-3 DataLens interface module which lets 1-2-3 users query and extract data from the server to a local spreadsheet. (See Chapter 9 for more details on DataLens.)

ExtendBase's real power arises from its Clipper interface. (Clipper is a popular dBASE-compatible programming environment and code compiler.) The ExtendBase Clipper Interface adds a few simple commands to the Clipper language; the programmer just modifies the code where needed to access the remote data and recompiles the program. Executable Clipper programs can then act as clients to the ExtendBase Server. Benchmark tests performed by *PC Magazine* and others have shown that moving .DBF files to an Extend-Base server generally reduces the time required to query or report on a database to a tenth of that required by dBASE or Clipper.

Advantage Xbase Server

Formerly known as XBase/Server from Megabase Systems, Advantage Xbase Server from Extended Systems is a Clipper-compatible .DBF database server that runs under DOS. Advantage Xbase Server, which requires a dedicated machine with at least 1Mb of RAM, runs on a Novell NetWare 3.11 or better LAN.

Databases on the Advantage Xbase Server can be accessed from any Clipper application. It adds a measure of data integrity through built-in security procedures, such as user IDs and an active database dictionary that implements some referential integrity features.

Because it's based on DOS, Advantage Xbase Server isn't designed for large databases or large numbers of users. Its low resource requirements make it ideal for small networks (generally under 20 users), which can benefit from the increased performance and security of a Client/Server system.

Quadbase-SQL Server

The most interesting of these three products is the Quadbase-SQL Server from Quadbase Systems. It brings sophisticated C/S and relational capabilities to .DBF files residing on the server. The databases can be accessed either through its own ANSI Level 2-compatible SQL language, or from any front-end that supports ODBC.

Quadbase-SQL also provides more data integrity support than the other products in this class. It does so by running in "catalog mode," which prevents other dBASE-compatible programs from accessing the .DBF files while Quadbase is running. "Noncatalog mode" lets Quadbase share its database files with other applications and programs. It also provides multiuser concurrency control, limited referential integrity, and true transaction processing through a transaction log.

Quadbase-SQL comes in two versions—a high-end version that runs under Windows NT, and a low-end version that runs under Windows 3.0 or higher. The NT version requires 8Mb RAM, 10Mb disk space, and a NetWare 3.11 or higher LAN. The Windows version needs 4Mb RAM and 3Mb disk space and runs on any LAN that supports NetBIOS.

- *Evaluating Client/Server Databases for UNIX Workstations and Minicomputers*
- *INGRES for UNIX and VAX/VMS*
- *ORACLE7 Server for UNIX and VAX/VMS*
- *SYBASE SQL Server 10.0 for UNIX and VAX/VMS*
- *Gupta SQLBase for UNIX*
- *INFORMIX-OnLine 6.0*

- *InterBase 4.0*

5

Client/Server Databases for UNIX Workstations and Minicomputers

SUPERSERVERS AND MINICOMPUTERS, REGARDLESS OF WHETHER they run UNIX or a proprietary operating system, fall into the middle of the computer spectrum with respect to power and number of users. With PCs at the low end and mainframes at the high end, it's convenient to refer to the systems discussed here and in Chapter 6 as midrange computers.

With two exceptions, all of the RDBMSs considered in this chapter have PC-based versions, so many of the features, advantages, and disadvantages are the same. Rather than duplicate information already covered, I'll highlight the differences between the two versions and the advantages, if any, of using the UNIX version over the PC version.

■ Evaluating Client/Server Databases for UNIX Workstations and Minicomputers

If you're thinking of adding a UNIX DBMS to an existing PC-based LAN, you'll find yourself confronted with a bewildering array of hardware and software choices. In addition to choosing the DBMS that fits your needs, you'll have to find a compatible platform. Then you'll have to determine the size of the platform, which can range from a desktop RISC workstation to a minicomputer or a superserver.

Or, if you already have UNIX systems, you may wish to extend their reach to the PCs in your organization. You'll find yourself faced with an entirely different set of considerations, not the least of which is choosing which of several methods to use to enable the UNIX and PC networks to talk to each other.

Either way, you'll find that adapting a UNIX-based DBMS to a Client/Server system can be a much more complex undertaking than setting up the same DBMS on a PC platform. Paying careful attention to both the general and the product-specific information in this chapter can help you successfully evaluate your options while avoiding some of the common pitfalls.

Advantages and Disadvantages

UNIX-based systems comprise less than a quarter of the C/S market. Why don't they have a larger market share, especially when most of the PC-based RDBMS servers were ported down from databases that ran under UNIX? No conclusive study has been done to date; however, based on both my experiences in designing and setting up C/S systems, and on numerous conversations with others doing the same, I can make some educated guesses.

One major reason is UNIX's reputation as a hard-to-learn, hard-to-use "techie" operating system, particularly among those most familiar with PCs. This poor reputation is not altogether undeserved, though the rise of UNIX-based GUIs such as Motif and Open Look have given UNIX the same easy-to-use advantages that Windows and OS/2 offer to PC users.

Another reason is cost, both in real dollars and in support resources. Prices for the entry-level (low-end) superservers and minicomputers generally start at around $20,000 to $25,000, and these systems are very limited in power and the number of users they support. High-end systems, which can support hundreds of users and/or multi-gigabyte databases, can run into the hundreds of thousands of dollars. As I mentioned in Chapter 2, the proprietary nature of these systems limits the market for third-party, add-on equipment, so options such as more RAM or disk space cost much more than the PC equivalents.

As for support, you'll find a smaller pool of UNIX-trained personnel to choose from, which means paying higher salaries for experienced personnel or spending more on training your existing technical staff.

UNIX software packages are also more expensive than their PC counterparts, due to both the smaller market (less demand) and the fact that the UNIX versions are multiuser. Another software problem is the lack of a standard version of UNIX (though this situation is slowly changing); every hardware vendor has its own customized version, and slight incompatibilities between different versions force the RDBMS vendors to maintain numerous versions of their products. Software costs are a factor for database servers too, because most of the Client/Server RDBMS vendors charge considerably higher prices for their UNIX versions.

Many RISC workstation vendors are touting models in the price range of high-end PCs as alternatives to PC-based systems. However, these RISC systems are really designed as single-user intelligent terminals on a network, rather than as database servers. They come with the bare minimum of RAM and hard-disk space needed to run UNIX. A standard RISC workstation would be acceptable as a client for a C/S database but not as a server. The high-end workstations that have the power to be database servers are more properly defined as RISC-based superservers.

The final reason for UNIX's smaller market share has to do with network protocols. The primary protocol for UNIX systems is TCP/IP and, until recently, the major PC LANs didn't support it as a native protocol. PCs on a network could use TCP/IP to communicate with UNIX systems, but only as intelligent terminals to the host system. In the early 1990s, Novell, Microsoft, and IBM began offering TCP/IP as a native protocol on their respective LANs, giving PC clients the ability to communicate with UNIX-based database servers. Soon the protocol problem will no longer be an issue.

However, some vendors's TCP/IP implementations take up a significant amount of RAM on PC/MS-DOS systems, so it may not be feasible (or even possible) to run TCP/IP all the time. There are gateways available that translate the common PC LAN protocols to TCP/IP, which can be used as an alternative solution.

With all these drawbacks, why would anyone want to use a UNIX system as a database server? There are a number of reasons; most important, superservers and minicomputers are still much more powerful than the top-end PCs.

This extra power translates into support for more users. Most PC-based C/S databases can realistically support no more than about 100 users per server, while a high-end UNIX system can support four to five times that number.

Speed is another reason. While the high-end PCs are closing the gap with RISC workstations, superservers and minicomputers are still much faster, which translates into faster response times for the same number of users. The higher speeds result from a number of factors, including the faster RISC chips or proprietary CPUs in the midrange systems. These systems can also use much more RAM than PCs—256Mb to 512Mb of RAM is not uncommon in the high-end minicomputers and superservers. This extra RAM provides the DBMS more room to work in memory, reducing the bottleneck of disk accesses for virtual memory paging or for querying commonly used data.

Another factor related to speed is the advanced forms of multiprocessing supported by most minicomputers and superservers. Multiprocessing means what the name implies—the system has more than one CPU, and the CPUs split different system tasks among themselves under the control of the operating system. There are two types of multiprocessing systems: asymmetrical and symmetrical. In an asymmetrical multiprocessing system, different CPUs handle different subsystems (that is, one CPU manages the central processing while another CPU runs the DBMS), and each CPU is dedicated to its own task. While asymmetrical multiprocessing systems are now available in all sizes of computers, symmetrical multiprocessing remains in the domain of midrange and mainframe systems.

In a symmetrical multiprocessing system, each CPU can handle any processing task independent of the other CPUs, as directed by the operating system. For example, a symmetrical DBMS will route a user query to any available CPU, which is obviously much faster than if one CPU has to handle all the queries. Symmetrical multiprocessing systems have recently been outpaced by parallel-processing systems in which single computation requests are split among different CPUs for processing; the answer arises from the combination of results received from the different CPUs. Parallel-processing systems are in the domain of supercomputers, which are the fastest computers available. While they hold great promise for the future as platforms for advances in artificial intelligence, currently they have little impact on the C/S market.

UNIX and the RISC versions of Windows NT are currently the only available operating systems that fully support symmetrical multiprocessing technology on a broad range of systems, offering advantages of power and speed for database servers. Just about all of the UNIX-based RDBMS vendors are committed to supporting multiprocessing in their software, so it appears that the midrange systems will retain their high-performance advantage in the foreseeable future. However, be aware that not all UNIX variants support multiprocessing. Applications have to include their own support for multiprocessing if the core operating system doesn't support it.

Another major advantage of midrange systems is their support for large amounts of disk space. Most PCs are currently limited to supporting less than 10G of disk space, and current PC-based C/S databases are limited by the operating systems to about 4G. Midrange systems usually start with 500Mb to 1G of disk space, and the higher-end systems easily support over 100G of hard-disk space. UNIX-based RDBMSs can take advantage of whatever disk space is available, so again, the midrange systems will have this advantage over PCs in the foreseeable future.

Security is also a factor in UNIX-based systems. When properly set up, a UNIX system can be as secure against unauthorized access as any proprietary minicomputer or mainframe operating system. The U.S. federal government is one of the largest UNIX users in the country. Under standards set by the Department of Defense, it has established a series of security ratings for use with classified data. The seven possible ratings are two-digit letter-number combinations, with the C-1 rating being the lowest and A-1 the highest. A UNIX system or DBMS must go through a rigorous certification process before it can claim one of the security rankings. Most UNIX systems qualify for one of the rankings, as does a special version of Windows NT.

The government has also created a standard API for programming applications, called POSIX. The POSIX standard is intended to make it easier to move an application from one platform to another. In theory, the source code for an application written using the POSIX API can simply be recompiled for a different platform without major modifications. In actual practice, though, the POSIX standard is still evolving, and incompatibilities still occur between different implementations. Also, the POSIX API only addresses character-mode applications, so it has fallen behind the market's move to GUIs somewhat. At some future point, every application written for government use will have to follow POSIX; however, it won't have a major impact on the DBMS market, as most vendors handle porting their product to other platforms, which bypasses the need for POSIX compliance. The POSIX standard will have more of an effect on front-end application development. Microsoft announced plans to include POSIX support in Windows NT, and IBM announced plans to release a POSIX version of OS/2, but neither company has fulfilled those plans as of this writing.

The concept of fault tolerance originated with the larger systems, and UNIX vendors were quick to add support for fault tolerant features such as disk mirroring, disk duplexing, and on-line backups. Many vendors also provide support for CPU fault tolerance, whereby a failing processor is locked out of the data stream, and tasks destined for the failed CPU are automatically directed to a different, still functioning CPU.

The final advantage of UNIX systems may, at first glance, not seem like an advantage at all—the fact that these systems are multiuser. While it may seem like heresy to say so in this book, not every database has to be a Client/Server database. There are many situations in which users only need access to the database and nothing more; a telephone order-taking department or warehouse inventory system comes to mind. The right solution for these circumstances may be a multiuser system with dedicated terminals; a full Client/Server system could possibly be overkill, and may well introduce unnecessary complexities and expense.

The UNIX-based RDBMSs covered in this chapter give you the best of both worlds: They can be directly accessed through terminals by those who need database access only; and, at the same time, they can act as a database server to the folks in the administrative departments, who use their PCs to track and analyze the whole company's business.

Special Considerations

Running a Client/Server system on a UNIX-based system presents an almost completely different set of considerations than running one entirely on PCs. Again, the information in this section should be considered only a starting point for the questions you need to ask when designing your own system.

- **Hardware:** Do you have an existing midrange system that you want to turn into a database server? Doing so may cause more problems than it's worth, as a number of studies of different Client/Server platforms have shown over the years. Many older minicomputers can't match the power of current high-end PCs, and the cost of upgrading them is too high when compared with the extra power gained in the upgrade. If your existing systems are more than five years old, you should consider replacing them completely or moving the database server to a different platform. However, the number of users you need to support may prevent a move to a smaller platform, so a newer version of the existing system is your only choice.

  If you're designing a completely new C/S system, getting the right hardware is less of a problem. Midrange system vendors and VARs usually have a lot of experience configuring complete systems that include all the necessary parts, such as sufficient RAM, disk capacity, and backup systems. However, configuring C/S systems may also be very new to some vendors, and they might not have a lot of experience in the field yet. It would be a wise move to contact other customers and talk to them about their experiences with the vendor before making a final decision.

- **Compatibility with existing networks:** This is the most critical area and the one where the most mistakes are made. First, be sure that the hardware you're going to use supports the same network topology (for example, Ethernet or Token Ring) that you run your LANs on. While there are bridges that can connect different topologies together, using one may be an unnecessary complication. The process is much smoother when all the systems share the same topology.

As mentioned previously, network protocol is a factor in setting up a C/S database on a midrange system. If your existing LANs can't support TCP/IP as a native protocol, you'll have to factor in the additional costs of either upgrading or replacing them. Upgrading may not be a big problem, but replacing them can carry many hidden costs, especially those involved in retraining both users and support staff on the new LAN software. If your LAN software does support a version of TCP/IP, make sure it's compatible with the TCP/IP used by the UNIX system. Every vendor implements TCP/IP in a slightly different way, and the differences can eventually cause problems that are hard to track down.

- **Support and training:** Most vendors of midrange systems have been around a long time and have extensive support operations that are well equipped to handle their customers's needs. Support plans usually include on-site vendor engineers who get the system up and running, and training classes for in-house staff to keep them running.

  However, such support doesn't come cheaply, so make sure you find out all the different plans the vendor has available. Support plans are usually based on response time—a plan that provides four-hour response time from support engineers can be considerably more costly to you than one that guarantees eight-hour response time. Make sure you factor in how much downtime you can afford when you're comparing the prices of these different plans.

  As with PC-based systems, find out where the vendor's training classes are held and include any transportation costs in your planning.

- **Performance monitoring:** This is much less a consideration with the midrange and large systems. These systems have been around for years (and even decades) in one form or another, and numerous third-party performance monitors exist to supplement those built into the operating systems.

- **Front-end software:** This is a much more critical factor with the midrange and large systems. Many PC-based front-ends work fine with the PC versions of the DBMSs but won't work (or require special software to work) with the UNIX-based versions. Many front-ends require an additional gateway system to communicate with the non-PC versions, which adds extra hardware and software costs to the price of the system. Make sure you find out which front-ends are supported before making a final decision on the DBMS software.

Advice and Tips

Given the state of the Client/Server market, the best advice I can offer about UNIX-based systems is to ascertain whether you really need the features such systems provide. Various benchmark tests run by *PC Magazine*, *PC Week*, and others have shown that PC-based systems are in many cases surpassing the performance of all but the higher-end superservers and minicomputers, at considerably less cost.

Midrange systems still offer the advantage of supporting a greater number of users per system, though this may diminish as distributed database technology makes further advances. This is where scalability can play a significant role in your decision. Choosing a DBMS that has a PC-based version will make it easier to migrate to a distributed system in the future.

The other advantage of midrange systems is database size. While advances in hard-drive technology have made it possible for some high-end PCs to support up to about 20G of disk space (though the PC operating systems haven't yet caught up with this amount), it will be quite a few years before PCs can approach the 100G+ disk space that high-end superservers and minicomputers support. If you expect to have such large databases, opt for a midrange system running UNIX.

I would also recommend a UNIX-based midrange system if you expect to have large amounts of highly confidential data in your databases or if you need to meet POSIX standards. Though Windows NT supports some of the DOD security standards, it may still be some time before any PC-based systems are certified as matching the security and POSIX capabilities of a UNIX system.

Finally, don't forget that these midrange systems are multiuser and can be accessed equally by both dedicated terminals and PCs. The extra cost of a midrange system can sometimes be offset by the savings accrued by not having to give a PC to everyone who needs access to the database.

■ INGRES for UNIX and VAX/VMS

UNIX and VMS are the primary (and currently preferred) platforms for the INGRES RDBMS and distributed processing tools. The features detailed in this section are those that the UNIX and VAX/VMS versions of INGRES have in addition to those found in the OS/2 version.

Significant Features

Depending on the hardware platform, INGRES for UNIX can support 300 or more users accessing the database from both client systems and dedicated terminals.

The real strength of the Class 2 UNIX/VMS versions of INGRES lies in their support for distributed processing, both with other midrange INGRES systems and with other VAX/VMS or mainframe-based databases. The INGRES/Star database-integration server distributes database queries to multiple INGRES databases, while appearing as a single database to the client system. INGRES/Star supports: a distributed database dictionary, which splits the dictionary across database servers; distributed query optimization, which optimizes the SQL statements and commands for the most cost-effective execution on databases split across different systems; and distributed transactions with full two-phase commit, which means a transaction isn't considered successful until all the individual modifications on the different databases are successfully completed.

INGRES/Star can also communicate with the INGRES/Gateway, which provides seamless access to DEC Rdb and RMS databases running on a VAX, Hewlett-Packard AllBase databases running on HP systems, and DB2 or IMS databases running on an IBM mainframe. INGRES/Star and INGRES/Gateway are available for VMS and various flavors of UNIX, including ULTRIX, SunOS, and AIX.

Hardware and Software Requirements

As with all UNIX and VMS systems, the amount of RAM and disk space needed by INGRES varies from platform to platform; the minimum requirements are 8Mb RAM and 75Mb disk space. In addition to VAX/VMS, INGRES runs on over 30 versions of UNIX, including AT&T's System V, SunOS, IBM's AIX, DEC's ULTRIX, HP's HP-UX, and SCO UNIX. Ingres also offers versions specific to the European and Asian markets; those run on systems from Bull, Nixdorf, Siemens, and Olivetti, among others.

Communications Protocols

Communications between the clients and the server are provided by INGRES/Net running over TCP/IP for the UNIX versions, and DECNet or TCP/IP for the VMS version. INGRES/Net also supports NetBIOS, Named Pipes, and SPX/IPX for accessing the server from DOS and Windows clients.

Native SQL Language

The UNIX/VMS versions of INGRES also support INGRES/SQL, Open SQL, and both QUEL and EQUEL.

Front-end Processors Provided

Ingres provides UNIX and VMS versions of the same front-end tools that come with the OS/2 version. In addition, any of the DOS-based front-ends can be used with the appropriate INGRES/Net drivers.

Version 6.4 includes the Interactive Performance Monitor (IPM), an additional administrative tool that allows the DBA to monitor the performance of any INGRES database server or INGRES/Star server on the network.

For an additional cost, developers can purchase UNIX versions of INGRES/Tools to create INGRES front-ends for RISC workstations. Also available is INGRES/Vision, an application generator that helps speed the process of developing both Client/Server and terminal applications on DOS and UNIX systems. INGRES/Windows4GL lets programmers create Windows 3.x front-ends for any INGRES back-end.

INGRES/Tools is regarded as one of the better application development tools in the industry, and many DBMS vendors have licensed versions that can be used for developing applications for their own products.

Advantages and Disadvantages

In the past, some INGRES users reported that the company had a reputation for providing only average support for their products. This situation probably hasn't changed now that Computer Associates owns the product. CA has been in the software business for many years, but they don't have a good reputation for providing support.

Ingres's strength lies in its midrange system versions, though they suffer from the same lack of third-party, front-end support that the OS/2 version suffers from. However, their distributed processing capabilities give the UNIX or VAX/VMS versions an edge over the OS/2 version for downsizing from mainframe systems. If you prefer to use INGRES as your DBMS, and particularly if you prefer QUEL to SQL, the UNIX version is your best bet.

Table 5.1

INGRES for UNIX and
VMS Quick Summary

PRODUCT INFORMATION	
Name	INGRES Server for UNIX and VAX/VMS
Vendor	Computer Associates International
OPERATING SYSTEMS	
On Database Server	30+ versions of UNIX, including AIX, SunOS, AT&T System V; VAX/VMS

**Table 5.1
(Continued)**

INGRES for UNIX and
VMS Quick Summary

OPERATING SYSTEMS	
On LAN Server	Any network that supports SPX/IPX, NetBIOS, Named Pipes, TCP/IP, or DECNet
On Workstations	DOS 3.1 or higher, Windows 3.1 or higher, RISC-based UNIX
MINIMUM REQUIREMENTS	
RAM on Server	8Mb
RAM on Workstation	2Mb DOS; 6Mb OS/2; 8Mb UNIX
Disk Space on Server	75Mb
UTILITIES PROVIDED	
Administration Utility	Yes
Interactive User Utility	Yes
Operating Systems/Environments Supported	UNIX or VAX/VMS; DOS versions part of client-side package
NATIVE LANGUAGES	
ANSI SQL	Level 2 with Integrity Enhancement
DB2 SQL Extensions	Subset
Other SQL Extensions	Yes
Non-SQL Language	Yes, QUEL
MAXIMUMS	
Database Size	Limited by disk space
Column Size	2,000 bytes
Row Size	2,008 bytes
# of Columns in Row	127 columns
# of Rows in Table	Limited by disk space
# of Rows per Database	Limited by disk space
# of Tables per Database	Limited by disk space
# of Views per Database	Limited by disk space
# of Tables per View	Unlimited, with maximum 127 columns per view

■ ORACLE7 Server for UNIX and VAX/VMS

I can't say much more about the midrange system versions of ORACLE beyond what I already stated in Chapter 4. ORACLE is the dominant RDBMS in the UNIX and VMS markets, and the company has made sure that all versions share the same features.

Significant Features

ORACLE7's scalability and portability features continue through the midrange systems. In addition to VAX/VMS (Oracle's primary platform), versions are available for over 30 versions of UNIX, including all the major variations such as SCO, AT&T System V, AIX, and SunOS. Oracle also offers a version that runs under Data General's proprietary AOS-VS minicomputer operating system. Any ORACLE version can be interconnected to any other version through SQL*Net, which makes Oracle the leader in the move to distributed databases.

Like Ingres, Oracle also has a number of products that let ORACLE7 users access data on non-ORACLE databases. SQL*Connect to DB2 and SQL*Connect to SQL/DS link ORACLE databases to IBM's mainframe-based RDBMSs, and SQL*Connect to RMS links ORACLE7 to DEC's VAX/VMS-based RMS database.

As with any midrange system, the number of users per ORACLE7 database depends on the hardware and software platform.

Hardware and Software Requirements

Oracle's RDBMS runs on over 80 platforms, including DEC's VAX/VMS, IBM's mainframe VM and MVS, and all the major versions of UNIX, ranging from PCs to the high-end superservers. The resources required vary depending on hardware and software configurations; as with the PC-based versions, though, ORACLE7 usually has higher system resource requirements than the other RDBMSs in this chapter.

Communications Protocols

Oracle's SQL*Net provides Client/Server communications for all versions. UNIX and VAX/VMS versions of SQL*Net support TCP/IP, DECNet, APPC, and asynchronous (dial-in) connections. The Data General version of SQL*Net only supports TCP/IP. DOS, Windows, OS/2, and UNIX-based clients can use any of the supported protocols to communicate with any ORACLE database on the network.

SQL*Net 2.0 enhances ORACLE7's distributed processing capabilities by implementing Oracle's Transparent Network Substrate (TNS), a common communications API that's protocol-independent. By using TNS-based versions of SQL*Net with Oracle's MultiProtocol Interchange, clients can access different ORACLE databases without regard for the underlying network protocol and without loading multiple copies of SQL*Net.

Native SQL Language

Oracle's SQL and PL/SQL are compatible across the whole range of supported server systems. As long as the proper version of SQL*Net is used, any front-end that relies on Oracle's SQL or PL/SQL can talk to any ORACLE back-end.

Front-end Processors Provided

All versions of ORACLE7 include a version of SQLDBA appropriate to the particular operating system the server is running on. Any version of SQLDBA can talk to any ORACLE server using the proper version of SQL*Net. All of the programming tools and front-ends available for the PC-based versions of ORACLE support any of the back-end versions through SQL*Net. UNIX versions of the programming tools are also available.

Cross-platform compatibility is an important feature in Oracle's development tools, though it sometimes works better in theory than in practice. The source code precompilers make it fairly easy to move PL/SQL applications from one platform to another. However, many application programmers report finding incompatibilities between different platform versions of some of the other application development tools, such as SQL*Forms and SQL*ReportWriter. While none of the incompatibilities reported were major, they do require the developers to redesign or re-create portions of the application.

Advantages and Disadvantages

All of the midrange and mainframe system versions of ORACLE7 share the advantages of the PC-based versions: significant third-party front-end support, portable applications, and platform scalability. They also share the problem of somewhat high resource requirements.

At this time, there are no ORACLE connections to DEC's Rdb or IBM's IMS, so Ingres wins out if you need to share data with these systems. Otherwise, ORACLE7 is the preferred platform for downsizing large-system databases to the midrange systems. It's also the best platform currently available for integrating databases across a wide variety of platforms.

Table 5.2

ORACLE7 Quick Summary

PRODUCT INFORMATION	
Name	ORACLE7 Server 7.0
Vendor	Oracle Corp.
OPERATING SYSTEMS	
On Database Server	VAX/VMS; DG AOS-VS; 30+ versions of UNIX, including AIX, SunOS, ULTRIX, and AT&T System V
On LAN Server	Any network that supports DECNet or TCP/IP
On Workstations	DOS 3.1 or higher, OS/2 2.0 or higher, Windows NT 3.1 or higher, RISC-based UNIX (including the Motif GUI)
MINIMUM REQUIREMENTS	
RAM on Server	Varies by platform
RAM on Workstation	640k DOS; 6Mb OS/2; 12Mb Windows NT; 8Mb UNIX
Disk Space on Server	Varies by platform
UTILITIES PROVIDED	
Administration Utility	Yes
Interactive User Utility	Yes
Operating Systems/Environments Supported	DOS 3.1 or higher, Windows NT 3.1 or higher, OS/2 2.0 or higher, RISC-based UNIX
NATIVE LANGUAGES	
ANSI SQL	Level 2 with Integrity Enhancement
DB2 SQL Extensions	Yes
Other SQL Extensions	Yes
Non-SQL Language	No
MAXIMUMS	
Database Size	Limited by disk space
Column Size	2G
Row Size	2G
# of Columns in Row	254 columns

**Table 5.2
(Continued)**

ORACLE7 Quick Summary

MAXIMUMS	
# of Rows in Table	Limited by disk space
# of Rows per Database	Limited by disk space
# of Tables per Database	Limited by disk space
# of Views per Database	Unlimited
# of Tables per View	Unlimited, with maximum 254 columns per view

■ SYBASE SQL Server 10.0 for UNIX and VAX/VMS

Like ORACLE, SYBASE SQL Server 10.0 for UNIX and VAX/VMS shares the same features as the NLM version covered in Chapter 4, so there's not much information to add here. SQL Server is Oracle's closest rival on midrange systems.

Significant Features

SQL Server's most significant feature is the Virtual Server Architecture (VSA), SYBASE's native support for symmetrical multiprocessing systems. First announced in 1990, VSA versions of SQL Server are available for various multiprocessing systems such as DEC VAXs, Sequent superservers, Sun 4/400 and 4/600MP SPARCServers, and AT&T StarServerE systems. Independent benchmark tests have shown that SQL Server VSA provides 30 to 50 percent performance increases over the regular UNIX or VMS versions, as well as the ability to support up to 1,000 simultaneous database users.

SYBASE can also integrate data from other DBMSs with data on an SQL Server through its distributed processing Open Client/Open Server APIs. Open Client provides support for client access through different network protocols such as DECNet, TCP/IP, IPX/SPX, and Named Pipes. Open Server is the basis for a number of SYBASE Open Gateways to non-SYBASE RDBMSs, including Informix, INGRES, ORACLE, DEC Rdb and RMS, and IBM's DB2. The Open Gateways allow any SYBASE client to access the other databases as if they were SQL Servers.

SQL Server shares ORACLE's portability and scalability, offering versions for VAX/VMS and most major UNIX versions, such AIX, AT&T System V, and the NeXT MACH operating system. Different versions can be linked together through a common protocol such as TCP/IP, and distributed processing is provided through both the Open Server facilities and SQL Server's support for Remote Stored Procedures (discussed in Chapter 4).

Hardware and Software Requirements

SYBASE SQL Server 10.0 runs on VAX/VMS systems and also supports over 30 major UNIX versions. It's unique in being the only RDBMS to have a version for the NeXT line of UNIX workstations. It's also the only one with full support for symmetrical multiprocessing systems such as the Sequent superservers. As always, the amount of RAM and disk space needed varies depending on the platform.

Communication Protocols

SYBASE's Open Client API supports DECNet, TCP/IP, Named Pipes, IPX/SPX, and IBM's SNA. DOS and OS/2 clients can use DECNet or TCP/IP to communicate with SQL Servers on midrange systems.

Native SQL Language

All versions of SQL Server use TRANSACT-SQL as their native language, which includes support for stored procedures and triggers. SYBASE provides a number of UNIX-based application development tools that use APT-SQL, an enhanced 4GL version of SQL designed to speed application development.

As part of the System 10 family of products, SYBASE released a series of GUI-based development tools under the common name Momentum. These tools run on Windows 3.x, Macintosh, and UNIX Motif systems.

Front-end Processors Provided

All versions of SQL server come with the character-mode ISQL utility. When used with the appropriate protocols, any front-end that supports the PC-based versions of SQL Server can be used to query and administrate midrange system versions.

The SQL Toolset uses both TRANSACT-SQL and APT-SQL, and includes: the APT Workbench, a forms-based development environment that lets the programmer create user query forms by painting them on the screen; Data Workbench, a report writer that programmers can use to create custom reports by again painting them on the screen; and APT-Build, a code generator and applications prototyping utility. APT-Build is particularly handy, as the code generator simplifies the application development process by letting the programmer describe the steps the application is to take through a series of menus and pick lists; the generator then translates the actions into source code that can be modified or compiled as is. The applications prototyping utility lets the developer test different actions and user screens prior to generating the code to make sure they work as expected.

Support is available for writing front-end programs on UNIX workstations in C, COBOL, and FORTRAN. SYBASE also sells SQL Debug, a UNIX-based, interactive, source-level debugger for TRANSACT-SQL applications.

Advantages and Disadvantages

SQL Server 10.0 on UNIX and VAX/VMS shares many of the same advantages as the PC-based versions, including the most third-party, front-end support of any of the Client/Server database systems. The one advantage unique to SQL Server is its support through VSA for true symmetrical multiprocessing, which can be a significant factor when you're looking for a high performance system that has to support up to 1000 users on a single server. However, many multiprocessing system vendors recommend ORACLE over SQL Server, because ORACLE works with the operating system's multiprocessing services, instead of providing its own multiprocessing support that bypasses the OS. The ORACLE method is generally better because it's always safer, for both the applications and the data, to work with the operating system instead of bypassing it. Bypassing the OS can lead to incompatibilities with the underlying hardware or to system crashes that occur when other applications don't know what the OS or DBMS is doing.

SYBASE's Open Client and Open Server facilities also make it Oracle's strongest competitor in creating distributed processing databases. SYBASE's gateway support for Informix, INGRES, and ORACLE databases gives it a slight edge; however, if you want to integrate existing systems into a complete database network, either SYBASE or ORACLE7 can do the job. I have no reservations about recommending either of them.

Table 5.3

SYBASE SQL Server 10.0
for UNIX and VAX/VMS
Quick Summary

PRODUCT INFORMATION	
Name	SYBASE SQL Server 10.0
Vendor	SYBASE, Inc.
OPERATING SYSTEMS	
On Database Server	VAX/VMS; most major versions of UNIX, including AIX, NeXT MACH, AT&T System V, and Sequent Dynix
On LAN Server	Any network that supports DECNet or TCP/IP
On Workstations	DOS 3.0 or higher; Windows 3.0 or higher; Windows NT 3.1 or higher; OS/2 1.2 or higher; RISC-based UNIX (including the Open Look and Motif GUIs)

**Table 5.3
(Continued)**

SYBASE SQL Server 10.0
for UNIX and VAX/VMS
Quick Summary

MINIMUM REQUIREMENTS	
RAM on Server	Varies by platform
RAM on Workstation	640k DOS; 4Mb Windows; 6Mb OS/2; 12Mb Windows NT; 8Mb UNIX
Disk Space on Server	Varies by platform
UTILITIES PROVIDED	
Administration Utility	Yes
Interactive User Utility	Yes
Operating Systems/Environments Supported	DOS 3.0 or higher; RISC-based UNIX
NATIVE LANGUAGES	
ANSI SQL	Level 2 with Integrity Addendum
DB2 SQL Extensions	No
Other SQL Extensions	Yes
Non-SQL Language	No
MAXIMUMS	
Database Size	Limited by disk space
Column Size	Normally 1,962 bytes; "image" and "text" data types store 2G through pointers to external data
Row Size	1,962 bytes
# of Columns in Row	255 columns
# of Rows in Table	Limited by disk space
# of Rows per Database	Limited by disk space
# of Tables per Database	2 billion
# of Views per Database	Unlimited
# of Tables per View	Unlimited tables, but only 250 columns per view

■ Gupta SQLBase for UNIX

SQLBase remains unique by being the only C/S database in this category to start as a PC-based RDBMS and move up to the UNIX platform. The UNIX version supports the SunOS operating system.

Significant Features

SQLBase for UNIX's most significant feature is its price; it's one of the two cheapest database servers for UNIX. Except for the additional performance and database size provided by the Sun SPARCStation platform, SQLBase for UNIX is 100 percent identical to the PC-based versions.

The UNIX version also supports the same gateways/routers as the PC-based versions, providing some distributed database capabilities.

Hardware and Software Requirements

SQLBase for UNIX requires a Sun SPARCStation or SPARCServer running SunOS 4.1.1 or higher, with at least 4Mb of RAM for the entry-level, five-user version. The software takes up approximately 10Mb of hard-disk space.

Communications Protocols

DOS and OS/2 workstations can communicate with a SQLBase for UNIX server via TCP/IP. The Gupta communications drivers have the same high RAM requirement as the PC-based server drivers.

Native SQL Language

SQLBase for UNIX uses the same SQLTalk as the PC-based versions.

Front-end Processors Provided

Again, SQLBase for UNIX provides the same front-end utilities and capabilities as the PC-based versions. A UNIX version of SQLTalk/Character is also provided, and API libraries are available for creating UNIX front-ends in C or COBOL.

Advantages and Disadvantages

Gupta's SQLBase for UNIX's low price and front-end compatibility with the PC-based versions are its most notable advantages. The UNIX version is ideal for "upsizing" existing PC-based versions when greater performance or database size is needed.

The lack of versions for other midsize systems is a very significant disadvantage, so at this time I recommend SQLBase for UNIX only as an upgrade to existing PC-based servers that are reaching their performance limits.

Table 5.4

Gupta SQLBase for UNIX
Quick Summary

PRODUCT INFORMATION	
Name	SQLBase 5.2; SQLBase 6.0
Vendor	Gupta Corp.
OPERATING SYSTEMS	
On Database Server	SunOS 4.1.1 or higher
On LAN Server	Any network that supports TCP/IP
On Workstations	DOS 3.1 or higher; Windows 3.0 or higher; SunOS 4.1.1 or higher
MINIMUM REQUIREMENTS	
RAM on Server	4Mb
RAM on Workstation	640k DOS; 4Mb Windows; 6Mb OS/2; 12Mb Windows NT; 4Mb SunOS
Disk Space on Server	10Mb
UTILITIES PROVIDED	
Administration Utility	Yes
Interactive User Utility	Yes
Operating Systems/Environments Supported	DOS 3.1 or higher; Windows 3.0 or higher; SunOS 4.1.1 or higher
NATIVE LANGUAGES	
ANSI SQL	Level 2 with Integrity Enhancement
DB2 SQL Extensions	Yes
Other SQL Extensions	Yes
Non-SQL Language	Yes (6.0)
MAXIMUMS	
Database Size	Limited by disk space

MAXIMUMS	
Column Size	Limited by disk space (LONG VARCHAR data type stores 2G)
Row Size	Limited by disk space
# of Columns in Row	250 columns
# of Rows in Table	Limited by disk space
# of Rows per Database	Limited by disk space
# of Tables per Database	Limited by disk space
# of Views per Database	Unlimited
# of Tables per View	Unlimited

■ INFORMIX-OnLine 6.0

Informix Software, Inc. was the first vendor to release a UNIX RDBMS, and
in the mid-1980s, it added support for SQL. Although it has since been ported
to other operating systems, UNIX remains INFORMIX's primary base.

Significant Features

Informix has two different Class 2 RDBMS which can serve as database servers: INFORMIX-SE and INFORMIX-OnLine. INFORMIX-SE is primarily
a multiuser DBMS designed for small to midrange databases which can be
used in a Client/Server system with the DOS- or Windows-based IN-
FORMIX-NET communications software. INFORMIX-OnLine has all the
features of the SE version and provides greater performance and capabilities. Of the two, OnLine is the better version for Client/Server applications,
so the remainder of this discussion will cover the more advanced version.

INFORMIX-OnLine Version 6.0 is designed for high-performance transaction processing systems, in which data integrity and high database availability are needed. One of the ways OnLine achieves its high performance is by
circumventing the native UNIX file system and replacing it with its own disk-
management routines that access the disk directly. This allows INFORMIX
to replace the UNIX disk-caching routines with its own internal disk buffers,
which are tuned for database performance.

OnLine also increases performance by providing limited support for parallel processing on a symmetrical multiprocessing system. Parallel processing
is part of the data-sorting routines; different aspects of the sorting process
are handled by different CPUs, and the results are combined before being

written back to disk. Version 6.0 added internal support for multithreading, which improves performance and provides a platform for more robust support of parallel processing in future versions.

Database availability is provided through disk mirroring and on-line, real-time database backups to tape. Version 6.0 added support for compressing the backups, which increases the amount of data that can be stored on a tape. Should the database system crash, INFORMIX-OnLine will automatically attempt to restore the database from the transaction logs when the system comes back up.

Data integrity is provided through a number of features, including stored procedures, business rules (similar to SYBASE's triggers), and referential and entity integrity. INFORMIX's stored procedures are implemented in much the same way as SYBASE's; the procedures are stored as part of the database and can be executed by any front-end application accessing the database. Business rules are user-defined stored procedures limited to functioning at the column level, unlike SYBASE's triggers, which can operate on a whole table or database. They can be used to specify such things as default column values or acceptable data values in a range.

Version 6.0 also has intelligent database recovery built into the database engine. The engine monitors the database and automatically detects corrupted data. It then isolates the bad data to prevent the corruption from spreading through the rest of the database.

While business rules can also be used to provide referential integrity, they're not necessary—INFORMIX provides full declarative RI that's compliant with the ANSI SQL Level 2 with Integrity Enhancements standard. Declarative RI is implemented as part of the table definition, along with options that determine how the RI is handled when a parent row is deleted (similar to Gupta's SQLBase implementation). In addition, INFORMIX provides entity integrity, in which the domain of a column is set when the column is defined. From that point on, the DBMS checks every INSERT or UPDATE action to ensure that the values being entered fall within the domain of the column.

INFORMIX-OnLine provides true support for binary large objects (BLOBs), which are text or graphics binary files up to 2G in size. Since BLOBs are implemented as pointers in the table columns to the external files, normal SQL commands can access the data. The BLOB data itself can be stored in a special disk area defined by the DBA. This provides additional performance, as the BLOBs are written directly to disk without going through INFORMIX's disk buffers. The INFORMIX-OnLine/Optical add-on lends OnLine the capability to store BLOBs on a write-once/read-many (WORM) optical drive. WORM drives, similar to CD-ROM drives, provide a large amount of storage space in a small package.

Client/Server capabilities and distributed databases are provided through INFORMIX-STAR, which provides full support for two-phase commits. INFORMIX-STAR lets the clients access, query, and modify multiple INFORMIX databases as if they were a single database.

Informix also sells INFORMIX-OnLine/Secure, a version designed primarily for government use. OnLine/Secure carries a Department of Defense B-1 security rating, which certifies it for use with top-secret data.

Hardware and Software Requirements

Version 6.0 of INFORMIX-OnLine is available for a limited number of UNIX systems, including SPARC systems running SunOS or Solaris, XENIX, AIX, AT&T System V, ULTRIX, and HP-UX.

INFORMIX-SE is also available for the same platforms, as well as for Windows NT.

Communications Protocols

INFORMIX-STAR uses TCP/IP to provide communications between On-Line systems and client systems. DOS- and Windows-based clients can use INFORMIX-NET over TCP/IP to communicate with the INFORMIX-STAR system.

Native SQL Language

INFORMIX-SQL is compatible with the ANSI Level 2 with Integrity Enhancements standard. INFORMIX uses a cost-based optimizer that can return information to the application about how the SQL statement will be optimized before actually executing it. This lets the DBA evaluate how the command will affect system resources and postpone executing it if the performance of the system will suffer.

Front-ends Provided

INFORMIX-OnLine offers a number of UNIX-based administration utilities. DB-Monitor is a menu-driven utility that lets the DBA monitor the system's resource usage, start and stop on-line backups and restores, and adjust system parameters.

Various command line utilities provide the DBA with information about disk fragmentation, and the abilities to both repair corrupted or damaged index tables and view the contents of the transaction logs.

Libraries are available for creating front-end applications in C, COBOL, and FORTRAN. Informix also has a number of application development tools available, such as INFORMIX-4GL, a forms-based tool that uses an enhanced 4GL version of SQL to create interactive applications, and ACE, a report writer.

Advantages and Disadvantages

INFORMIX-OnLine suffers from the same disadvantage as INGRES—a lack of support by third-party front-end vendors. While this situation may improve now that a Windows NT version of INFORMIX-SE is available, potential INFORMIX users are currently limited to custom-programmed client applications. Informix also has a reputation among users for providing poor support for its products.

Another disadvantage is that Version 6.0 currently runs on only a few versions of UNIX. This situation may change over time; however, the lack of wide platform support limits INFORMIX-OnLine's market appeal. Until more versions are available, OnLine will continue to have only limited support from third-party vendors.

INFORMIX's greatest advantage is its OnLine/Secure version. OnLine/Secure's high security rating makes it one of the few RDBMSs that can be used for top-secret government applications. This advantage is enhanced by the distributed processing capabilities provided by INFORMIX-STAR, which seamlessly ties multiple INFORMIX databases together.

Despite its advanced technology, I hesitate to recommend INFORMIX-OnLine for ordinary Client/Server use until Version 6.0 supports more platforms and third-party front-ends.

Table 5.5

INFORMIX-OnLine 6.0
Quick Summary

PRODUCT INFORMATION	
Name	INFORMIX-OnLine 6.0
Vendor	Informix Software, Inc.
OPERATING SYSTEMS	
On Database Server	SunOS 4.1.1 or higher, AIX, ULTRIX, XENIX, AT&T System V, and HP-UX
On LAN Server	Any network that supports TCP/IP
On Workstations	DOS 3.1 or higher; RISC-based UNIX
MINIMUM REQUIREMENTS	
RAM on Server	8Mb
RAM on Workstation	640k DOS; 8Mb UNIX
Disk Space on Server	5Mb

**Table 5.5
(Continued)**

INFORMIX-OnLine 6.0
Quick Summary

UTILITIES PROVIDED	
Administration Utility	Yes
Interactive User Utility	No
Operating Systems/Environments Supported	SunOS 4.1.1 or higher, AT&T System V, and HP-UX
NATIVE LANGUAGES	
ANSI SQL	Level 2 with Integrity Enhancement
DB2 SQL Extensions	Yes
Other SQL Extensions	Yes
Non-SQL Language	No
MAXIMUMS	
Database Size	Limited by disk space
Column Size	32,767 bytes; BLOB stores 2G
Row Size	65,271 bytes
# of Columns in Row	2,000
# of Rows in Table	Limited by disk space
# of Rows per Database	Limited by disk space
# of Tables per Database	4,096
# of Views per Database	4,096
# of Tables per View	4,096

■ InterBase 4.0

After letting it languish for years, Borland International finally released a new version of InterBase in late 1994. InterBase 4.0 represents a major upgrade to the product Borland inherited with its purchase of Ashton-Tate. It includes a number of technological features that make it a serious contender in the Client/Server marketplace. On the other hand, relatively poor marketing and Borland's recently signed agreements with SYBASE may once again push InterBase into obscurity.

Significant Features

InterBase's most significant feature is that it offers a lot of advanced database technology for a low price. It shares the honors with SQLBase for being the least expensive UNIX-based C/S database available.

It's also tightly integrated with Borland's two Windows-based DBMSs, dBASE for Windows 5.0 and Paradox for Windows 5.0. In fact, these two products manage their data files with a stripped-down version of the InterBase engine, which makes it easy to move dBASE and Paradox applications to a C/S system as your needs grow. Of course, InterBase support's Borland's IDAPI as well as ODBC.

The time between Borland's acquisition of InterBase and the release of Version 4.0 wasn't entirely wasted—InterBase features some of the latest Client/Server technology, including declarative referential integrity, stored procedures and triggers, user-defined functions, and BLOB support. It also provides an event alerter that can notify the applications when a specific portion of the database changes.

InterBase supports two-phase commits across multiple servers and can dynamically tune its performance based on the number of users and available resources on the server. Version 4.0 also adds support for the full Level 2 SQL standard (prior versions used a proprietary query language), fully scrollable cursors, and a cost-based optimizer.

Hardware and Software Requirements

InterBase 4.0 is available for a limited number of UNIX systems, including Alpha OSF1, SunOS and Solaris, and HP-UX. It's resource requirements are rather low—it only needs 250k RAM and 6Mb minimum disk space. Of course, its performance and ability to support more users increases with the amount of RAM available.

Versions for NetWare and Windows NT have been announced and should be available by the time you read this. Windows 95 and OS/2 versions have also been announced for release in mid-to-late 1995.

Communications Protocols

InterBase uses TCP/IP as its native protocol. The NetWare and Windows NT versions will support SPX/IPX, NetBIOS, and Named Pipes.

Native SQL Language

Version 4.0 supports the ANSI Level 2 SQL with Integrity Enhancements standard. It also provides support for GDML, InterBase's proprietary query language, for backwards compatibility with applications written for Version 3.2.

Front-ends Provided

InterBase comes with Windows 3.1-based administration tools. In addition, Borland also sells InterBase bundles: The decision support bundle includes a copy of the ReportSmith report writer, and the enterprise bundle includes a copy of Delphi95, Borland's recently announced front-end development toolkit.

Advantages and Disadvantages

Though Borland is positioning InterBase as a competitor to SQL Server and ORACLE, it strikes me more as a competitor to Gupta's SQLBase. Once versions are available for all the PC-based operating systems, InterBase will have scalability capabilities similar to Gupta's products.

InterBase's real advantage lies in its close ties to dBASE for Windows 5.0 and Paradox for Windows 5.0. Its natives support for applications written in these two products makes it ideal as a growth path and upgrade from a traditional LAN-based database system to a C/S system. It support for ODBC provides InterBase access to a number of other front-end applications as well.

Unfortunately, InterBase doesn't provide the same integration with Borland's dBASE for DOS 5.0. DOS application developers have to first upgrade their applications to Windows before they can move the application to a C/S environment.

In the wake of the split between SYBASE and Microsoft, Borland and SYBASE signed a joint agreement to provide tighter integration between the two companies's products. This could have a negative impact on Borland's efforts to market InterBase as both the upgrade path from its PC-based DBMSs and as a competitor to SQL Server. Only time will tell if InterBase can survive and flourish as a major player in the C/S marketplace.

Table 5.6

InterBase 4.0 Quick Summary

PRODUCT INFORMATION	
Name	InterBase 4.0
Vendor	Borland International, Inc.
OPERATING SYSTEMS	
On Database Server	Some versions of UNIX, including Alpha OSF1, SunOS and Solaris, and HP-UX
On LAN Server	NetWare 3.11 or higher; Windows NT Advanced Server 3.1 or higher; any network that supports TCP/IP
On Workstations	Windows 3.1 or higher

**Table 5.6
(Continued)**

InterBase 4.0 Quick
Summary

MINIMUM REQUIREMENTS	
RAM on Server	250k
RAM on Workstation	4Mb Windows
Disk Space on Server	6Mb
UTILITIES PROVIDED	
Administration Utility	Yes
Interactive User Utility	Yes
Operating Systems/Environments Supported	Windows 3.1 or higher
NATIVE LANGUAGES	
ANSI SQL	Level 2 with Integrity Enhancement
DB2 SQL Extensions	No
Other SQL Extensions	No
Non-SQL Language	GDML for backwards compatibility
MAXIMUMS	
Database Size	Limited by Disk Space
Column Size	32k
Row Size	65k (excluding BLOB data types, which are unlimited)
# of Columns in Row	16,000
# of Rows in Table	Limited by Disk Space
# of Rows per Database	Limited by Disk Space
# of Tables per Database	64,000
# of Views per Database	64,000
# of Tables per View	64,000

- *Evaluating Client/Server Databases for Proprietary Minicomputer Systems*

- *Rdb/VMS Version 6.0*

- *AllBase/SQL*

6

Client/Server Databases for Proprietary Minicomputer Systems

MANY PEOPLE IN THE COMPUTER INDUSTRY SAY THAT THE DAY OF the large computer systems (minicomputers and mainframes) has passed and that the future belongs to the PCs and RISC-based workstations and superservers. For the most part, I agree with this sentiment when it comes to Client/Server DBMSs; the previous two chapters have shown that the majority of the activity and advances in this arena are taking place on the smaller systems.

During the period from the early 1970s to the mid-1980s, minicomputer companies such as Hewlett-Packard, Digital Equipment Corporation (DEC), and Data General dominated what was then the low end of the computing market. These systems were proprietary, because they primarily ran the operating systems provided by the hardware vendor, and the vendor's operating system didn't run on anyone else's hardware. You could only access the computers through dedicated terminals. So, for example, if you wanted to run a VMS application, you had no choice but to purchase a VAX minicomputer and the VAX/VMS software from DEC.

The rise of microcomputers and UNIX-based RISC systems (usually referred to as "open systems") broke the stranglehold that the minicomputer vendors had on the low end of the market. The vendors scrambled to provide versions of UNIX for their hardware and to open up their systems to connections with PCs and workstations through LANs. Proprietary minicomputers were eventually squeezed into the narrow (and rapidly shrinking) portion of the computing spectrum between the superservers and the mainframes. In the late 1980s and early 1990s, the minicomputer vendors realized that their only hope of staying in the marketplace at all was to shift their focus from proprietary systems to open systems and reposition their minicomputers as superservers.

■ Evaluating Client/Server Databases for Proprietary Minicomputer Systems

Deciding whether to use a proprietary minicomputer as a database server boils down to one fundamental question: "Do I already have one of these systems running a database that LAN users need access to?" If the answer is no, there's really no need to look at these systems any further—you'll be better off investigating the systems covered in Chapters 4 and 5.

Advantages and Disadvantages

The proprietary minicomputers offer the same advantages as the UNIX-based superservers when it comes to the number of users supported and the potential database size. The larger minicomputers can support 500-plus users and databases well into the hundreds of gigabytes in size. However, the hardware required to do this is generally much more expensive than the same amount of computing power provided by the superservers (even those superservers sold by the same minicomputer vendor).

These minicomputers primarily support access through dedicated terminals, so you can mix dedicated and C/S database access on the same system.

In this way, they share the mixed-use advantage of the larger UNIX systems discussed in Chapter 5.

Software license costs are also a factor. Not only are the proprietary operating systems more expensive, but they're usually licensed for a monthly fee instead of being purchased outright like the versions of UNIX operating systems. This can add significantly to the cost of maintaining a proprietary minicomputer.

You should also consider the problem of support personnel. A programmer or system administrator familiar with one version of UNIX can usually adapt to another without too much additional training. Someone whose entire computer experience is with a proprietary operating system would probably have to be formally retrained on a different operating system, which increases the support costs. The pool of potential technical support employees is also predictably smaller; however, the decline in proprietary systems means fewer jobs available for those who haven't yet switched to a different system, so more experienced technicians and programmers may be available for hire.

The vendors of proprietary systems have also been somewhat slow in adapting their DBMSs to Client/Server capabilities. The independent DBMS vendors have beaten the minicomputer vendors to the market with versions of their own C/S DBMSs that run on the vendor's proprietary OS or have produced gateway software that lets users of the third-party DBMS access data from the minicomputer's proprietary DBMS. For the most part, the proprietary systems fall into the Class 5 rating, supplemented by Class 3 capabilities provided by both the system vendor and third-party vendors.

In the long run, the major advances in Client/Server technology will primarily take place in the PC and UNIX systems and not with the proprietary systems. This should be particularly true for front-ends as the third-party vendors expand their support of the more popular DBMSs.

The minicomputers have an advantage that they share with the high-end RISC and superserver systems: built-in CPU and disk fault tolerance. The systems, designed to stay up and running as long as possible, automatically correct or compensate for failures in most of the subsystems. PC and RISC system vendors are rapidly adding fault tolerant features though, so this advantage won't exist too much longer.

Here's the bottom line: You'll only benefit from these systems if you already have one that's loaded with critical data. You can then extend the system's reach to include Client/Server capabilities without having to transplant the data to a different DBMS.

Special Considerations

Once you've decided that you want to stay with an existing proprietary system rather than move your database processing to an open system, the main item to consider is network protocol. TCP/IP is the most common and is supported by the three systems discussed in this chapter, as well as by all the UNIX- and PC-based systems. However, expect to pay a premium price for the hardware and software needed to add TCP/IP to an existing proprietary system. Also don't forget that the TCP/IP protocol stack usually takes up more RAM on the client systems than other protocols, though this is less of a problem with Windows-based systems. A gateway can be used in most cases to translate between the LAN's native protocol and TCP/IP, though this adds a level of complexity to the system.

In general, networking between proprietary systems and PCs wasn't a priority for the system vendors until recently. The steadily growing market forced them to add network support; however, such support is usually grafted onto the minicomputer, instead of being designed as part of the system. This almost guarantees that problems will occur when you're setting up a Client/Server system between a minicomputer and PCs. Make sure your PCs can connect easily and efficiently with the DBMS you're thinking of using before committing time and resources to developing the C/S system.

Unless you already have the vendors SQL-based RDBMS software, make sure that your existing data can be imported into the DBMS's format without major modifications.

Finally, be prepared to develop your own front-end software; the majority of the front-ends available for these systems are provided by the minicomputer vendor. There aren't many direct (non-gateway) third-party front-ends available for the three DBMSs described in this chapter.

While the minicomputer vendors usually have good technical staff ready to support customers, I have found that getting information about their products can be an exercise in frustration if you're not already a customer (which is reflected in the scarcity of information in some of the quick summary tables in this chapter). This situation hasn't appreciably changed since the first edition of this book. The problem seems to lie in the layers of bureaucracy that have built up over the years in the vendors' internal organizations. Local sales offices seem to be geared more toward buyers than shoppers, so in most cases they refer information inquiries to the national office. The national offices don't have one person responsible for simply providing information, and in every case they suggested contacting the local sales office. If you're already a customer, you shouldn't have too many difficulties obtaining information on DBMSs from local vendors. If you're not, be prepared to spend some time tracking down the information you need to make an intelligent comparison between these products and the third-party RDBMSs.

Advice and Tips

At the risk of sounding like a broken record, the best advice I can give is to avoid using a proprietary system for a Client/Server database if you can. The disadvantages of using one far outweigh the advantages. Unless you're already locked into one of the three systems discussed here (perhaps because of a non-DBMS application that only runs on the proprietary system), your best course of action would be to build your C/S system around one of the DBMSs in Chapter 4 or 5.

Alternatively, consider using one of the third-party RDBMSs that supports the minicomputer's OS. As I mentioned in Chapter 5, Ingres, Oracle, and SYBASE have VAX/VMS versions of their DBMSs which can be integrated into a distributed system with other platforms through TCP/IP or DECNet.

Ingres, Oracle, SYBASE, and Informix also have versions for Hewlett-Packard's HP-UX variant of UNIX—these are better alternatives to HP's own AllBase on HP-UX. The same is true for IBM AS/400 systems running IBM's AIX. However, if you're running HP's proprietary MPE/XL or IBM's OS/400 operating systems on their own minicomputers, you're out of luck—your only choice is the respective vendor's SQL-based RDBMS.

■ Rdb/VMS Version 6.0

Digital Equipment Corporation (DEC) is the market leader in proprietary minicomputer systems, most of which run its VAX/VMS operating system. Both the ORACLE and the INGRES RDBMSs were initially written for VMS, and it remains their primary home. In an effort to remain a player in the database market, DEC created the Relational Rdb/VMS in the mid-1980s.

Significant Features

DEC's strength has always been VAX/VMS, which was designed from the ground up as a multiuser, real-time access operating system. (When VMS was initially released, the dominant operating systems were designed for batch processing on mainframes.) The latest version is OpenVMS, which runs on any DEC system—from the Alpha-based workstations to MicroVAXs to the DECStations to the mainframe-size VAX 9000 series. Because of this scalability, OpenVMS has become a popular platform for a wide variety of multiuser applications, and DEC has become the largest minicomputer vendor in the world. DEC was also an early pioneer in local area networks, using the Ethernet topology and DECNet protocol to link any number of VAX systems together.

Rdb/VMS runs on any OpenVMS system, and a run-time version is included with the operating system. This lets Rdb/VMS applications run on any VAX without requiring you to purchase the full product. The full Rdb system is necessary for developing applications and providing Client/Server access to the database.

Rdb/VMS uses a concept called storage maps to store its data, which lets the DBA allocate data space in a number of ways. Of particular interest is a storage method called horizontal partitioning. Horizontal partitioning lets the DBA create rules governing where Rdb stores particular types of data, providing a measure of automatic load balancing on the data disks and increasing data-retrieval throughput.

Also available is SERdb Version 6.0, an add-on to Rdb/VMS that provides U.S. Department of Defense security levels for federal government use. The enhanced security features are also useful for businesses dealing with highly confidential data, such as patient medical records.

Another interesting module is Rdb/ELn, which provides real-time data capture capabilities for Rdb databases. Real-time data capture is useful, for example, in a laboratory to automatically gather test data from specialized testing machines or in a weather bureau to gather continuous radar updates.

DEC also sells their own version of UNIX, called ULTRIX, but doesn't offer a version of Rdb for it. ULTRIX users can purchase a version of INGRES that DEC has customized called ULTRIX/SQL. DEC also sells ULTRIX/SQL Remote Access to Rdb/VMS, a module that lets ULTRIX/SQL users access Rdb databases, and a cross-compiler that lets programmers convert ULTRIX/SQL applications to Rdb/VMS applications.

DEC also supports the multimedia market with the SQL Multimedia for Rdb/VMS module, which lets client applications running on VMS, ULTRIX, PC/MS-DOS, and Macintosh systems store and access large data objects, such as graphics and video, in an Rdb database.

Hardware and Software Requirements

DEC developed the Alpha RISC CPU and released the first Alpha systems in 1993. They have continued to move their entire line of computers and operating systems to an Alpha-based architecture, lead by the release of OpenVMS, which runs on both traditional VAXs and Alpha-based systems.

Rdb/VMS runs on any DEC computer that uses the OpenVMS operating systems, including the DECStation workstations, MicroVAX superservers, and VAX minicomputers. The number of users supported depends on the capacity of the hardware platform.

A run-time version of Rdb is included with every VMS operating system package. The full Rdb/VMS system is available separately.

Communication Protocols

Rdb/VMS uses the DECNet protocol to communicate with other VAX systems running OpenVMS or ULTRIX. The full Rdb package includes the VAX SQL/Services communication protocol, which provides network access to Rdb/VMS databases from applications running on DEC systems using OpenVMS or ULTRIX. It also provides access from PC's running PC/MS-DOS connected to the VAX over a DECNet LAN.

DEC provides their own gateway-like software, called SQL/Services, to assist third-party vendors in creating front-end applications for Rdb. One of the more notable products that uses SQL/Services is Novell's NetWare for VMS, a version of their popular LAN operating system that runs on VAXs. NetWare for VMS lets PC clients use the IPX/SPX protocol to access Rdb/VMS.

A few front-end vendors provide their own gateways to Rdb. Gateways are also available from other DBMS vendors, such as Ingres, which use TCP/IP to communicate with Rdb. DEC supplies TCP/IP for the VMS systems as an additional cost module.

DEC was also the first third-party DBMS vendor to provide support for the Microsoft/SYBASE Open Database Communications (ODBC) protocol. ODBC support has made more third-party front-ends available for Rdb.

Native SQL Language

Rdb/VMS's current SQL implementation is compatible with the ANSI Level 2 with Integrity Enhancements standard. DEC also provides their own relational language, called RDML (Relational Database Management Language); however, it was never very popular, and DEC provides cross-compilers and program translators to help developers move RDML programs to SQL.

Rdb uses dynamic optimization to optimize SQL statements. Dynamic optimization is unique to Rdb (DEC has patents on the process); it can dynamically switch between different search techniques based on the initial responses to a query. For example, Rdb starts a search by using the appropriate index for the table. If the number of rows that satisfy the query criteria exceeds a certain percentage of the total number of rows in the table, Rdb will switch to just scanning the whole table to complete the search. This method ultimately improves response time, since Rdb doesn't have to search in two separate places (the index and the actual table) for the data.

Front-end Processors Provided

The VAX SQL/Services included with Rdb/VMS provide an interactive character-mode administration utility for OpenVMS, ULTRIX, and PC/MS-DOS systems. Also included are a number of programming libraries for creating custom front-end applications on PC/MS-DOS, Macintosh, and Sun systems.

DEC has licensed a number of the Ingres application development tools and adapted them for creating Rdb/VMS applications using the SQL/Services gateway. DEC also provides InstantSQL for Rdb/VMS, an ULTRIX-based development package that runs on the Motif GUI. The graphical interface allows users to create applications that access Rdb without having to learn SQL.

Advantages and Disadvantages

The major advantage to Rdb/VMS is that DEC includes a run-time version with every copy of the VMS operating system. So anyone who has one or more VMS systems needs only one copy of the full version to create applications that can run on all their systems. The security enhancements and real-time data collection modules are also an advantage for those who need such capabilities.

Another advantage is the architecture of the VAX hardware systems. One of the primary features of the VAX/VMS systems is called clustering, in which multiple VAX computers can be linked together into one complex, and each computer has full access to all the disk drives and communications resources of the cluster. This offers users the ability to expand the processing power of the computer system without purchasing full VAX systems with their own disk drives and communications hardware. This option can amount to a significant cost savings. OpenVMS automatically balances the workload between the different systems in the cluster to improve performance.

DEC provides fairly complete Client/Server capabilities for Rdb/VMS. There are a number of third-party front-ends available (though far fewer than for the DBMSs described in Chapters 4 and 5) that use either SQL/Services or their own proprietary gateways. Of particular interest is the number of Macintosh-based client applications available; there are at least twice as many for the Macintosh as there are for PCs. This is probably due to co-development agreements between Apple and DEC, which are designed to improve Macintoshes's access to VAX/VMS systems. A number of third-party gateways are also available, and DEC's ODBC support has increased the number of front-ends that can access Rdb/VMS directly.

However, unless you absolutely have to run Rdb/VMS (for example, if you already have a significant amount of data in an Rdb database), your best bet for integrating OpenVMS systems into a company-wide Client/Server network is to use one of the third-party RDBMSs that have a VMS version. I recommend using ORACLE (which is the most popular VMS database), instead of Rdb, because it offers better built-in distributed processing capabilities, multi-platform support, and greater front-end support.

Table 6.1

Rdb/VMS Quick Summary

PRODUCT INFORMATION	
Name	Rdb/VMS Version 6.0
Vendor	Digital Equipment Corp. (DEC)
OPERATING SYSTEMS	
On Database Server	DEC OpenVMS
On LAN Server	DEC Pathworks (DEC version of MS LAN Manager)
On Workstations	PC/MS-DOS; ULTRIX; OpenVMS
MINIMUM REQUIREMENTS	
RAM on Server	Varies depending on platform
RAM on Workstation	640k DOS
Disk Space on Server	Varies depending on platform
UTILITIES PROVIDED	
Administration Utility	Yes
Interactive User Utility	Yes
Operating Systems/Environments Supported	PC/MS-DOS; ULTRIX; OpenVMS
NATIVE LANGUAGES	
ANSI SQL	Level 2 with Integrity Enhancements
DB2 SQL Extensions	No
Other SQL Extensions	Yes
Non-SQL Language	RDML
MAXIMUMS	
Database Size	Varies depending on platform
Column Size	32,767 bytes; LIST data type up to 2G
Row Size	65,291 bytes
# of Columns in Row	2,000
# of Rows in Table	Limited by disk space

**Table 6.1
(Continued)**

Rdb/VMS Quick Summary

MAXIMUMS	
# of Rows per Database	Limited by disk space
# of Tables per Database	4,096
# of Views per Database	4,096
# of Tables per View	4,096

■ AllBase/SQL

Hewlett-Packard (HP) was one of DEC's early competitors in the minicomputer market. They have the distinction of being the first vendor to release a minicomputer-based DBMS, called Image. Image was based on the Network Database model and ran on HP's 1000 and 3000 series computers.

HP moved their entire line to the RISC architecture in the late 1980s. They replaced the HP3000 operating system with their proprietary MPE/XL (which was backward-compatible with the earlier OS) and HP-UX—their own version of UNIX. At the same time, HP released AllBase, an RDBMS that runs under either operating system.

Significant Features

HP is unique in that it provides two different interfaces to AllBase/SQL. An Image interface presents the relational AllBase's data as though it were still based on the Network Database model; this gives it backward compatibility with Image applications. It also has an SQL interface for use in applications and Client/Server systems.

AllBase provides some distributed database processing by letting users of one AllBase database query data on remote AllBase databases as though they were part of the local database. HP still markets TurboIMAGE, the current version of their Network model DBMS, and also provides AllBase TurboCONNECT, which lets AllBase users transparently access Image-based databases.

The HP3000 and HP9000 RISC-based microcomputers have gained a reputation for providing an excellent price-to-performance ratio, and HP markets them as alternatives to superservers for use as database servers. HP has aggressively pursued third-party vendors to provide Client/Server applications, front-ends, and development tools for AllBase. They've also encouraged other RDBMS vendors to port their products to HP-UX and to date, Oracle and Informix have answered the call. Ingres also provides a gateway to AllBase databases.

Hewlett-Packard's minicomputers are a hybrid of proprietary and open systems, as HP pushes both the proprietary MPE/XL operating system and the more open HP-UX UNIX variant. The only reason I've classified them as proprietary is that AllBase itself only runs on HP systems. Though they've not yet announced any plans to do so, HP's targeting of the Client/Server market suggests they may provide versions of AllBase for other UNIX systems.

Since the first edition of this book, HP has extended AllBase/SQL to support both ODBC and the Gupta SQLBase APIs. This opened AllBase/SQL to a wider variety of front-end applications and development environments.

HP has also extended AllBase/SQL's distributed database capabilities with AllBase/Replicate, which provides replication services for AllBase databases. The databases can be replicated on local or remote systems.

Hardware and Software Requirements

AllBase runs on any HP3000 or HP9000 series minicomputer. Both the MPE/XL and HP-UX operating systems are supported. The number of users and the size of database supported depends on the underlying hardware platform.

Communications Protocols

HP supports TCP/IP for communications between clients and AllBase. User-transparent distributed database communications between different AllBase databases are provided by HP's own Network System (NS) protocol. Transparent communications lets a user send a query to an AllBase server without considering where the data actually resides. The server passes the query on to the proper database and passes the response back to the user.

In 1991, HP introduced AllBase/SQL PC API, through which PC/MS- DOS applications communicate with AllBase databases over TCP/IP.

Native SQL Language

HPSQL is AllBase's native language, which is ANSI Level 2 compatible. Support is also available for accessing AllBase databases through the Image language, retaining the Network model interface and backward compatibility with Image applications.

Front-end Processors Provided

No real Client/Server front-end is provided; the administration utility that comes with AllBase runs on a directly connected terminal. However, HP has a number of development tools available, including AllBase/4GL (designed for creating on-line transaction processing applications) and AllBase/Query (a terminal-based query tool for creating ad hoc queries and reports).

HP's aggressive marketing has also led to an increasing amount of third-party front-end support, including such PC-based front-ends as Gupta's SQL Windows and PowerSoft's PowerBuilder (covered in Chapter 10). Other front-ends can access AllBase/SQL through the appropriate ODBC drivers. A UNIX-based version of INGRES/Tools is also available for creating All-Base client applications on RISC-based workstations.

Advantages and Disadvantages

AllBase continues to be the rising star of the proprietary Client/Server RDBMSs, and Hewlett-Packard's continuing efforts to line up third-party support make it a strong challenger to the third-party UNIX-based C/S systems. DEC's Alpha-based Rdb/VMS systems are HP's only serious competition in the UNIX market for proprietary C/S database servers.

The downside is that AllBase is still a proprietary product, because you're limited to running it on HP computers. HP's continued encouragement for porting third-party RDBMSs to their HP3000 and HP9000 platforms makes me wonder if they're as serious about making AllBase a contender in the Client/Server market as their marketing approach makes them appear.

While AllBase is the second-best overall of the three databases in this chapter for Client/Server applications, I'd really like to see HP announce plans for supporting it on other platforms before giving it any kind of recommendation. Until then, you're better off using Oracle's or Informix's RDBMS on the HP platforms.

Table 6.2

AllBase/SQL Quick
Summary

PRODUCT INFORMATION	
Name	AllBase/SQL
Vendor	Hewlett-Packard Company
OPERATING SYSTEMS	
On Database Server	MPE/XL, HP-UX
On LAN Server	Any LAN that supports TCP/IP
On Workstations	PC/MS-DOS; Windows; HP-UX
MINIMUM REQUIREMENTS	
RAM on Server	3Mb

**Table 6.2
(Continued)**

AllBase/SQL Quick
Summary

MINIMUM REQUIREMENTS	
RAM on Workstation	640k DOS, 4Mb HP-UX
Disk Space on Server	10Mb
UTILITIES PROVIDED	
Administration Utility	Yes (terminal-based)
Interactive User Utility	No
Operating Systems/Environments Supported	HP-UX, MPE/XL
NATIVE LANGUAGES	
ANSI SQL	Level 2 with Integrity Enhancements
DB2 SQL Extensions	No
Other SQL Extensions	No
Non-SQL Language	Image
MAXIMUMS	
Database Size	Varies depending on platform
Column Size	Not available
Row Size	Not available
# of Columns in Row	Not available
# of Rows in Table	Limited by disk space
# of Rows per Database	Limited by disk space
# of Tables per Database	Not available
# of Views per Database	Not available
# of Tables per View	Not available

SQL/400

Even though it's the largest computer company in the world, IBM hasn't had as great an impact (or market share) as DEC and HP when it comes to minicomputers. IBM's most successful minicomputers were the System/36 and System/38, released in the late 1970s. The System/3x computers were unique in that a DBMS was built into the operating system. Many of these systems were (and are) used in applications requiring dedicated database processing, for example, in warehouse inventory and point-of-sale (POS), cash-register-type applications.

In 1990, IBM announced and released the first of the AS/400 line of minicomputers, which they've positioned as enhancements to and replacements for the System/3x line. The AS/400s are (for the most part) backward-compatible with System/3x applications and continue the System/3x tradition of having a DBMS as part of the operating system.

Significant Features

It's impossible to talk about the large IBM systems without briefly discussing IBM's System Application Architecture (SAA). During the mid-to-late 1980s, IBM found itself losing some of its large-system market share to DEC, primarily because IBM's systems lacked the ability to interconnect between the different-sized computers. DEC's VAX/VMS has built-in networking capabilities; these capabilities combined with VMS's ability to run on virtually every size of DEC's computers gave customers an easy way to link different department and corporate computers into a coherent company-wide system.

In an effort to counter DEC's networking advantage, IBM announced SAA in 1987. SAA isn't a particular application or operating system—it's a design specification for creating applications that can run on and access any of IBM's computers, no matter which platform was used to develop them. Along with SAA, IBM announced the SNA-based (System Network Architecture, the native networking protocol for IBM's mainframes) Application Program-to-Program Communications (APPC) protocol, which runs on any of their systems and allows applications running on one system to talk to those running on other systems. APPC is clearly designed as IBM's attempt to enter the Client/Server computing market.

SAA generated a lot of excitement when it was first announced, particularly among folks in MIS and IS departments whose entire computing power was tied up in IBM's mainframes. Their users were clamoring for a way to interconnect their desktop PCs with the companies's central hosts, and SAA seemed to answer the MIS departments's prayers. However, it hasn't worked out quite so smoothly in practice, as IBM has been slow in implementing SAA across their entire range of systems.

So how does this relate to SQL/400? Well, one of the motivations for developing the AS/400 systems was to provide an SAA-compatible line of midrange computers to fill in the gap between OS/2 (the desktop portion of SAA) and IBM's DB2 (the only SAA mainframe DBMS to date). SQL/400 provides a nearly SAA-compatible SQL interface to the data on an AS/400, as well as some distributed processing and C/S capabilities.

The initial version of SQL/400 provided SAA-compatibility more in theory than in practice. Version 2.1.1, released in early 1992, significantly closes the gap by providing 98 percent compatibility with IBM's major SAA application, DB2. Unfortunately, the missing pieces make SQL/400 less capable as a Client/Server system than IBM's OS/2-based DB2/2 (covered in Chapter 4). For example, one missing piece is the SQL command ALTER TABLE, which lets the database administrator change the structure of a table. Under SQL/400, the only way to change a table is to create a new one with the desired structure, copy the data from the old table to the new one, and delete the old table. This is not only time-consuming, but it violates some of the database structure independence rules specified in the Relational model. This hasn't changed in the last three years—IBM hasn't released a significant upgrade to SQL/400 since 1992.

Otherwise, SQL/400 provides the same database structures as DB2 and the OS/2 DB2/2, so PC-based databases can be moved to the larger system as processing needs warrant. The additional power and disk-size capabilities of the AS/400 systems place them in between PCs and mainframes in user capabilities and maximum database size.

IBM also sells a version of their AIX UNIX variant that runs on the AS/400 systems. Ingres, Oracle, and SYBASE all have AIX versions of their RDBMSs.

Hardware and Software Requirements

SQL/400 only runs with OS/400, the native operating system for the AS/400 line. The AS/400 systems range in size from the 9402 Model C04 that supports 12 users to the 9406 Model E90 that supports 240 users. OS/400 includes native DBMS capabilities; SQL/400 is an additional-cost module that provides an SQL interface to the underlying data.

Both AIX and OS/400 can run at the same time on the same AS/400, provided the system has enough RAM to support both operating systems. SQL/400 doesn't run on AIX, but the separately available AIX Viaduct for AS/400 module provides interprocess communications between AIX applications and SQL/400 databases.

Communication Protocols

SQL/400 communicates with other IBM systems through APPC. Unfortunately, APPC is memory intensive and takes up too much RAM on PC/MS-DOS-based systems (over 300k) to be practical for DOS-based client systems. TCP/IP is also available for the AS/400 systems and can be used by AIX and other TCP/IP workstations to communicate with SQL/400. IBM also sells the AIX AS/400 3270 Connection Program, which lets AS/400 systems running both

AIX and OS/400 communicate with other SNA systems, such as an IBM mainframe or RS/6000 RISC workstation.

Native SQL Language

As I mentioned previously, SQL/400 is 98 percent compatible with IBM's DB2 SQL. This would make it mostly compatible with the ANSI Level 2 with Integrity Enhancement standard, as well as providing the DB2 SQL extensions. However, the missing 2 percent can cause complications when an application from another IBM SQL system is moved to SQL/400.

The native language of OS/400 is the 3GL RPG/400, which was initially developed for the System/3x line. Support for COBOL is also available. The data on an AS/400 system can be accessed through applications outside of the SQL/400 interface, which implicitly violates the Relational model's data integrity principles. The system administrator can optionally prevent applications from reaching data without going through SQL/400, which partially resolves this problem.

Front-end Processors Provided

The AS/400 series is still primarily designed as a host system for dedicated terminals, so the only SQL/400 administration tools provided are terminal-based. Front-end PC-based client support is available only through the Query Manager that comes with IBM's OS/2-based DB2/2.

Because of APPC's high RAM requirements, no PC/MS-DOS-based front-ends are available at this time. While TCP/IP can be used by a DOS PC to communicate with an AS/400, there has been little demand for such products, so none exists.

Advantages and Disadvantages

At this time, an AS/400 system can serve as an upgrade to an existing System/3x minicomputer, which is the only real advantage to AS/400s. Upgrading to an AS/400 will provide additional processing capabilities and a limited form of Client/Server access to data formerly residing on the System/3x. The lack of 100 percent SAA and DB2 SQL compatibility prevents SQL/400 from neatly fitting into the midrange slot between the OS/2 DB2/2 and DB2.

IBM still hasn't really clarified how the AS/400 systems fit into their product line, other than as replacements for existing System/3xs. IBM's line of RISC-based RS/6000 workstations and superservers provide as much (if not more) processing power as the AS/400s. The RS/6000s are generally less expensive and have the advantage of running AIX, so they're compatible with many third-party UNIX-based RDBMSs. The only advantage that the AS/400s have over the RISC systems is that IBM has not yet announced how

AIX will fit into SAA. SQL/400 maintains the advantage in providing some distributed database capabilities in a predominantly IBM environment.

Unless you're replacing a System/3x or need a midrange, terminal-based system that fits into an existing SAA environment, I'd recommend using one of the RS/6000 superservers with a third-party RDBMS over an AS/400 if you're looking for an IBM minicomputer.

Table 6.3

SQL/400 Quick Summary

PRODUCT INFORMATION	
Name	SQL/400
Vendor	IBM, Inc.
OPERATING SYSTEMS	
On Database Server	OS/400
On LAN Server	IBM LAN Server or any network that supports APPC; TCP/IP support optional
On Workstations	OS2 2.0 or higher
MINIMUM REQUIREMENTS	
RAM on Server	8Mb
RAM on Workstation	8Mb OS/2
Disk Space on Server	10Mb
UTILITIES PROVIDED	
Administration Utility	Yes (terminal-based)
Interactive User Utility	No
Operating Systems/Environments Supported	OS/2 2.0 or higher
NATIVE LANGUAGES	
ANSI SQL	Level 2 with Integrity Enhancements (98% compatible)
DB2 SQL Extensions	Compatible
Other SQL Extensions	No
Non-SQL Language	RPG/400

Table 6.3 (Continued)

SQL/400 Quick Summary

MAXIMUMS	
Database Size	Varies depending on platform
Column Size	4,000 bytes, or 32,700 characters in LONG VARCHAR
Row Size	4,005 bytes
# of Columns in Row	255 columns
# of Rows in Table	Limited by disk space
# of Rows per Database	Limited by disk space
# of Tables per Database	Limited by disk space
# of Views per Database	Limited by disk space
# of Tables per View	15

- *Evaluating Client/Server Databases for Mainframes*
- *DB2*
- *SQL/DS*
- *ORACLE7 Mainframe Versions*

7

Client/Server Databases
for Mainframes

Iᴛ ᴍᴀʏ ꜱᴇᴇᴍ ᴏᴅᴅ, ᴀᴛ ꜰɪʀꜱᴛ, ᴛᴏ ᴄᴏɴꜱɪᴅᴇʀ ᴍᴀɪɴꜰʀᴀᴍᴇꜱ ᴀꜱ ᴀ ᴘʟᴀᴛꜰᴏʀᴍ for Client/Server databases, since the common reason for moving to a C/S platform is to rightsize corporate databases from large, expensive computers to smaller, less costly ones. However, the reality is that mainframes still make up a significant portion of the C/S market. The reason is simple: In many businesses, mainframes are the primary computer resource; it's easier to integrate them into a company-wide Client/Server system than to toss them out and start from scratch.

Another inescapable fact is that currently no other computers can handle the quantity of data and simultaneous users that a mainframe can (though some of the high-end minicomputers and superservers are starting to come close). Mainframe architecture has evolved over the last 30 years to include support for multiple CPUs linked through high-speed data channels, attached to hundreds, if not thousands, of large capacity disk drives. Anyone who has ever been in a mainframe computer room containing rows upon rows of disk-drive cabinets can understand why they're commonly referred to as "disk farms."

For this reason, mainframes, expensive as they are to maintain, aren't going to disappear in the foreseeable future. However, their role in corporate computer operations is changing; increasingly, mainframes are viewed less as the primary computer resource and more as the central storage facility for data access through Client/Server or distributed database processing. Even IBM (the world's largest mainframe vendor) recognizes this and refers to their mainframes as the "data warehouses" of large corporations.

Although I primarily discuss IBM mainframes in this chapter, it's important to remember that companies such as Ahmdal, Hitachi, and others also make mainframes that run the same operating systems and software as IBM. However, since IBM has the largest share of the market and all mainframe software is written to the IBM standard, it's simpler to refer to mainframes as though they all came from IBM.

■ Evaluating Client/Server Databases for Mainframes

Evaluating a mainframe as a Client/Server platform is very different from evaluating the other platforms in this book. First, we have to work on the assumption that you already have a mainframe. With all the less expensive alternatives available, there's no reason to purchase a mainframe for the database server function alone—it just isn't cost-effective. With the advances being made in C/S databases available for the smaller platforms, it makes more sense to expand their capacity or add more database servers than to move all the data to a costly central platform.

Second, mainframe-based databases are, with one exception, designed primarily for access via dedicated terminals, with little built-in support for Client/Server communications. The primary way to access data on a mainframe from a PC or RISC client is through a gateway system. This system translates the communications across the different network protocols used by the client and the mainframe. Gateways also translate the client's SQL commands into a form of SQL which the mainframe databases understand and translate the responses from the database into a form the clients can use.

The exception to this is ORACLE7, which has versions for the two major mainframe operating systems, VM and MVS. ORACLE7 databases on the mainframe can share data with other ORACLE databases and can be accessed by clients, just like any other version of ORACLE, using the appropriate version of SQL*Net and network protocols.

Advantages and Disadvantages

The clear advantage of mainframe databases is the potential quantity of data and number of users supported. It's not unheard of for a mainframe database to hold terabytes (one trillion bytes) of data, which can be accessed by a thousand or more users at the same time. While advances in computing power and distributed databases may someday give the less expensive systems the same capabilities, the mainframes should continue to hold this advantage through the rest of the 1990s, and possibly into the early part of the twenty-first century.

Of course, such power comes at a very high cost. It's not just the mainframe CPUs and disk drives that are expensive; there are numerous necessary add-ons, such as communications processors to connect to the dedicated terminals, banks of tape drives to back up all that data, and high-speed printers to produce reports from the data. There's also the cost of maintaining the special environment a mainframe requires: a raised floor in the "data center" for all the cabling and pipes to pass under; special air conditioning systems to keep the computer room at a constant temperature; water pipes for cooling the CPUs; and large generator-driven backup power supplies to prevent the computer from crashing when the main power goes out.

Then you must consider the personnel costs. Most MIS departments grew up around mainframes because of the number of different technical support staffs needed to keep the system running. There are systems programmers who tune the operating system and balance the load between different applications to obtain the best performance; systems analysts and application programmers who design, develop, and support the user applications; system operators who monitor the system and perform day-to-day maintenance tasks such as data backups; and network technicians who support and maintain the communications portion of the system.

There are also the complexities of sharing the data on a mainframe with client systems. Mainframe databases are just not geared toward C/S applications, so the previously mentioned gateways are usually needed to communicate between the client systems and the mainframe. IBM is making moves in the Client/Server direction with its two mainframe RDBMSs, but the problem is that the majority of mainframe databases are still running under the hierarchical IMS database (discussed in Chapter 1) or similar DBMSs and not under the relational DB2 or SQL/DS DBMSs. Special gateway systems are needed to translate the SQL commands into a form IMS can understand and respond to.

In addition to the need for gateways to handle the different communications standards or access non-SQL databases, there's the problem of character coding. Mainframes and other computer systems simply don't speak the same language when it comes to how standard characters are coded in binary form. Character coding is the way the letters, numbers, and symbols of the standard alphabet are assigned unique binary data values. By using a standard coding (usually referred to as a character set), every system that follows the standard agrees (for example) that a certain value represents a capital *A*, while another value represents a lowercase *a*. PC, UNIX, and VAX/VMS systems use a form of text coding called ASCII (American Standard Code for Information Interchange), while mainframes use EBCDIC (Extended Binary-Coded Decimal Interchange Code). Database gateways must translate the ASCII-coded SQL requests from the client systems into EBCDIC-coded SQL to pass requests to the mainframe, and then must reverse the process with the response. While this translation process sounds complex, it's actually based on common technology that has been available for years. So the process itself is fairly trivial to implement, and the net effect is a slight increase in processing overhead.

Mainframes do have an advantage when it comes to security. Decades of experience with mission-critical and/or confidential data translates into the highest security capabilities of any computer systems available. Mainframe hardware and software vendors provide a number of security packages that control access to the different applications and databases, and most of these packages meet the U.S. Department of Defense security standards. Mainframe support personnel also have the experience needed to maintain the security systems that are in place, and they are usually more aware of potential security problems than the majority of those who support the smaller systems—especially those who support PCs.

Finally, mainframes remain the most reliable computer systems currently available, primarily due to the large number of redundant components in the system. Mainframe designers have years of experience in determining which components are most likely to fail, and they have built-in automatic systems that lock out a failed component and activate its backup. Many high-end minicomputers and superservers are closing the gap though, as their designers add the reliability features pioneered on the mainframes. I expect that most of these systems will match the mainframe's reliability within the next few years, reducing this advantage to a common feature.

Special Considerations

In various respects, mainframes and potential client systems don't speak the same language. Mainframes use the IBM System Network Architecture (SNA) protocol to communicate with dedicated terminals, with PCs acting as dedicated terminals through modems, or with terminal emulation boards. SNA isn't designed to accommodate the complex two-way communications necessary for true Client/Server applications.

One solution is the gateway systems mentioned earlier. A gateway system is generally a node on the LAN consisting of specialized software that talks to the mainframe through a terminal emulation board. The gateway is usually a dedicated system, due to the amount of processing needed to handle the translations between the different protocols and character codes. The clients either talk directly to the gateway or send the query to the local database server, which then passes it on to the gateway. Client communications use the normal LAN protocols, and the gateway translates the requests and sends them to the mainframe in the SNA protocol. A software application is usually running on the mainframe that's part of the gateway system; the software handles the interface between the data in the DBMS and the SQL commands passed along by the gateway. Needless to say, gateways are expensive and add a tremendous amount of complexity to the communications between the clients and the database.

Another alternative is to use a common network protocol, such as TCP/IP, to provide communications. While this may seem to be a better solution, it's not without its own complexities and costs. Adding TCP/IP to a mainframe involves using an expensive hardware/software combination. And some type of gateway application on the mainframe must still handle the application communications and character-set translations between the client and the database.

The real price for all this complexity is generally slower response time to database queries. Because of the number of layers a client request goes through to be processed, it takes longer to get a response from a mainframe database than to get the same response from a local database server.

I also encountered the same problems in acquiring information I mentioned in Chapter 6: Getting information from IBM about their two mainframe database products was almost impossible. Most of the information about DB2 and SQL/DS in this chapter was gathered from third-party sources—the "new," more open IBM may be in charge of the PC-based products, but the old IBM is still very much in control when it comes to large systems. Getting information from Oracle about their mainframe version provided a pleasant contrast to IBM's silence. Oracle's representatives were more than willing to provide any information I requested about their products; only IBM's OS/2 products division showed the same level of cooperation.

Advice and Tips

The whole point of moving to a Client/Server DBMS is to rightsize from a large, expensive system, so your first step should be to closely examine your current database processing system to see if it can be replaced by smaller, and possibly distributed, systems. It's entirely possible that you don't need to keep all the data in the mainframe active; you may be able to archive most of it on tapes and to restore it only for special processing runs such as quarterly or annual reports. It may also make sense to break up the data contained in one large database into smaller databases dedicated to a particular department or function. The data can then be combined through some type of distributed processing capabilities when needed for complex analysis or reports. However, be aware that breaking up a large database requires careful planning, including a complete rethinking of the database's structure. Such planning requires a great deal of expertise in database theory and design; in most cases, you'll be better off hiring a qualified consultant who has experience in downsizing large systems to help you in your efforts.

Distributed processing is really the preferred method of implementing a Client/Server system, whether you choose to archive or break up the data. If it's not possible to do either, the next step to consider is building a semi-distributed system. You can do this by maintaining parts of the database on superservers or high-power PC servers that the users actually access. At scheduled times during the day, the database servers can communicate with the mainframe and transfer any data modifications for integration into the central database. The mainframe can then replicate the appropriate updates to the databases on the servers, so that users always work with the latest data.

Many companies with existing mainframes use a variation on this method. Instead of maintaining multiple copies of the database, the MIS department sets up a system that downloads the relevant portions of the data to a PC (usually in ASCII format). The user can then import the data into a PC-based application such as a spreadsheet or word processor, where he can further manipulate the data or create custom reports. This practice reduces the overhead of performing a number of queries on the mainframe itself. More importantly, it reduces the need to have expensive application programmers spend time and resources developing custom reports on the mainframe—reports that a user can easily create in a matter of minutes or hours with a familiar PC application.

The next alternative is to use a gateway system to allow direct client access to the mainframe databases. While this solution is complex and somewhat expensive, it may be the only choice if there's no logical way to break down the database or if confidentiality and security concerns require that all the data be maintained in a central place.

Finally, there's the same alternative that exists with the proprietary mini-computers—keep the mainframes, but switch to a DBMS more suited for Client/Server applications. Oracle sells a version of their RDBMS that runs on mainframes and can be connected to other ORACLE databases to share data and client access. IBM sells AIX (their version of UNIX) for their mainframes, and many of the UNIX-based DBMS vendors have versions that run under it.

The bottom line, though, is that the best way to approach using a mainframe for a database server is as a short-term solution. In the long run, it makes the most sense from both technological and cost perspectives to right-size your databases from the big systems in the "glass house" (slang for the computer center) to distributed servers running DBMSs that are designed for Client/Server computing.

■ DB2

Both the Relational model and SQL were developed at IBM, and IBM did most of the early research in implementing a Relational database with their System/R project in the mid-1970s. However, Oracle beat them to the market with a commercial RDBMS by almost two years. It wasn't until 1981 that IBM announced their first RDBMS (SQL/DS, covered later in this chapter). In 1983 IBM announced the first version of Database 2, more commonly known as DB2, and it has since become their flagship database product.

Significant Features

The current version of DB2 is Version 4, which became available in 1993. All of IBM's current research and development advances in the Relational model and SQL are based on DB2, so it's the first to implement any new features that will eventually be added to IBM's other RDBMSs. Because of IBM's influence in the computer industry, DB2's SQL has become the de facto standard—the ANSI Level 2 and ANSI 92 SQL standards are predominantly based on the DB2 implementation of SQL, and many third-party database vendors make a point of supporting the extensions IBM has added to DB2's SQL since 1989.

DB2 was initially designed for multiuser access from dedicated terminals and that remains its primary market. Until recently, the only way to access DB2 from a Client/Server system was through third-party gateways, which made it a Class 3 database.

In late 1991, IBM announced its "Information Warehouse" concept, a strategic plan for tying all its RDBMS products together with Client/Server capabilities. The basis of the Information Warehouse is the Distributed

Relational Database Architecture (DRDA) specification, a portion of IBM's SAA network strategy (see the SQL/400 section in Chapter 6 for more details on SAA). DRDA describes how RDBMSs on different platforms can communicate with each other in a Client/Server or peer-to-peer server capacity. These capabilities are implemented through a function IBM calls the Remote Unit of Work (RUOW), a fancy name for the simple process of creating a query on a client system and sending it to the database to be processed. With RUOW the client can either be a workstation or another RDBMS, blurring the line a bit in defining a client system under the C/S architecture. Confusing terminology aside, RUOW is IBM's first significant step toward implementing a distributed database system.

DB2 Version 2.3 was the first IBM database to implement DRDA. A significant number of third-party vendors have announced support for DRDA, and IBM is implementing RUOW capabilities in its other RDBMSs, so DB2 should continue its move toward becoming a true Class 2 C/S back-end over the next several years.

Location independence is another distributed database concept implemented by IBM in DB2 2.3. Simply described, *location independence* means that a user can query one or more tables in one or more DB2 databases at the same time, regardless of the data's location in the network. In standard SQL, a user can specify a particular table in a particular database by using both names in the query, separated by a period: *<database>.<table>*. Location independence extends this by adding a third name which specifies the database server plus the user's ID:

```
<server>.<authorizedID>.<database>.<table>
```

As you can see, specifying four names can become unwieldy, so DB2 includes support for aliases which let the DBA identify the *<database>.<table>* combination with a single name. This cuts the location identification down to a slightly more manageable construct:

```
<server>.<authID>.<table alias>
```

DB2 includes support for read-only databases, which prevents users from accidentally modifying the data. It also lets the DBA create and grant security permissions to groups of users (similar to SYBASE), making it easier to administrate the database.

DB2 Version 4 has added a number of features common on other databases. It includes support for stored procedures on the mainframe. It also supports true parallel processing by splitting the database processing between the various processors in the mainframe (earlier versions could only use one processor at a time). Version 4 also includes native ASCII support for easier connections with other platforms and databases.

Hardware and Software Requirements

DB2 runs on the most recent versions of IBM's MVS mainframe operating system, MVS/XA, MVS/ESA, and MVS/SP. MVS runs on any of IBM's System/370-compatible mainframes, but it requires a lot of system resources to get decent performance. The majority of MVS systems are IBM's largest mainframes, the 3090 series or the high-end ES/9000 models.

DB2 itself also has a reputation as a resource hog, and the majority of users I've talked to say they wouldn't run it on anything but the most powerful of the 3090 or ES/9000 computers. However, the prices for just the mainframe range from about $3.5 million for a 3090 model 250J to over $22 million for an ES/9000 Model 900, so you can see why many businesses are seriously considering downsizing.

Communications Protocols

DRDA is a part of SAA, so all native communications are done through IBM's Advanced Peer-to-Peer Communications (APPC) protocol. APPC runs on any network protocol that supports it, though the dominant implementations are in IBM's LAN Server NOS and the SNA protocol used by the mainframes.

APPC requires a lot of RAM on the client, so it's not normally used on PC/MS-DOS systems. DOS clients can access data in a DB2 database through a roundabout method, using NetBIOS to communicate with a DB2/2 server on an OS/2 system. The Database Manager can then pass the SQL statements to DB2 using APPC, which effectively makes it a type of gateway system for DB2.

Gateways

Though support is improving for DRDA, the primary medium for client access to a DB2 database is still a gateway. Many Client/Server DBMS vendors have their own gateways, such as Gupta's SQLHost/DB2, Oracle's SQL*Connect for DB2, and the INGRES/Gateway for DB2. These gateways run in conjunction with the vendor's respective database servers and translate the user's request for data from the SQL used by the third-party RDBMS to DB2's SQL before passing it on.

The best known third-party DB2 gateway is marketed by Micro Decisionware Inc. The gateway consists of two parts: the Database Gateway for DB2 that runs on a LAN-based OS/2 system, and the DB2-CICS Access Server that runs under MVS on the mainframe. This combination lets users of Microsoft's SQL Server query a DB2 database as if it were an SQL Server database. Database Gateway uses Microsoft's Open Database Connectivity (ODBC) API, so any front-end application that supports ODBC or SQL Server can use it to communicate with DB2. It supports data compression between the gateway and the host to cut down on transmission times, and it also lets the DBA transfer data from DB2 to an SQL Server in order to reduce mainframe network traffic and processing costs. The gateway automatically translates SQL Server remote stored procedures into DB2 RUOWs, and it provides SQL access to data stored in IBM's nonrelational databases, such as IMS and VSAM.

Information Builders, Inc., the vendor of the non-relational Focus DBMS, has taken an interesting approach to providing client access to DB2. Their Enterprise Data Access/SQL (EDA/SQL) gateway is database-independent on both the client and server side, providing transparent access to over 50 different DBMSs. EDA/SQL provides this access through its own API, called API/SQL. Any client system that supports API/SQL can talk to any DBMS that EDA/SQL supports. The client-access portion of EDA/SQL runs on an OS/2 system and communicates with EDA software running on the DBMS host system. EDA/SQL is the first non-IBM product to fully support DRDA, and IBM is marketing it as one of its Information Warehouse products. EDA/SQL's database-independence may have an enormous impact on the Client/Server market over the coming years, as it gains support among front-end application vendors.

Using a gateway is an acceptable but expensive method of providing Client/Server access to DB2. For example, the Micro Decisionware Database Gateway for DB2 costs over $3,000—which doesn't seem like much until you add the $24,000 to $70,000 for the DB2-CICS Access Server. A complete EDA/SQL setup can run as high as $115,000.

Native SQL Language

As I mentioned previously, DB2's SQL is the de facto standard by which all other SQL implementations are judged. The ANSI Level 2 with Integrity Enhancements and ANSI 92 SQL standards are based in large part on DB2's SQL, and many third-party SQL databases are compatible with the DB2 SQL extensions. DB2's SQL query optimizer has a reputation for providing good performance, even though it's still syntax-based. DB2 also provides a number of other SQL performance enhancements to speed response time. However, these enhancements come at the price of requiring more system resources, particularly CPU processing power and additional memory.

Front-end Processors Provided

No front-end processors are provided. Instead, DB2 administration is handled through a dedicated terminal, which uses applications that run directly on the mainframe. IBM's OS/2-based DB2/2 provides the only native client support for accessing and administering a DB2 database using RUOWS.

Advantages and Disadvantages

DB2's only advantage is that it runs on a mainframe—which gives it capabilities far beyond most other RDBMSs in terms of database size and the number of simultaneous users it supports. A few of the high-end superservers are beginning to approach mainframe capabilities at considerably less cost, but no system yet matches the computing power a mainframe provides.

But this power comes at enormous expense in terms of hardware, software, environment, and personnel costs. While IBM is to be commended for finally "seeing the light" and making an effort to provide Client/Server access and distributed processing capabilities to their large-system DBMSs, the costs involved in maintaining a mainframe completely outweigh any capacity advantages. The C/S architecture was specifically designed for downsizing databases from the large systems while best utilizing the computing power of desktop PCs and RISC workstations.

DRDA may have a significant impact on the development of true distributed databases, primarily because of IBM's backing. However, using DRDA or a third-party gateway to provide client access to DB2 is at best a short-term solution for most companies. Granted, there are databases that are, and will remain, so large that for the foreseeable future only a mainframe can provide the necessary processing power and disk capacity. Careful analysis of your current database processing needs is the only way to determine whether you absolutely need a mainframe. If not, your ultimate goal should be to move your databases to smaller Client/Server systems and pull the plug on the mainframe.

Table 7.1

DB2 Quick Summary

PRODUCT INFORMATION	
Name	Database 2, Version 4.0
Vendor	IBM
OPERATING SYSTEMS	
On Database Server	MVS/XA, MVS/ESA, MVS/SP
On LAN Server	Any network that supports APPC, or an appropriate gateway

**Table 7.1
(Continued)**

DB2 Quick Summary

OPERATING SYSTEMS	
On Workstations	OS/2 2.0 or higher, with IBM's DB2/2; other operating systems through an appropriate gateway
MINIMUM REQUIREMENTS	
RAM on Server	Varies based on platform and number of users
RAM on Workstation	16Mb under OS/2
Disk Space on Server	Varies based on platform
UTILITIES PROVIDED	
Administration Utility	Terminal-based
Interactive User Utility	No; OS/2 DB2/2 needed
Operating Systems/Environments Supported	MVS; OS/2 2.0 or higher for DB2/2
NATIVE LANGUAGES	
ANSI SQL	Level 2 with Integrity Enhancements
DB2 SQL Extensions	Yes
Other SQL Extensions	No
Non-SQL Language	No
MAXIMUMS	
Database Size	Varies according to system capacities
Column Size	4,056 bytes; 2G in various LONG data types
Row Size	32,767 bytes
# of Columns in Row	750
# of Rows in Table	Limited by disk space
# of Rows per Database	Limited by disk space
# of Tables per Database	Unlimited
# of Views per Database	Unlimited
# of Tables per View	Unlimited tables, but only 750 columns per view

■ SQL/DS

SQL/Data System (SQL/DS) is the direct descendent of IBM's System/R prototype RDBMS and was IBM's first commercial Relational database when it was released in 1983. It remained IBM's primary relational platform until the 1989 release of DB2 Version 2. Since then, SQL/DS has faded into the background, though many mainframe shops still prefer it to DB2.

Significant Features

The latest version of SQL/DS is Version 3.3 for the VM and DOS/VSE operating systems. DOS/VSE is an early mainframe operating system that still has widespread user support, despite IBM's best efforts to retire it. VM is IBM's preferred operating system for the smaller mainframes (the 438x series and the lower-end ES/9000 models), though there are some companies that prefer VM to MVS because VM offers better real-time transaction processing capabilities.

IBM has continued to enhance SQL/DS for VM to the point that it is, for all intents and purposes, a VM version of DB2. Released in March of 1992, Version 3.3 supports IBM's Distributed Relational Database Architecture (DRDA) and Remote Units of Work (RUOW), making it DB2's full partner in the Information Warehouse concept. It also provides 100-percent compatibility with DB2's SQL, so applications written for one can easily be moved to the other. However, it is still DB2's "little brother," so any advances IBM makes to RDBMS technology will show up first in DB2 and then be added to a later release of SQL/DS.

SQL/DS for DOS/VSE still bears a strong resemblance to the System/R prototype, and IBM had implied in 1992 that the VSE version will not become part of SAA nor will it support DRDA. However, there was a significant outcry from DOS/VSE users, so IBM relented and brought the DOS/VSE version up to the same level as the VM version. SQL/DS for VM is the preferred platform for bringing the smaller mainframes into a C/S system, though.

Hardware and Software Requirements

IBM's VM and DOS/VSE operating system runs on any size System/370 mainframe, from the smallest 4381 and ES/9000 to the high-end 3090s and ES/9000s. However, its predominant market is the smaller systems ranging in price from about $400,000 to $4 million. Both VM and SQL/DS require fewer system resources than MVS and are better suited for smaller organizations with less than 500 users.

Communication Protocols

SQL/DS uses the same protocols as DB2, so everything discussed in that section of this chapter applies here.

Gateways

Oracle is the only third-party RDBMS vendor to provide a gateway to SQL/DS. Their SQL*Connect to SQL/DS supports both current versions of SQL/DS as well as older Version 2 databases, and it provides Client/Server capabilities from any front-end compatible with an ORACLE7 Server.

Micro Decisionware's Database Gateway for SQL/DS is virtually identical to their DB2 gateway. Information Builder's EDA/SQL supports all versions of SQL/DS.

Native SQL Language

As I mentioned earlier, SQL/DS is 100-percent compatible with DB2 SQL. It also maintains support for the native SQL found in older versions of SQL/DS for DOS/VSE to ease the transition between DOS/VSE and VM versions.

Front-end Processors Provided

Again, everything described in the DB2 section on front-end processors applies to the VM version. The only user and administration tools provided for the DOS/VSE version are terminal-based.

Advantages and Disadvantages

SQL/DS for VM has only two advantages: It provides DB2 capabilities on a smaller system with fewer resources, and it's a part of IBM's DRDA. Unfortunately, SQL/DS's primary market is the smaller mainframes, which are rapidly being surpassed in power and capabilities by less expensive minicomputers and superservers. You should only use SQL/DS as a Client/Server database if you already have a significant amount of data in it. SQL/DS systems are prime candidates for downsizing to a less expensive platform.

Table 7.2

SQL/DS Quick Summary

PRODUCT INFORMATION	
Name	SQL/Data System (SQL/DS) Version 3, Release 3
Vendor	IBM

**Table 7.2
(Continued)**

SQL/DS Quick Summary

OPERATING SYSTEMS	
On Database Server	VM/SP, VM/XA, VSE/AF, VSE/VSAM
On LAN server	Any network that supports APPC, or an appropriate gateway
On Workstations	OS/2 2.0 or higher, with IBM's DB2/2; other operating systems through an appropriate gateway
MINIMUM REQUIREMENTS	
RAM on Server	Varies based on platform and number of users
RAM on Workstation	16Mb under OS/2
Disk Space on Server	Varies based on platform
UTILITIES PROVIDED	
Administration Utility	Terminal-based
Interactive User Utility	No; OS/2 DB2/2 needed
Operating Systems/Environments Supported	VM, DOS/VSE; OS/2 2.0 or higher for DB2/2
NATIVE LANGUAGES	
ANSI SQL	Level 2 with Integrity Enhancements
DB2 SQL Extensions	Yes
Other SQL Extensions	Yes
Non-SQL Language	No
MAXIMUMS	
Database Size	Varies according to system capacities
Column Size	4,056 bytes; 2G in various LONG data types
Row Size	32,767 bytes
# of Columns in Row	750
# of Rows in Table	Limited by disk space
# of Rows per Database	Limited by disk space
# of Tables per Database	Unlimited

Table 7.2
(Continued)

SQL/DS Quick Summary

MAXIMUMS	
# of Views per Database	Unlimited
# of Tables per View	Unlimited tables, but only 750 columns per view

■ ORACLE7 Mainframe Versions

You've probably noticed by now that Oracle is prominently mentioned in all four chapters of this book that cover Client/Server back-ends. The reason is simple: Oracle is dedicated to providing database solutions for every major computer platform available.

Significant Features

The only difference between ORACLE7 on a mainframe and ORACLE7 on other platforms is the operating systems they each support and the data capacities a mainframe provides. In every other respect, the ORACLE7 RDBMSs are the same.

The mainframe version of ORACLE7 runs under the MVS and VM operating systems. Like other versions, it uses SQL*Net to communicate with both clients and other ORACLE databases, providing both C/S and distributed database capabilities. Oracle's two mainframe gateways can run on the same system and provide ORACLE users with transparent access to SQL/DS and DB2 databases. Client systems simply send their SQL commands to the ORACLE7 database, and it passes the data requests through SQL*Connect for processing. Users can also communicate directly with the SQL*Connect gateways using ORACLE-compatible front-ends, bypassing the need for an ORACLE database on the mainframe.

By using various versions of the ORACLE RDBMS and one of the SQL*Connect gateways, an MIS department can create the most complete distributed database system available today. IBM's DRDA has just started providing what Oracle has offered for four years or more. And ORACLE7 enhances Oracle's lead in the Client/Server market by providing tighter links between different platforms, as well as their own support for DRDA.

Ironically, one of Oracle's greatest weaknesses is having so many different platforms to support. New versions are always released for the VAX/VMS platform first, and the expanding Client/Server market demands that Oracle will concentrate on porting new versions to PC-based and UNIX platforms next. There's usually a time lag of more than a year between the initial VMS release and the release of the mainframe versions.

For a more complete discussion of ORACLE's features and capabilities, see the ORACLE sections of Chapters 4 and 5.

Hardware and Software Requirements

Oracle's mainframe versions run on both VM and MVS, so they support the entire range of mainframe systems. A version for IBM's AIX is also available, though it's fairly unusual for an MIS shop to run UNIX on a mainframe. The mainframe versions share the same problem as the other versions: They tend to be resource hogs, and the system requirements are similar to those needed by DB2.

Communications Protocols

Every version of ORACLE7 uses SQL*Net to provide client access to the DBMS. The mainframe version of SQL*Net supports the APPC, TCP/IP, DECNet, SNA, and asynchronous network protocols, lending it the widest networking support of any RDBMS available. Other protocols are supported through links between different ORACLE databases; for example, a PC/MS-DOS client can access ORACLE on a mainframe by using Named Pipes to talk to an OS/2 ORACLE database, which can then transfer the request to the mainframe over one of the other supported protocols.

Gateways

No gateways are needed for client access to an ORACLE database running on a mainframe, unless you need to interface between different network protocols. As noted previously, Oracle provides their own gateways to other databases, including DB2 and SQL/DS.

Native SQL Language

ORACLE7's mainframe versions use the same SQL and PL/SQL as the other versions. Applications and front-ends written for one version can access any other ORACLE database through the proper SQL*Net drivers.

Front-end Processors Provided

The mainframe versions of ORACLE7 come with the version of SQL*DBA appropriate for the operating system. SQL*DBA is terminal-based on a mainframe, but any other platform's version can be used to query and administrate a mainframe-based ORACLE database through the proper SQL*Net drivers.

Advantages and Disadvantages

ORACLE7 is currently one of the best solutions for bringing a mainframe into a Client/Server system, due to its built-in distributed processing capabilities. Even with the advent of DRDA, it's still much easier to communicate with an ORACLE database than with IBM's RDBMSs, and the savings generated by the reduced complexity may be substantial. And Oracle doesn't charge an additional monthly license fee on top of the software costs, which saves even more money over the long run.

Using ORACLE7 on a mainframe will make it easier to move the data to a smaller platform when you decide to downsize your databases. Or, if you use Oracle's SQL*Connect gateway products, you don't even have to migrate data from your DB2 or SQL/DS databases to take advantage of ORACLE's communications capabilities. The gateways also ease the processes of downsizing a DB2 or SQL/DS database to an ORACLE database on a smaller platform.

Of course, the mainframe versions are expensive (as is everything else associated with a mainframe), but the software's cost may well be offset by the savings in personnel costs. If you absolutely have to have a database on a mainframe, ORACLE7 may be your best choice. If you already have DB2 or SQL/DS databases, ORACLE provides Client/Server capabilities that surpass those currently available from DRDA or EDA/SQL. The combination of ORACLE and SQL*Connect is the best solution currently available for integrating your mainframe into a distributed database system. I fully expect Oracle to do everything they can to maintain their lead over other systems in the Client/Server and distributed database market.

Table 7.3

ORACLE7 Server Quick Summary

PRODUCT INFORMATION	
Name	ORACLE7 Server 7.0
Vendor	Oracle Corp.
OPERATING SYSTEMS	
On Database Server	MVS, VM, AIX
On LAN server	Any network supporting APPC, DECNet, or TCP/IP
On Workstations	Any operating system supported by ORACLE7 front-ends
MINIMUM REQUIREMENTS	
RAM on Server	Varies depending on platform and operating system

**Table 7.3
(Continued)**

ORACLE7 Server Quick
Summary

MINIMUM REQUIREMENTS	
RAM on Workstation	640k DOS; 6Mb OS/2; 12Mb Windows NT; 8Mb UNIX
Disk Space on Server	Varies depending on platform and operating system

UTILITIES PROVIDED	
Administration Utility	Terminal-based
Interactive User Utility	Terminal-based
Operating Systems/Environments Supported	MVS, VM, AIX, or any platform supported by ORACLE7 front-ends

NATIVE LANGUAGES	
ANSI SQL	Level 2 with Integrity Enhancement
DB2 SQL Extensions	Yes
Other SQL Extensions	Yes
Non-SQL Language	No

MAXIMUMS	
Database Size	Limited by disk space
Column Size	2G
Row Size	2G
# of Columns in Row	254 columns
# of Rows in Table	Limited by disk space
# of Rows per Database	Limited by disk space
# of Tables per Database	Limited by disk space
# of Views per Database	Unlimited
# of Tables per View	Unlimited, with maximum 254 columns per view

- *What Is Groupware?*
- *Evaluating Groupware*
- *Lotus Notes*
- *DCA OpenMind*
- *C/S Groupware Add-ons*

8

Client/Server Groupware

IN THE PAST COUPLE OF YEARS, CLIENT/SERVER DATABASES AND applications that can be described as *groupware* have gained a lot of attention from both the computer press and potential users. The best-known product of this type is probably Lotus Notes, but there are many products that fall under the groupware description.

But what exactly is groupware? What groupware products fall into the Client/Server marketplace? And how does it differ from typical C/S database applications? The answers to these questions are the key to understanding and appreciating the capabilities of these applications.

■ What Is Groupware?

The rise of LANs naturally led to the rise of applications that are designed to make it easier for groups of people to work together. Electronic mail applications were an early implementation of this principle, though they're rarely referred to as groupware. The next step came in the late 1980s, with the release of such products as the Higgins group scheduling and e-mail program, and Mustang Software's Brainstorm, an early attempt at a group discussion package. Due to the limited number of LANs in use at the time, and the lack of a robust GUI-based interface, these products only had limited success and eventually faded away. But the ideas behind them didn't, and the concept of group applications lay dormant until PC platforms became powerful enough, and LANs widespread enough to reawaken interest.

Sometime in the early 1990s, the term groupware started being used to describe such applications. Today, it's primarily used to describe three classes of LAN-based applications:

• Scheduling programs designed to assist in scheduling meetings, travel, and conference rooms and resources

• Document and image management applications that assist in tracking documents and images through the development and revision process

• Group conferencing or discussion software, which provides a central place for on-line discussions in an organization

All three classes share a common underlying concept: making it easier for groups of people in an organization to work together, whether they're all in the same physical location or scattered around the world.

No one is really sure who originated the term, but the first relatively successful groupware software was Lotus Notes Version 1.0, which was released in the early 1990s as an OS/2-based C/S application. Version 1.0 was very expensive, which kept it from being widely accepted at the time, though it did receive good reviews in the computer press. However, its capabilities, limited though they were, caught the imagination of other application developers. Document management programs, which originated on minicomputers and mainframes, were moved to PC-based platforms, and were enhanced with groupware features. Other vendors developed and released group discussion packages designed to reduce the need for face-to-face meetings. And of course, Lotus continued developing Notes into the premiere groupware application available today.

Most groupware applications use (or are similar to) traditional databases, where the common data is stored on a LAN file server, and all the data is sent back and forth over the cable to the workstations. But there are a number that either use their own C/S technology, or include and use a standard C/S database as their data engine. The rest of this chapter will discuss these C/S-based groupware applications.

■ Evaluating Groupware

As is not the case with the other products in this book, evaluating a groupware application can't be boiled down to a simple list of what to look for. Groupware applications are the Swiss Army Knives of the LAN application world—they are as much a development platform for creating the application you want as they are a solution in their own right. They can be used as is, right out of the box, or as the foundation for a series of applications you didn't even know you needed.

Such versatility can be both a blessing and a curse. Once you start using a groupware application, you'll begin to see other ways to use it that make life easier in your organization. What may start out as a simple on-line discussion about a project may eventually grow or mutate into a complete management system for the project. Or you may find that with minor modifications the application lets you also track in-house resources, or schedule meetings or vacations. The uses to which you can put a groupware application may only be limited by your imagination (and programming skills).

And therein lies the curse. It's possible to become so enamored with the technology that you begin to apply it to situations where it's not appropriate. Just because you *can* track all the resources in your organization doesn't mean that you *should*. Keeping track of overhead projectors and PCs is fine; keeping track of every pencil and box of paper clips would be overkill. You also have to remember to manage the groupware databases you build, so they don't overload your computer resources. Unless you still need them for current research, there's usually no need to keep discussions or documents on-line and available for more than a few months. Judicious archiving of older materials becomes an important part of using a groupware application.

With that in mind, what should you look for in a groupware application? The answer depends on how your organization works.

- **Meetings:** Does your organization have a lot of meetings? Do you lose a lot of your personnel's time to planning and holding meetings? If so, you should consider a conferencing application that lets your people hold their meetings at their own pace, right from their offices. Few meetings are so time-critical that the discussions held at them can't be spread out over a number of hours or even days. A conferencing package also gives your users the time to do the research they need to do before responding to a point raised in the discussion. And finally, many conferencing packages support remote users, so you don't have to worry about getting everyone to the same location to take part in the discussion.

- **Scheduling:** Do your employees travel a lot? Schedule a lot of meetings or service calls at client sites? A groupware application can help your employees keep track of where they have to be, and it can also help your in-house support staff keep track of where your field staff is at any time.

- **Resource planning and tracking:** Every organization has in-house resources—conference rooms, for example, and the equipment usually used in them—that it needs to keep track of. A groupware application can help you track who's using what conference areas at what time. It can also help you track where the equipment is, and schedule it for the appropriate times and places.

- **Document management:** Document management applications were among the earliest implementations of the groupware concept. Document creation and revision tracking is vital to many organizations, such as law offices, publishers, and even software developers creating manuals for their applications. A document management application lets you keep track of who created the document, who modified it, what revisions were made and when, and can even control who has access to it. Document management applications also provide varying levels of indexing, ranging from just the description of and keywords about the document to indexing every word in the document. This indexing makes it easier to find the appropriate documents for later reference, or for use as boilerplates for new documents.

- **Image management:** Managing images has become an important application need in recent years due to the increasing availability of image producing applications, such as fax-capable modems and communication applications, multimedia, and image/document scanners. Image management applications are similar to and an enhancement of document management applications. In fact, some applications provide both capabilities, which is something you should keep in mind when you're looking to purchase one.

- **Research and support:** Does your organization do a lot of research from on-line or other computer database sources? Do you provide telephone support to your clients? Some groupware applications make it easy to create a knowledge base for your support personnel, where they have immediate access to technical documents and problem reports and solutions. Text files from outside sources can be imported into the application and indexed for later research.

These are just some of the ways you can use a groupware application. You'll most likely find more after you start using one. So long as you keep the "groupware curse" in mind, and don't try to shoehorn the application into situations where it's not appropriate (or is overkill), you may find that the groupware application becomes the most-used software on your LAN.

■ Lotus Notes

As I mentioned earlier, Lotus Notes was the first relatively successful groupware application. Notes was designed as a Client/Server application from the very beginning, and in many ways bears a resemblance to the typical C/S databases discussed in earlier chapters. However, its focus is quite different. First of all, Notes includes both the client and the server software; though other front-end applications now have the ability to access Notes databases, the server is primarily designed to be accessed by Notes clients.

Second, and most important, is Notes's text orientation. The databases support a number of data types, but they're mainly designed to store, index, and retrieve text. Notes's text processing capabilities make it ideal for creating any of the groupware application types discussed in the previous section.

The current version is Notes 3.2. The client software is available for Windows, OS/2, UNIX, and Macintosh platforms; the server runs on a number of platforms, including OS/2, Windows, Windows NT, and NetWare.

Significant Features

Notes comes with a number of predefined databases and database types (the types are called *templates*), including an e-mail database and discussion databases. Most users will never need more than these predefined capabilities.

However, Notes is also a complete application development platform—it has a number of design capabilities, and it also has a full-featured macro language that can be used to automate the application processing. Notes can be the foundation for any number of groupware applications.

Notes's main screen is the Workspace, as shown in Figure 8.1. The Workspace resembles a set of file folders, with the databases represented as icons in each folder. Every user has three databases automatically created—the user's EMail database, outgoing mail database, and local address book. The user can add other databases to the Workspace by opening the database and adding the icon to one of the folders. The icons can either be plain, or can show the number of unread messages or documents in the database.

Figure 8.1

Lotus Notes's main
screen is the user's
Workspace, where the
user can organize the
databases into file
folders.

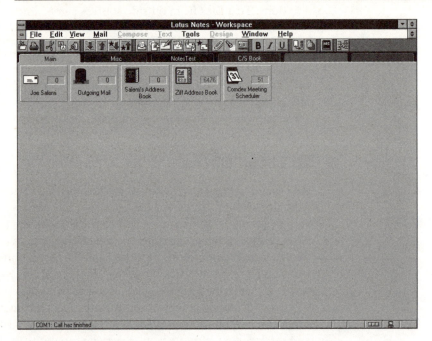

Notes databases can be local (kept on the user's PC), or they can be
stored on one or more servers. Any Notes user can create a new database,
and the person who creates it automatically becomes the database's manager. Notes supports a number of security levels, which are set in access control lists (ACLs). Database users can be assigned read-only access, read-
write (author) access, or manager access. Databases can be created from an
existing template, as shown in Figure 8.2, or designed from scratch.

Group discussions can be created with the default discussion template,
or you can create your own discussion format using Notes's form design capabilities. Discussions can be displayed in hierarchical format by topic category,
or by message date or author. Notes includes full support for attaching files
and linking or embedding OLE objects. You can even link a message in one
discussion database with a message in another, reducing the need to duplicate information.

Notes includes a complete e-mail system. External e-mail links are available through gateways to other mail systems, including commercial providers
such as MCI Mail. The user's mailbox is just another database, and can be
modified or replicated like any other Notes database (I'll be covering replication later in this section).

Figure 8.2

Notes databases can be
created from a
predefined template and
stored on the user's PC
or on a server.

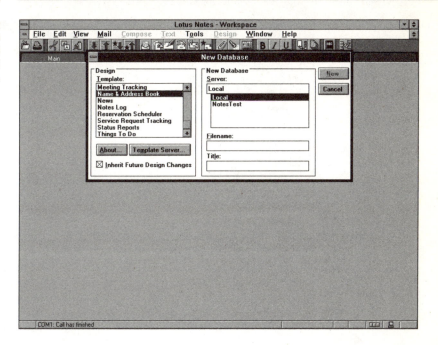

Notes is primarily forms-based. Designing a new database is as simple as creating the appropriate form or forms for the database. The first form determines the structure of the database; additional forms created for the database can display it in different ways using some or all of the elements created in the first form. Figure 8.3 demonstrates the address book form, which is one of the default forms that comes with Notes. You can select different forms through the View menu option, which also controls how the user views the overall database (for example, by topic, date of message, and so on).

Notes's greatest strength is its replication capabilities. *Replication* is the process where an exact copy of a database is created and maintained on another server, or in the case of Notes, a remote user's local system. The replicated database is automatically updated based on a user- or administrator-defined schedule, or manually updated as needed. With replication, enterprise-wide databases can be created on one server, and automatically replicated to other servers in the organization. Remote users can dial in to their main server and automatically create local replicas of the databases. Remote users can also dial in and work with the server-based copies of the database, though this method is obviously slower than working with a local copy.

Using replication for remote support has both advantages and disadvantages. The biggest advantage is that connection time is reduced, as only

Figure 8.3

Notes uses forms to view
and manipulate the
databases.

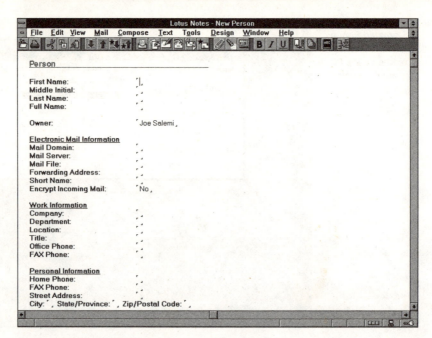

changed information is passed between the remote client and the server
(after the initial replication, of course). On the other hand, the remote client
has the disadvantage of needing a complete copy of the client software on
the local system, which can take up an enormous amount of disk space—a
bit over 32Mb if you install the entire Notes client, less if you use the Notes
Express client (described in the next section). Active discussion databases
can quickly expand to 2Mb or more in size, so make sure you have a lot of
free disk space if you're going to run Notes as a remote client.

Notes also provides the ability to add external applications to the base
system. These applications are known as Lotus Notes Companion Products,
and provide such capabilities as voice-mail links to Notes databases, document imaging, Optical Character Recognition (OCR) for scanned documents, and incoming and outgoing fax processing. Gateways are available to
link the built-in EMail system with Lotus's cc:Mail, Novell Message Handling System (MHS) compatible systems, and Internet e-mail users.

Hardware and Software Requirements

The Notes server software is available for Windows 3.x, Windows NT, OS/2,
NetWare, Sun's Solaris (UNIX) operating system, HP-UX, and IBM's AIX.
Full client software is available for the same platforms.

Lotus released the Notes Express client software in 1994. Express is a stripped-down version of the client package that includes EMail and four pre-written database applications. Express doesn't have the application development capabilities found in the full package; however, it can run most custom-designed Notes applications. Express comes in Windows 3.x, OS/2, and Macintosh versions.

Advantages and Disadvantages

Notes's biggest advantages are its text orientation, application development, and database replication capabilities. Notes can be used to develop sophisticated groupware applications such as group discussions, scheduling, resource management, knowledge bases, and document management. The pre-written templates included with the full package cover most of these application types, and can be used to create complex applications without modification. However, if you need to do something not included in the templates, you can quickly and easily create a custom application using Notes's built-in development capabilities.

Replication is a powerful feature that makes it easy to create and support applications for wide-spread organizations. The corporation-wide EMail system and discussion and scheduling databases in use at Ziff-Davis are a prime example of this capability. Databases are shared between servers in New York, California, and Massachusetts, and with remote editors and writers (such as yours truly) scattered around the U.S.

These capabilities do have their downside, though. Once you become accustomed to Notes's power and flexibility, you may feel a strong temptation to use it to computerize in-house processes that really shouldn't be computerized (or at least, not computerized with Notes). The ability to create custom applications can also lead to the phenomenon I described earlier, where databases are created to manage or track things that don't really need to be managed or tracked. Careful planning and forethought can help prevent your making this common mistake.

Another disadvantage is the size of the client software, especially for remote users. The full package can take anywhere from 15Mb to 32Mb of disk space, and replicated databases can also be quite large. Using Notes Express can alleviate some of this; judiciously choosing which databases to replicate and which to work with on-line also helps.

■ DCA OpenMind

DCA's OpenMind 1.0 is a client/server conferencing application that takes a unique approach to displaying and managing discussions. It uses a hybrid of a hierarchical display of the message threads, with a conversation display that shows part or all of the text of the messages in those threads on the same screen. It also has sophisticated document management features, including revision tracking and control, and a number of built-in file viewers. Version 1.0 has some limitations, but future versions have the potential to be serious contenders in the groupware market.

OpenMind's biggest limitation at this point is that the server only runs on Windows NT Advanced Server, and the client is only available for Windows 3.x.

Significant Features

The database on the OpenMind server is referred to as the Mind (a bit of corporate humor that you don't see too often these days). You can either install the default Mind, or create your own empty Mind. Automatic backups are supported, and can be run as a background task, even if users are logged in.

The primary view in the client software is the Explore view, shown in Figure 8.4. It displays the name of the current Mind and the topics in that Mind as icons on the top of the screen. When you open a topic, any subtopics are displayed in a similar manner. The Mind also provides each user with a default area for personal private topics and conferences.

Figure 8.4

OpenMind displays the available topics as icons, with the threads in a topic displayed in collapsed form at the bottom.

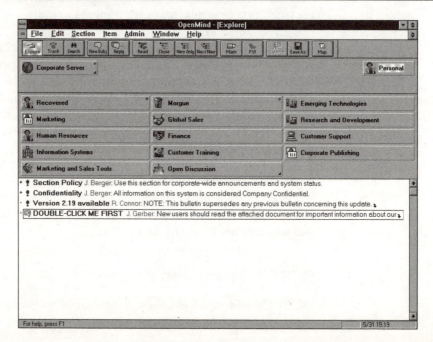

The bulletins, messages, and file folders in a topic are displayed in the bottom window. Bulletins are flagged with a exclamation point and messages with an icon that looks like a printed page. OpenMind displays the title, author, and first line of a bulletin or message, with a small arrow at the end of the line to indicate that the message continues. You can read the full message by double-clicking on the line or the icon. Figure 8.5 shows the complete message that starts a thread, with the first line of each reply shown in the hierarchy below it.

Figure 8.5

OpenMind displays message threads as a combination of full message displays and hierarchical trees.

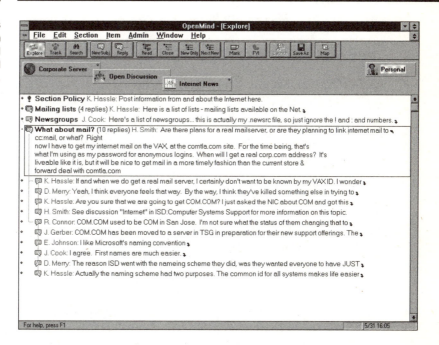

Files can be attached to messages, or included as linked or embedded OLE 2.0 objects. You can also launch the appropriate application from the viewer menu or icon bar. The built-in viewers are used to display file types that don't match the applications installed on your system.

OpenMind's document management features are part of the *folder* item type. Folders are part of a topic, and any user can add files. The person adding a new file or opening an existing file specifies whether or not other users can make changes. If they can, OpenMind automatically keeps track of the different versions of the file. The current version of OpenMind doesn't support indexed searching through folder documents, though this capability is planned for a future release.

You can use the Track view to see only those messages you marked for later retrieval, or which were highlighted by another user for your attention. The Search view lets you search for text in messages, bulletins, sections, or the entire database. OpenMind also has a navigation map that shows the sections and subsections in a tree format.

OpenMind supports server-to-server replication. Remote users can access the Mind by dialing directly into the server. Unlike Notes, remote users can't replicate the database on their local system—the Mind can only be accessed through real-time connections. It also doesn't support access to discussions through an external e-mail system at this time. DCA plans to add this capability in a future release.

Hardware and Software Requirements

The OpenMind server only runs on the Windows NT Advanced Server operating system, with at least 16MB RAM. The client software runs under Windows 3.x.

Advantages and Disadvantages

OpenMind is primarily a group discussion package, with limited, though useful, document management features. OpenMind's closest competitor is probably Lotus Notes. While Notes also provides document management features, they aren't as accessible and easy-to-use as OpenMind's, and some custom programming is usually required to take full advantage of them. OpenMind's conferencing capabilities make it very useful for discussions, and its search and file viewing features make it a good platform for knowledge base applications.

OpenMind's document management features are useful for tracking revisions; however, its real strength lies in combining the document management with on-line discussions. This is ideal for creating documents that require input from a large group of people, such as software manuals or support documents. For example, your technical writers can use the document management to keep track of the revisions while getting comments on the manual from the programmers in the conference database.

OpenMind's greatest disadvantage is its limited platform support. An NT Advanced Server can be added to most LANs, but you may not want the hassles of supporting more than one NOS. The lack of support for clients other than Windows also limits the package's usefulness in organizations that have a variety of systems.

The lack of replication support for dial-in users can be either an advantage or a disadvantage, depending on your point of view. The ability to replicate databases on a remote user's machine can improve performance, and also means you may not need as many dial-in lines. However, replicated databases can take up a big chunk of disk space, and can get severely out of synch with the main database. There are pros and cons to both approaches, though I personally prefer the way Notes does it. You may find OpenMind's approach more suitable to your organization's needs.

■ C/S Groupware Add-ons

There's a class of groupware products that use one or more of the standard C/S database engines to provide data management and indexing capabilities. For lack of a better term, I'm calling these products *groupware add-ons*. However, these add-ons aren't quite like the ones discussed in the next chapter—these products are usually sold as a complete application system, and include the database software as part of the package.

There are two types of groupware add-on products: document management and image management.

Document Management

Document management applications do just what their name implies—they manage documents. Document management takes a number of forms:

- Revision control

- Document security

- Full-text indexing and searching

- Document summaries and keywords

- Archiving inactive documents

Originally, document managers just worked with text files and files from only one or two word processors. Over the years, the term document has been expanded to include some nontext files, such as spreadsheets and traditional database files. Today's document managers can usually index and search files from all the major word processing applications, most spreadsheets, and common database formats such as .DBF files. There are three groupware add-ons that fit in this category: Mezzanine, Saros Document Manager, and PC Docs Open.

Saros Mezzanine and Document Manager

Saros Corporation produces two document management systems. Mezzanine is their original product, and was first written for a number of UNIX-based minicomputers. In the early 1990s, Saros created a LAN version, using the Microsoft SQL Server as the database engine. The database server is primarily used to track document locations, manage document summaries and keywords, and create full-text indexes of the documents themselves.

Mezzanine is more an API than a full-fledged application. Saros provides their own Windows front-end, called ViewZ, which supports a number of Windows-based documents, but not full-text searches. The majority of Mezzanine-based document management applications come from third-party developers and value-added resellers (VARs), who use the Mezzanine API to create custom document management applications. Since they're based on the API, these third-party applications support a number of popular platforms and document file types. The Mezzanine server runs on both the OS/2 and Windows NT versions of MS SQL Server; a version that runs on the NetWare version of SYBASE SQL Server is under development.

Saros Document Manager represents Saros's full entry into the document management field. It's based on the Mezzanine engine, and provides a complete document and image management system for DOS, Windows 3.x, OS/2, Macintosh, and UNIX clients. It supports word processing, spreadsheet, database, graphic, bitmap, and Adobe Acrobat files, and includes full-text search capabilities for documents that contain text.

Saros Document Manager is designed to handle the needs of large organizations, and can easily support 500 or more users. It uses SQL Server's Remote Procedure Call (RPC) capabilities to distribute the workload across multiple servers, reducing the performance hit that can result from a large number of users simultaneously indexing or searching documents.

PC Docs Open

PC Docs Open from PC Docs Inc. is the C/S version of the popular proprietary document management system. PC Docs Open runs with most database servers, including SQL Server and ORACLE. It's sold as both an add-on for your existing database servers, or as a complete bundle that includes the server software. The server can import document information and indexes from PC Docs, which gives users an upgrade path as their document management needs grow.

The client software comes in DOS, Windows 3.x, and Macintosh versions. The DOS version only supports WordPerfect files; the Windows and Macintosh versions support all the popular word processing and spreadsheet applications on those platforms, including WordPerfect, Microsoft Word and Excel, and Lotus's Ami Pro and 1-2-3.

Image Management

Image management applications are a variation of document management applications, designed primarily to manage bitmapped images. These images can come from fax applications, OCR scanners, CAD/CAM programs, and

PC-based image design and painting applications. Image managers provide most of the same features as document managers, with one big exception— since the information is stored in a bitmap, the image manager can't create full document text indexes. Image managers compensate for this lack by providing extensive profiling and summary features that index the image descriptions and keywords provided by the users.

As GUI environments become more prevalent, the line between document managers and image managers is becoming less distinct. As we've already seen in the previous section, Saros includes some image management capabilities in the Saros Document Manager. I fully expect these two categories to merge into one by the time the third edition of this book hits the presses.

At this time, there's only one image manager based on a C/S database— IBM's ImagePlus/2.

ImagePlus/2

IBM's ImagePlus/2 is an OS/2-based C/S image management and workflow system that's designed to import and manage paper forms and graphic images. *Workflow applications* are a relatively new class of applications designed to replace paper forms with their electronic equivalents. The electronic forms can then be routed through the organization using either a proprietary routing system or a common e-mail system. ImagePlus/2 is actually more of a development platform for vertical market image management systems than a product that end users can set up and use right out of the box.

Paper forms are imported into the program as bitmaps from a scanner or fax. It can also handle any other graphic images that can be converted to the OS/2 bitmap format. The images for a particular task or project are stored in a common folder called a *workbasket* (it even has an icon that looks like a little basket). ImagePlus/2 uses this workbasket metaphor to route the images from task to task.

ImagePlus/2 version 1.0 doesn't provide its own built-in support for scanning or faxing images; however, it easily links to a number of Windows-based scanning and fax programs through OS/2's DDE capabilities. ImagePlus/2 2.0 will have built-in scanning, fax, and e-mail capabilities; it should be available by the time this book hits the shelves.

Users and application developers can create customized profile screens that store information about the image. The profile screens can be indexed and searched, and can also include routing information for moving the image through the organization. ImagePlus/2 also lets you add voice annotations to the profile form if you have a sound board that OS/2 supports. The voice annotations are saved in .WAV files that become part of the image profile.

ImagePlus/2 had three main interfaces to the system. The Service Facility is used by the system manager or developer to import the images, create the profiles, and create the workflow workbaskets for storing each image and task. It's also used to set up the workflows for the image. Users access the workbaskets through one of two programs: the full-featured Application Facility, or the simplified Store and Retrieve Facility. The Application Facility lets the user browse through and work on all the workbaskets and file cabinets (ImagePlus/2's term for a set of related workbaskets) the user has access to. The Store and Retrieve Facility takes the user directly to a particular workbasket, bypassing the overhead involved in the Application Facility.

ImagePlus/2 uses IBM's DB2/2 database as the indexing engine. It requires OS/2 2.x or higher on both the server and the workstations, and only runs on the IBM LAN Server 2.0 or better NOS. Its resource requirements are rather large. The server must be at least a 33MHz 80486 system with 16Mb RAM and 320Mb disk space, and IBM recommends at least 24Mb RAM for the best performance. The recommended workstation configuration is a 33MHz 80386DX with 12Mb RAM and 100Mb disk space.

- *How Front-ends Work*
- *Types of Front-ends*

9

User Front-ends

A CLIENT/SERVER DATABASE IS A WASTE OF HARDWARE AND software if there's no way to access its data. The database vendors usually provide an interactive administration tool and user front-end, but the real power in C/S systems arises from the variety of third-party client applications and development software.

Front-end packages can be divided into four broad categories based on their primary function: add-ons to existing products, query/reporting programs, application development tools, and data integration and analysis tools. Add-ons are modules that enable existing PC applications such as dBASE or Lotus 1-2-3 to query the database server. Query/reporting tools make it easy for non-programmers to create queries for and reports from the data on the back-end. Application development tools, used primarily by programmers, are designed to ease the process of creating custom front-end applications. Finally, data integration and analysis tools are designed for managers and executives who need to examine data from a number of sources in order to make complex business decisions.

While front-end applications are available for just about every desktop platform currently sold, the vast majority support the Intel-based PCs and environments: DOS, Windows, and OS/2. In fact, just about all the front-ends available today run under Windows. The next two chapters concentrate primarily on these products, but the general principles of front-end operations apply to all platforms. Further, since many front-end vendors are porting their products to other platforms (a trend I fully expect will continue), this chapter will help you evaluate future products as they become available for other environments.

The number of front-end applications has significantly increased since the first edition of this book. Because of this, I've split the discussion about front-ends into two chapters for this edition. This chapter will cover a representative sampling of the add-ons and query/reporting tools, and the next chapter will cover the application development toolkits and data integration and analysis programs. Because of rapid market changes, the best sources for current information are magazines and trade publications such as *PC Magazine* and *PC Week*.

After describing the products here and in Chapter 10, I'll provide some advice and tips on deciding which ones best meet your needs. Chapter 10 closes with a table listing all the front-end applications covered and the back-ends they support. Use this information to evaluate both the products listed here and others that you may come across. Also, please bear in mind that the presence or absence of a front-end application in Chapters 9 and 10 implies neither an endorsement nor a silent critique; every client application has its strengths and weaknesses, and only you can decide which ones are right for you.

■ How Front-ends Work

Front-end applications can be either standard off-the-shelf software or custom programmed applications for a particular company or user. In either case, the client application looks and runs just like any other application the user has on his PC, Macintosh, or UNIX workstation. If the client software is designed properly, the only hint to the user that she's using a front-end to a remote database server occurs when she enters her security log-on ID and password.

The sequence of events that takes place when the user accesses the database server can be generalized into the six basic steps illustrated in Figure 9.1. For the sake of simplicity, the term *query* represents any action the user can take on the database, such as updating the data, inserting new data, deleting data, or requesting data from the database.

Figure 9.1

The general sequence of events that occurs when a user accesses a database server

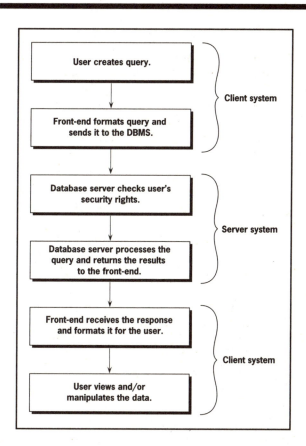

First, the user creates the query. It can either be created on-the-fly, frequently called an ad hoc query, or the user can run a preprogrammed or saved query that's part of the application. Next, the front-end application formats the query into the SQL used by the target back-end server and sends it out over the network to the server.

The server first verifies that the user has the proper security rights to the data being queried. If so, it then processes the query and sends the appropriate data back to the front-end. The client application receives the response data and formats it for presentation to the user. Finally, the user sees the response on the screen and can manipulate the data or modify the query and start the process over again.

In the case of add-on front-ends, the process is usually more complicated at the user end. As Figure 9.2 shows, the add-on module first translates the query from the client's native language or menu format to SQL and then sends it on to the server. When the data is returned, the add-on processor translates the response data into the client's native file format. The user then views and manipulates the data as if it came from the front-end's own data files (which it now in fact does). All these translations add overhead to the process. This usually means that add-ons require more resources on the client system, particularly additional RAM and CPU power.

Many folks investigating Client/Server systems wonder why a particular front-end application can't access data on any vendor's database server. There are two reasons for this: the variations in SQL and communications protocols. As noted in Chapters 4 through 7, SQL isn't quite as standard as it should be; every DBMS vendor adds unique extensions or interpretations to SQL that make their version slightly incompatible with any other vendor's version. The developers of the front-end packages have to know every command used by a particular back-end in order to add support for that DBMS to their package.

In addition, every DBMS uses a different communications protocol between the client systems and the database server. It isn't sufficient for a client to speak the proper dialect of SQL; the front-end developers must also include the proper application programming interface (API) calls in their software to enable it to talk to the DBMS's communications driver.

Needless to say, front-end vendors are sometimes reluctant to invest the time and resources necessary to support every Client/Server DBMS available, so they support a few (or even just one) of the more popular back-ends. That's why it's relatively easy to find client applications that support the Microsoft or SYBASE SQL Server or ORACLE, while front-ends for DBMSs like INFORMIX-OnLine are somewhat rare.

Fortunately, this situation is changing. Client/Server database vendors recognize the advantages of working closely with the third-party front-end vendors and encouraging them to support the vendor's DBMS. The rise of database-independent APIs, such as the Microsoft ODBC and Information Builder's EDA/SQL or IBM's DRDA, has helped front-end vendors broaden their support for different back-ends.

Figure 9.2

When the client software is an add-on to an existing application, the sequence of events in processing a query is slightly more complex.

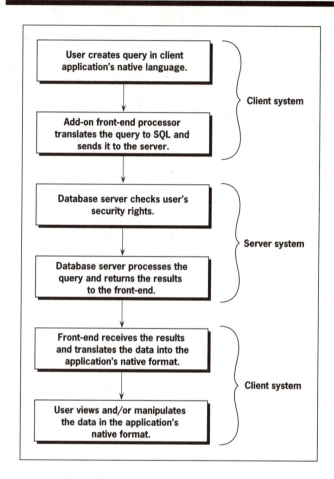

Open Database Connectivity (ODBC) and Other Common APIs

The proliferation of different RDBMSs from various vendors has resulted in efforts to create a common, database-independent Application Programming Interface (API). A common API would make it easier for developers and vendors of front-end applications to support any number of database servers, without having to write specific drivers for each DBMS. At this time, there are three competing versions of a common API, each with its own backers and capabilities.

The first common API was Microsoft's Open Database Connectivity (ODBC). Database applications talk to the ODBC driver, and the driver handles the necessary translations to access the back-end database. ODBC is currently the most popular of the common APIs, and is rapidly becoming the

Relate to Access

standard. Microsoft only provides ODBC drivers for its own database products; other RDBMS vendors have to write their own ODBC interface for their own products. Many were reluctant to do so until support for ODBC reached a critical mass, which happened in 1994. Now, the majority of front-end vendors provide ODBC support.

Information Builders took a slightly different approach with their EDA/SQL common API. EDA/SQL uses a gateway system to access over 50 different DBMSs, including all versions of SQL Server. The gateway system is a type of database server that doesn't actually store any data; instead, it processes incoming EDA/SQL statements, determines what the destination database server is, and translates the statements into the appropriate SQL dialect. It also handles any data translations needed between the front-end application and the database server. The gateway is completely independent of whatever platform the database server is running on, provided they can use a common network protocol to communicate.

Information Builders doesn't sell a database server, so their product is independent of any one back-end. They've also taken it on themselves to write the interfaces for the different DBMSs, instead of leaving the job to the vendors. Though this gave EDA/SQL the potential to become the standard cross-platform database API, the reality is that it hasn't caught on with front-end vendors.

Borland, IBM, Novell, and WordPerfect announced the Integrated Database API (IDAPI), a competitor to ODBC, in the Fall of 1992. IDAPI supports databases created by Borland's dBASE, Paradox, and InterBase database server, as well as IBM's Database Manager and DB2/2, NetWare Btrieve and NetWare SQL, and WordPerfect's DataPerfect database. Other companies announced support for IDAPI, but few actually carried through with their plans to do so. Today, only Borland, Novell (WordPerfect merged with Novell in 1994) and SYBASE provide any measure of support for IDAPI.

In fact, SYBASE may have topped everyone with the release of SYBASE Open Client 10. Open Client 10 provides native support for ODBC and IDAPI, as well as continuing support for SYBASE's own API. Though it seems to add an additional layer of overhead to the translation process, Open Client 10 has the potential to provide the same database-independent features as EDA/SQL. Even it if doesn't live up to that potential, Open Client 10's support for the existing standards ensures current and potential users that it won't become obsolete.

The bottom line, though, is that ODBC support has become very important if a vendor wants its front-end product to be widely accepted by the marketplace. You can't go wrong choosing a front-end that includes ODBC capabilities.

■ Types of Front-ends

Client/Server front-end applications fall into four general categories: add-ons to existing products, query/reporting programs, application development products and toolkits, and data integration and analysis tools. I'll be covering the first two categories in the rest of this chapter and the remaining two in Chapter 10.

No hard-and-fast rules determine which category a product belongs in, and it's not uncommon for a front-end to have features that overlap different categories. For example, a good data analysis program can also have excellent reporting features, or an application that uses an add-on module to access a Client/Server DBMS can be the best query and reporting program for those familiar with its features.

There's been one major change in front-ends since the first edition of this book—the vast majority are now Windows 3.1 applications. With the PC market as a whole moving to the GUI platforms, I suspect that DOS-based front-ends will fade away in the next couple of years. Even if they don't, it's highly unlikely that the vendors will continue spending a lot of time and resources updating their DOS applications.

I've categorized the front-end products according to their primary strength and features. Wherever possible I'll point out product features that properly belong to other categories.

Add-ons to Existing Products

It's only natural that the majority of add-ons exist for PC-based databases: After all, the majority of client systems are PCs, and just about every organization that has PCs also has PC databases. PC database vendors are eager to ensure that their products continue to be useful (and in demand) as more and more businesses move to the C/S architecture.

PC database add-ons also make it easier for those designing and developing Client/Server systems to integrate their existing databases into the new system. Front-end application development costs may be lower, because the users and programmers are already familiar with the existing database. With minimal training, they can usually adapt their existing skills to access the data from the server.

A PC database is also one of the more versatile front-end applications, primarily because it's a full DBMS in its own right. Most PC databases have a user-friendly interface, featuring menu-driven queries and complete reporting capabilities. PC databases also have fairly complex programming or script languages, which make it easy to create complete applications that can access and combine data from both native databases and database servers. The front-end features of a PC-based database could relegate it to any of the four categories.

In fact, the trend has been towards opening up the PC database architectures to support numerous data file types in their native formats. In most cases, this is being accomplished through support for ODBC drivers. The net result of this increasing openness, especially when it's combined with the move to GUI platforms, is to give PC databases a new lease on life as powerful and sophisticated front-end applications and development platforms.

On the other hand, a database add-on usually requires more system resources (particularly RAM) than a product designed as a front-end, due to the extra translation steps involved in converting queries and responses to the native format (see Figure 9.2 earlier). It's not uncommon for the database front-end to require 1Mb or more of extended or expanded RAM (4Mb under Windows) on the client system. The extra overhead also slows down the response time between the front-end and the database server.

However, when compared to the cost of developing an entirely new front-end application, the extra overhead of an add-on may be worth it. PC-based databases can serve as permanent solutions for creating client systems, if you realize problems may arise because these products are not primarily designed to be clients. The add-ons may not be tightly integrated into the product, which may require changes in how your applications function, though this is becoming less of a problem as more vendors support ODBC. PC databases can now serve as both a short-term solution while new front-ends are developed and the data is moved from the PC database to the database server, or as complete front-ends in their own right.

Add-ons fall into three subcategories: external modules that are added to a product; modules that are included in the base version of the product; and modules that are released as part of a special version of the product.

Access

In November 1992, Microsoft released their first (and long awaited) database product, Microsoft Access; it has since been upgraded to Version 2.0. Access is a Windows 3.1 database that makes excellent use of Windows's graphic interface, and provides a number of interesting features. Version 2.0 can directly read from and write to Btrieve, dBASE, FoxPro, and Paradox files, and can access data on Microsoft and SYBASE SQL Servers and ORACLE through the included ODBC drivers.

Microsoft Access introduced two features that have since been added to all of Microsoft's Windows applications (and a number of other vendor's applications as well): Cue Cards and Wizards. Cue Cards are a type of real-time help system that offer step-by-step instructions for performing common tasks. Wizards are a system of intelligent help facilities that use icons and pick-lists to help the user through complicated tasks, such as creating a form or report.

Access also makes full use of Windows's drag-and-drop capabilities; for example, the user can place fields on a report form by simply dragging the field box to the proper location with the mouse. Other GUI facilities include an icon bar for calling up common tasks, numerous pick-lists and dialog boxes, and support for displaying various types of graphic images as part of the on-screen forms and reports. Users can create links between different tables by simply drawing a line between the two dialog boxes representing the tables and linking the appropriate field names. Access also includes a copy of Microsoft Graph for creating charts and graphs based on the database data.

Access has a macro language composed of over 40 functions that let users and programmers automate database access. It also comes with Access Basic, a subset of the BASIC language that lets developers write custom functions, and Access SQL, a subset of SQL Server's TRANSACT-SQL language that can be used to query both Access and external databases. The main limitation of Access SQL is the lack of the SQL DDL and DCL statements ALTER, CREATE, DROP, COMMIT, GRANT, and LOCK. The functions provided by these statements are replaced in Access with some menu commands and Access Basic statements.

Data can be mixed and matched from multiple external data files by attaching them to the current database, as Figure 9.3 demonstrates. Microsoft Access runs under Windows 3.1 or better, and requires at least 6Mb RAM, with 8Mb recommended. A Windows NT version is under development.

Figure 9.3

Access can mix and match data from multiple sources by simply attaching the external data to the current database.

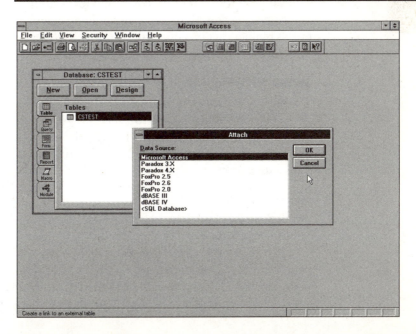

Approach

Lotus Development Corp. purchased Approach in late 1993, and released version 3.0 in 1994. Approach gives you easy access to a number of data formats and database servers right out of the box through its PowerKey technology. It defaults to dBASE IV .DBF files, and can create and access dBASE, FoxPro, Access, and Paradox files in their native formats. It can be integrated with 1-2-3 to provide access to spreadsheets, and can also access and modify Notes databases. Approach also includes drivers for connecting to Microsoft and SYBASE SQL Server and ORACLE database servers directly; to mainframe-based DB/2 databases through the MicroDecisionware gateways; and to any ODBC compatible database. It also has full support for DDE and OLE 2.0, so you can use other Windows programs as your data source.

Approach achieves this flexibility by storing everything but the data itself (that is, reports, forms, and so on) in Approach files. The Approach file also contains the information on the data source, and you can use multiple data sources in the same Approach file. This allows you to create relational-like forms and reports that combine data from dissimilar formats.

Approach defaults to two basic data views when you open a new file—a form containing all the fields in the database, and a worksheet that gives you a tabular view of the data. From there, you can design your own forms and worksheets, or use the included SmartMaster layouts to quickly create custom views and reports. Like the Wizards and Experts in other programs, Approach's Smart Assistants guide you through the process of creating sophisticated forms, reports, labels, and form letters.

Approach doesn't have a programming language, but it does have a macro builder that can be used to automate common tasks. It runs under Windows 3.x, and requires at least 4Mb RAM (6Mb recommended).

dBASE for Windows

The big news in the database world in 1994 was the release of Borland's dBASE for Windows 5.0. dBASE has always been the workhorse of PC-based databases—the release of the Windows version finally brought it into the 1990s. dBASE for Windows can access dBASE and Paradox data files in their native formats, using Borland's IDAPI (Independent Database Application Programming Interface). Access to ORACLE, SYBASE, and Microsoft SQL Servers, InterBase and ODBC compliant database servers is provided through the Borland SQL Links package, the new name for the old Paradox SQL Links modules.

dBASE for Windows is backwards-compatible with applications and data files created under dBASE III PLUS and IV. You can run these applications unchanged, though you'll be limited to seeing the forms and reports in a text-based window. dBASE for Windows gives developers two interlinked approaches to creating applications—the Command Window and various GUI designers. The Command Window replaces the familiar dot prompt, and is split into two sub-windows. You enter code in the top window, and the bottom window displays the results. The Query Designer, Form Designer, and Menu Designer use Windows's point-and-click capabilities to create their respective elements, and automatically generate the appropriate program code.

The two design approaches are tightly interlinked. If you have the Command Window and a designer open at the same time, you can watch the code being written in the Command Window as you make changes to the application element in the designer. Conversely, any changes made to the code in the Command Window are reflected in the designer. Figure 9.4 shows the various dBASE windows in action.

Figure 9.4

dBASE for Windows lets you create new databases, forms, queries, and menus in GUI-based designers, or by using regular dBASE code in the Command Window.

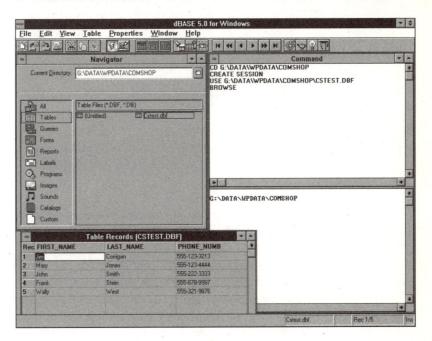

dBASE for Windows includes an integrated version of Crystal Reports 3.0, which makes it easier to create reports and mailing labels. It also provides support for multimedia objects such as graphics, sound files, and other BLOB (Binary Large Object) type data. dBASE for Windows also supports OLE 1.0 and DDE. Users can access and integrate any of the supported data sources from within the same application.

dBASE for Windows runs under Windows 3.1 or higher, and requires at least 6Mb RAM.

Programmers who want to use the dBASE language to access a database server, but prefer not to use dBASE itself, can use Microsoft's FoxPro for Windows. FoxPro can access any DBMS that supports ODBC through the add-on Client/Server connectivity kit.

Paradox for Windows 5.0

Ironically, dBASE's closest competitor in the PC database market is Borland's Paradox. Paradox is well-known for its user-friendly Query-by-Example (QBE) interface and semi-relational capabilities. In 1994 Borland released Paradox for Windows 5.0, with support for direct access to both Paradox and dBASE files, and for the Borland SQL Links. These are identical to the ones used by dBASE for Windows, which gives Paradox for Windows the same ability to access external data sources. In fact, both Paradox and dBASE use Borland's IDAPI-based database engine to access files created in the other's format.

Paradox has always been known for its excellent Query-by-Example interface, and the Windows version maintains this tradition. Its ease-of-use has been enhanced through the addition of a real-time help and guidance system that's a combination of Experts and Coaches. The Form Expert is similar to the one found in dBASE for Windows; the Mailing Label and Report experts are unique to Paradox. Experts use a combination of dialog boxes to step you through the respective tasks. Coaches are similar to Access's Cue Cards, and are designed to help you perform common tasks by guiding you through the process with a real-time on-line help system.

Version 5.0 also includes a number of features designed to make application development easier. The Experts can be used to create the basic objects, which can then be customized and programmed through the Integrated Development Environment (IDE). The IDE includes a built-in editor for creating and modifying ObjectPAL (Paradox's native language) applications. It also has a built-in debugger that lets programmers set breakpoints and watch points and trace an application while its executing. Developers can also create custom application experts, and use SQL to query local databases.

Paradox for Windows supports OLE 2.0 for linking databases with other Windows applications. Version 5.0 also adds support for a number of data types that were noticeably absent in prior versions, including time, logical, and auto-incrementing fields. It also supports BLOB fields that can contain graphic images, sound files, or other binary data files.

Paradox for Windows also provides support for sending and receiving data, query results, files, and messages through a number of e-mail systems. This support is provided through a separate application called OBEX, for Object Exchange, which is included in the standard package.

Paradox for Windows runs under Windows 3.1 or higher, and requires 6Mb RAM, with 8Mb recommended.

DataEase SQL

DataEase is also known as an easy-to-use but powerful PC-based DBMS that uses query forms as its primary user interface. In 1990, DataEase International released DataEase SQL, a full version that provides access to ORACLE, SQL Server, Database Manager, and DB2 back-ends, as well as to native files and applications. DataEase SQL transparently integrates database server access into the forms-based DataEase environment. For example, when a user first creates a form, he specifies the data source with which a form is associated; from that point on, the links to the data are made without user intervention.

The secret behind this is a DataEase facility called PRISM, the Processing Router for Integrated SQL Management. PRISM converts the DataEase functions and DataEase Query Language (DQL) statements into optimized SQL statements and transmits them to the database server. Application developers can also include native SQL statements in a DQL application.

Both DOS and OS/2 character-mode versions are available. A Windows 3.x version is under development, and should be released by mid-1995. It will be backwards-compatible with the DOS and OS/2 versions, and will support the same external databases. DataEase SQL's forms-based environment makes it an able query and reporting tool. It can access multiple database sources from the same application, so it can also be used for data integration and analysis applications.

Superbase95

Superbase, Inc.'s Superbase95 Version 3.0 has had a long and somewhat checkered history. It was originally developed by a small software company as one of the very first Windows-based DBMSs. It was later purchased by Software Publishing Corp. (SPC), who made it their flagship product—at least until they tried to enter the Client/Server market with their InfoAlliance system. InfoAlliance was less than a stellar success, and was finally discontinued shortly after the first edition of this book went to press. SPC then planned to roll InfoAlliance's reporting and data analysis features into Superbase, but ultimately ended up selling it to the present owners.

The latest version of this veteran Windows-based DBMS maintains Superbase's reputation as an application development environment while enhancing its end-user capabilities. Superbase95 can directly access .DBF files, and can connect to any database server that supports ODBC.

Superbase95's end-user features have been improved through the addition of SuperSteps, Superbase's name for its real-time user help system. SuperSteps guide the user through a number of common tasks, such as creating databases, forms, queries, and reports. It also includes a number of designers and editors that automatically generate the appropriate code, and it uses Windows's drag-and-drop capabilities to place objects on forms and reports. Its default data view is a form, and it also includes a table browser and a QBE interface for quick queries.

Object SBL is Superbase95's object-oriented programming language. Object SBL is similar in structure and features to Visual Basic. It also supports direct SQL, and has some additional enhancements to SQL that make it easier to include SQL statements in SBL programs. It supports DDE and OLE 2.0 for linking to other Windows applications. Users and developers can create reports that combine data from different sources.

Superbase has always supported graphic objects in databases, forms, and reports through the "external" data type. Superbase95 adds support for any type of external binary file, such as video images, sound files, DDE links, and OLE objects.

Superbase95 runs under Windows 3.1 or better, and requires 4Mb RAM, with 6Mb recommended.

Q&A

Symantec's Q&A is a DOS-based flat-file database, or non-programmable database, that's primarily designed for managing simple tasks such as maintaining mailing lists or small databases. It also hasn't substantially changed since the first edition of this book. Like most non-programmable databases, its menu-driven primary interface allows users to easily create and manipulate databases. Unique among the non-programmable databases, its add-on module enables it to query and report on data from ORACLE and Microsoft and SYBASE SQLBase servers. Figure 9.5 shows the streamlined menu interface that Q&A presents to the user. The Link-to-SQL module is available directly from Symantec; just send in a card that's included in the package.

Q&A can also perform data lookups from external Q&A databases or directly from dBASE III and dBASE IV data files without having to import the data into the current database. Q&A has a complete built-in word processor that makes it easy to incorporate information from a database into letters and documents. It supports multiple printer fonts and has a built-in spell checker and thesaurus, all of which makes it ideal for creating professional mail merge letters.

Another of Q&A's unique features is its Intelligent Assistant, a natural language interface to the database that lets the user enter queries in plain English. With the Intelligent Assistant's Query Guide, users choose the data operators, the field names, and unique values for the fields from pop-up menus, greatly simplifying the process of creating an ad hoc query. Q&A is a great tool for users who have limited database needs, but who occasionally have to access a database server.

Figure 9.5

Unique among the non-programmable databases, Symantec's Q&A lets the user access data from an ORACLE or SQLBase server

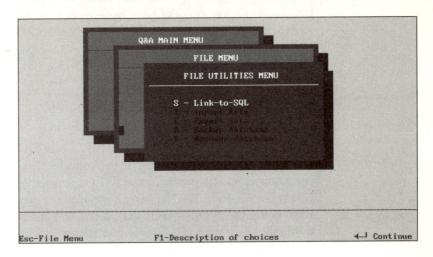

A Windows 3.1 version of Q&A is available, but it doesn't support access to external databases at this time.

Advanced Revelation

A number of PC-based database packages are designed for application developers rather than end users, and their vendors have jumped on the Client/Server bandwagon. Advanced Revelation is one example of a programmer-oriented database, and SQL is only one of the four programming languages it supports. Its primary language is R/BASIC, which has a wide range of functions for manipulating both the data and the Advanced Revelation environment. It also includes a variety of debugging routines and tools. Reports can either be designed directly through programming in R/LIST (the report writer language) or through the EasyWriter report generator, which creates R/LIST routines from your design. The Command Language (TCL), the master control language for all of Advanced Revelation, is a combination command line and job control language. TCL routines control the overall execution of applications by displaying windows and calling the appropriate R/LIST and R/BASIC modules.

Environmental Bonding refers to Advanced Revelation's ability to incorporate optional modules that let users access data files from other database systems (including database servers) in the external product's native format, using the standard Advanced Revelation languages and programming environment. Environmental Bonds for ASCII and dBASE III files are included in the product. Bonds for SQL Server, ORACLE, NetWare SQL, and DB2 are available from Revelation Technologies at an additional cost.

Clarion

Clarion is another PC-based database application development package that has a small but loyal following. Its add-on drivers allow application developers to access a wide variety of Client/Server DBMSs, including SQL Server, XDB-DBMS, INGRES, and ORACLE. Clarion has an IMAGE data type that's similar to Superbase 4's external file data type; it lets the programmer add graphics to the database.

PC/Focus and PM/Focus

Information Builders, Incorporated (IBI) is best known as the vendor of Focus, a DBMS based on the Network model that was designed for mini-computers and was ported down to PCs. Rather than creating their own Client/Server RDBMS, IBI is making its mark on the C/S market with EDA/SQL, the common SQL API discussed in Chapter 7. IBI is now positioning its PC/Focus (DOS) and PM/Focus (OS/2) databases as environments for creating front-end applications for the database back-ends supported by EDA/SQL. The two Focus versions can also access data on a SQL Server. PC/Focus and PM/Focus almost cross the line to being pure application development tools, but their continuing support for Focus databases keeps them in the add-on category for now.

Spreadsheet Add-ons

I can't close this section on add-on front-ends without mentioning the add-on modules that let spreadsheets query data from a Client/Server database. Spreadsheets are commonly used for analyzing, charting, and reporting on data, so they're a natural choice for users who are already familiar with the products and who need to analyze data that resides on a database server. The add-on modules translate the spreadsheet's requests into SQL and send them to the server. They then convert the server's responses into the spreadsheet's native format; the user can then manipulate the query's results just like any other spreadsheet.

Lotus Development Corporation has added this support to the DOS, OS/2, and Windows versions of 1-2-3 through its DataLens drivers. DataLens drivers for SQL Server, dBASE, and Paradox are included with 1-2-3 for Windows (Figure 9.6) and are available for the other versions for an additional cost. Lotus has made it easy for other vendors to provide DataLens drivers for their own DBMSs, and Oracle Corporation sells a DataLens driver for their ORACLE DBMS.

Microsoft has also added support for querying SQL Server to Excel, their Windows-based spreadsheet. Excel accesses the server through Microsoft Query, a stand-alone query tool that comes with Excel and uses ODBC to connect to external databases.

Figure 9.6

Lotus includes DataLens
drivers for dBASE, SQL
Server, and Paradox with
its 1-2-3 for Windows.

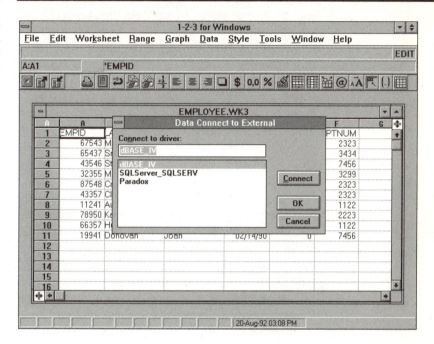

Informix, more widely known as a DBMS vendor, has an interesting spreadsheet called Wingz. Wingz is unique in the spreadsheet market because versions are available for all the major GUI environments, including Windows 3.x, OS/2 2.0 and higher, Macintosh, the NeXT system's NeXT-Step, and the UNIX-based Motif and Open Look. Informix provides back-end links through additional modules called DataLinks. Informix sells a DataLink for their own INFORMIX-Online DBMS and NetWare SQL. Fusion Systems Group is a third-party vendor that provides other DataLink modules that let Wingz access ORACLE and SQL Server databases.

Query/Reporting Programs

Query and report writing programs are primarily end-user tools, designed to make it easy for the casual user and non-programmer to access data on a Client/Server database. Querying, which requests data and presents the response on the screen, and report writing, which sends the response to a printer, are actually two different functions, though just about every front-end program does both.

This type of front-end application usually doesn't have a built-in programming language, but may have a scripting or macro language that records the user's keystrokes so that common queries can be automated for later reuse. It may also save a query to a file so that it can be rerun when needed or used in a report.

Query and reporting front-ends vary in their abilities. Some have excellent query interfaces with only minimal reporting capabilities, while others are more suited to report writing. As with any other application, which function you need more will determine which query/reporting program you should use.

Quest

Gupta's Quest is the little brother to Gupta's SQLWindows, an application development toolkit covered in Chapter 10; it's available as a stand-alone program, or comes as part of the SQLWindows Corporate Edition package. Quest is a Windows-based query and reporting tool that uses dialog boxes to insulate the user from the underlying SQL requests. It also has a number of built-in functions to assist in analyzing the data, and can be used as a tool to pass query results to other Windows programs for further analysis.

Like SQLWindows, the single-user base package comes with a stand-alone version of SQLBase, which lets the user create and use a local database or access an existing SQLBase server. It can also directly access dBASE-type and Paradox data files, so it can be used for some limited data integration. Support for SQL Server and other back-end databases is supplied through the various routers and gateways that Gupta sells.

Quest's main feature is its easy-to-use interface. A series of dialog boxes, pick lists, and drop-down menus leads the user through the process of choosing the database, tables, and columns to query, as shown in Figure 9.7.

Figure 9.7

Gupta's Quest lets the user choose the tables to query from a pop-up pick list.

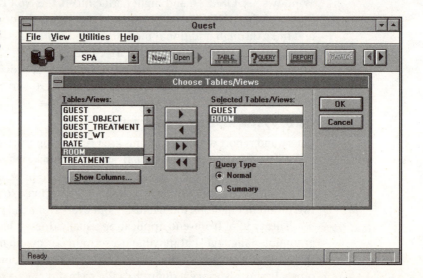

Other dialog boxes, lists, and menus let the user set the sort order and conditions for the query. Multi-table joins are created through a dialog box that displays a graphic link between the columns of the tables to be joined. Quest's built-in intelligence automatically displays a link between columns in different tables that have the same name. The user can either go with that link, add more links, or create a completely different one.

Quest also provides a dialog box-driven function editor with a large number of math, string, date, and time functions that can be used to create new columns in the result set to analyze the data. Queries can be saved for reuse or reports once the user is satisfied they're working properly. All of this can be done without the user knowing a single line of SQL.

Quest isn't strictly a query tool; users can modify the columns and data in local tables, create new tables, and import data into the local database from an external dBASE or Paradox file. Quest can also create local tables using the data returned from a query that the user can further manipulate without affecting the data stored on the server. These capabilities give Quest the ability to also serve as a stand-alone DBMS that can be expanded to a C/S system as your needs grow.

Reporting is another of Quest's strong features. It includes a full-screen report painter that uses dialog boxes to set the report size and format. Reports are based on existing saved queries or local database files, and can be previewed on the screen prior to printing. A number of formatting options are provided, including adding graphic borders to fields, controlling blank lines, and printing different fields in different fonts. Bitmap (BMP) graphics such as a letterhead can be added to a report for viewing or printing.

In addition to the numerous query functions, Quest has a set of aggregate and non-aggregate functions that can be used in a report. The report functions let the user do data analysis on the components of the report through statistical functions such as minimums and maximums, sums, and data counts. They also proved numerous string functions for extracting portions of text fields, or converting fields between numeric and text formats. Quest's reporting functions also make it easy to create mailing labels or form letters that use the data in a database for the fill-in information.

Quest doesn't have a native programming or scripting language. It can be indirectly programmed through DDE links with Visual Basic programs, or through macro languages such as those in Microsoft's Excel or Word for Windows.

Quest's biggest limitation is that it doesn't directly support joins or views from multiple data sources, because it can only access one database at a time. The only way to create multi-database joins is to query each database and save the results to a local database. Joins can then be done on the tables in the local database.

Other features include a forms-based interface, which supports QBF (query-by-form) applications, and the Query Estimator, which application developers and DBAs can use to limit the number of rows that can be accessed in a query. Finally, it includes a number of built-in business graphics features, including pie, bar, and line charts.

Quest is only available for Windows 3.x. It's available as a stand-alone package, or as part of Gupta's SQLWindows Corporate Edition Package. It directly supports Gupta's SQLBase database server; a single-user version of SQLBase is included in the package. Microsoft SQL Server, ORACLE, DB/2, Database Manager, and Informix can be accessed through the appropriate Gupta SQLGateway or SQLRouter.

Quest Reporter

Gupta introduced Quest Reporter in early 1994. Quest Reporter is a stripped down version of Quest, and has all the same query and reporting features. It's also 100-percent compatible with reports and queries saved in Quest. However, Reporter lacks the ability to update the database or enter new data.

Quest Reporter requires Windows 3.x. It's a good alternative query tool for application developers who like the Quest interface, but want to prevent users from modifying the database.

Impromptu

Impromptu 3.0 is a Windows 3.x query tool that has native support for dBASE and Paradox files, and can directly access ORACLE, Interbase, and Cognos's Starbase.

Impromptu bases its queries and reports on catalogs, which are its representation of the tables and columns in a database. Its catalogs present a somewhat object-oriented view of the data so the user doesn't have to be concerned with the actual structure of the database. Impromptu includes a snapshot function that keeps a local copy of the database's structure, allowing the user to create queries and reports off-line, and then connect to the database to run them.

Impromptu includes full support for Windows 3.x, including DDE, OLE, drag-and-drop editing, and dynamic pick lists. It has a number of built-in reporting and summary functions, including totals, subtotals, averages, and counts.

Personal Access

Spinnaker Software's Personal Access is a Windows-based application that extends the concept of hypermedia card stacks to user-oriented database access. Users can create cards that access data from a number of sources, including SQL Server, ORACLE, dBASE-type .DBF files, and Paradox data files.

Personal Access is actually an integrated front-end to Spinnaker's PLUS, a hypermedia applications development and management engine that also comes in a script-compatible Macintosh version. PLUS, an object-oriented system, lets users create stacks of cards that contain data objects such as text fields, data fields, graphics, and control buttons. However, the combination of Personal Access and PLUS is very resource intensive, requiring at least a 80386 system with a minimum of 4Mb of RAM.

A PLUS stack, illustrated in Figure 9.8, consists of one or more cards that contain the actual data queries. Cards are created by placing various objects on either the foreground (present only on the visible card) or background (present on all cards in the same stack). A series of floating toolboxes makes designing and placing objects easy. By itself, PLUS can only access data entered directly into the card stack.

Figure 9.8

Personal Access and PLUS use hypermedia card stacks to provide access to a variety of data sources.

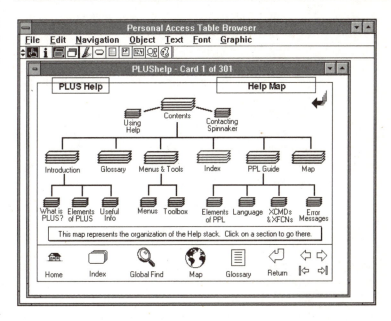

Personal Access extends PLUS's cards utility by accessing external databases. Users can create queries through dialog boxes and pick lists, and a single card can contain queries from multiple databases. Up to 500 databases can be accessed through a single card to create complex lookups and interrelationships, which means Personal Access can perform data integration and analysis as well. The user isn't limited to working with only one type of back-end or database file at a time; if a common field exists, stacks can access data from different database formats at the same time.

Cards can be designed to show only one record at a time or to display multiple records in a table format. When a link exists between two or more databases, later cards in a stack can contain other fields that are linked to the fields on the first card, which gives the user the means to further examine the databases's contents. For example, the first card can contain a query of all the departments in a company; when a particular department is highlighted, the second card in the stack can contain the results of a query of all employees in that department.

Designing database card stacks is very easy using the point-and-shoot toolkits. Personal Access and PLUS also provide on-screen navigation menus that let the user move quickly around the stack. Floating toolboxes such as Quick Tools give the user easy access to the basic tools for creating and browsing through card stacks, adding fields to existing cards, or placing predefined action buttons on the card. All the toolkits can be toggled on and off, so they're not in the way when you're browsing data.

The PLUS Programming Language (PPL) is an event-driven scripting language that consists of over 200 command statements and functions that control Windows message handling, properties, navigation, visual and sound effects, menus, and other user-interaction tools. PPL scripts are automatically created when the cards are designed, and a built-in editor is included for more advanced customizing of precreated scripts or for custom programming of card stacks.

PPL also provides support for DDE with other Windows applications and can access external Dynamic Link Libraries (DLLs) for more complete control over the Windows environment. When used with PLUS, Personal Access adds additional PPL commands to the language to support external database access.

PPL scripts can be used with any version of PLUS, making it easy to create applications for both IBM and Macintosh systems that access the same database servers.

External utilities assist in database management and can be run directly from Windows or through Personal Access. The Table Maintenance utility lets the user create and change database files, and Joiner lets the user precreate links between different database tables for later use in PLUS card stacks. Index Finder manages dBASE-type indexes, creating the associations needed for accessing .DBF files through Personal Access.

The included PLUS Reports module is a full-screen WYSIWYG report designer that lets the user create custom row-and-column or free-form reports, mail-merge letters, and forms from data contained in card stacks. Bitmap graphics from the clipboard can be included in reports, but only after they're copied to the clipboard from a card stack with a custom script. Reports can be printed or viewed in a window on the screen.

Also included in the package is PLUS View, which lets the user create dynamic row-and-column views of all the data contained in a particular stack. Views can be used as navigation tools or as a basis for quick summary reports of a stack.

Personal Access and PLUS are a powerful team for the easy creation of complex hypermedia card stacks for accessing existing databases. If you prefer a hypermedia interface or need to create database access applications that run on both the IBM and the Macintosh, the Personal Access/PLUS combination is a good choice.

Oracle Card

Oracle also provides Oracle Card, their own version of a hypermedia interface that uses the PLUS engine. Its scripting language, called Oracle Talk, is an enhancement of PPL which allows users and developers to issue PL/SQL and SQL commands from within a script. Oracle Card is similar to Personal Access, but is limited to accessing ORACLE databases. Many developers also feel that Oracle Card isn't as powerful as the Personal Access/PLUS combination and recommend using Personal Access instead of Card if you want to create hypermedia applications.

ClearAccess

ClearAccess from ClearAccess Corporation is a Windows and Macintosh-based query tool that's also designed to be a data link between a back-end database and Windows or Macintosh applications such as Microsoft Excel and Lotus 1-2-. for Windows. Its ad hoc query capabilities are very easy to use, and can be stored for reuse through script recording. The latest version also includes a report writer module. ClearAccess only supports ORACLE servers directly; SYBASE SQL Server is accessed through SYBASE Open Client, and Microsoft SQL Server through ODBC. Other servers can be accessed through EDA/SQL, DAL (Data Access Language, Apple's standard API for connecting to Macintosh-based databases), or a number of database gateways. ClearAccess now includes a local database server called Clear-Base, which allows ClearAccess to act as a stand-alone DBMS.

ClearAccess's main screen, called the Dashboard, consists of icons that give the user access to the various modules, such as the Query Builder and ClearReports. The Dashboard can be customized so that the icons can automatically run queries or reports.

The Query Builder is the heart of ClearAccess. Once a connection is established to a database, the Query Builder presents pick lists of all the accessible tables in the database; when a table is chosen, the columns in the table are displayed in a second pick list window. Queries are built by clicking on the columns and dragging them to a window on the right side of the query screen. The conditions and sorting options for the query are then chosen and entered, and the query is run. Other query options let the user format the results, create joins, and edit the various conditions prior to running the query. ClearAccess doesn't provide any statistical or mathematical functions beyond those provided by the supported back-ends.

The results can be returned either to the screen or to the Windows clipboard. Screen results are shown in a separate window that can be scrolled or enlarged; the results can also be saved to a file in ASCII, SYLK, or WKS format for importing into other applications. Users can join results from different databases by storing the different results sets in a local ClearBase database (similar to Quest and its local copy of SQLBase), and creating a JOIN on the local tables. Or the results can be sent directly to the Windows or Macintosh clipboard to be manually or automatically pasted into another application.

ClearReports is the reporting module that lets the user create reports using the GUI's drag-and-drop capabilities. Reports can be based on queries created in the Query Builder, or on queries created as part of the report. A number of default report styles are included such as columnar, mailing labels, and envelopes.

ClearAccess's real power comes from ClearScripts, the name for its scripting module. The script language has over 50 commands, and scripts can be created by recording an ad hoc query, or by direct editing in a text editor. Existing scripts can be edited through the built-in editor, and are run from the RUN button on the main menu. Simple debugging is supported through its ability to pause scripts during execution, or to watch the actual back-and-forth dialog between the script and the database server in a separate window. The script language also lets the developer prompt the user for values during script execution, which lets ad hoc queries be created and run through scripts.

The included ClearLinks modules let ClearAccess act as a direct automatic query link for Excel, 1-2-3, HyperCard, and other applications using DDE. Other Windows or Macintosh applications can be started and stopped by a ClearAccess script, which lets the developer completely automate the process of querying the database and moving the results to another application for reporting or analysis. Excel is supported directly through an included Excel Add-In document that lets Excel macro sheets access and run Clear-Access scripts to query databases and return the results to a spreadsheet. A similar facility is provided for Wingz and 1-2-3 for Windows. ClearLinks for other applications are under development.

ClearAccess Corporation's ClearManager 1.0 is a database manager and monitoring application for Windows 3.x and the Macintosh. ClearManager can be used by a DBA to track database accesses, control ClearAccess applications, manage libraries of ClearScripts, and schedule queries for execution when the database isn't in heavy use.

ClearAccess's best feature is its linking capabilities; its strength lies in its ability to automate database access and automatically pass the results to other GUI applications for further reporting or analysis.

ClearAccess and ClearManager are available for Windows 3.x and the Macintosh. They use SYBASE Open Client to connect to the SYBASE SQL Server, and ODBC to connect to Microsoft SQL Server. They can directly access ORACLE and ClearBase databases, and can use DAL, EDA/SQL, and various database server gateways to connect to other databases.

DataPivot and DataPrism

Brio Technology's DataPivot and DataPrism are designed to work together; DataPivot is a reporting tool and DataPrism provides the query capabilities and database links. Both programs originated on the Macintosh and were eventually ported to Windows.

DataPivot uses Apple's System 7.0 Subscribe feature (similar to the DDE links in Windows) or DataPrism to get the data for its reports. DataPivot for Windows uses DDE and can also directly access Excel and Lotus 1-2-3 spreadsheets, text files, and data received from DataPrism for Windows queries. Both versions of DataPrism support direct access to ORACLE databases, as well as databases that can be accessed by DAL or SYBASE Open Client.

DataPivot and DataPivot for Windows include the common reporting functions such as averages, counts, and totals. They also let the user create custom formulas that can be included in the report. Their strong point is the ability to create multilevel cross-tabulation reports, giving the user a handy data analysis tool. They can automatically recalculate a report when the data the report is based on is updated.

DataPrism and DataPrism for Windows make it easy to create queries by taking full advantage of the GUI's drop-down menus, dialog boxes, and pick lists. Queries can be edited and saved for future use. They can export the results of the query to external programs for further analysis through System 7.0's Publish feature on the Macintosh, and DDE in Windows.

DataPivot and DataPrism run on the Macintosh. DataPivot for Windows and DataPrism for Windows run on Windows 3.x. The Windows version of DataPivot can directly access Excel and 1-2-3 spreadsheets, as well as import data in text format. Both versions of DataPrism can connect SYBASE SQL Server though Open Client, as well as directly connecting to ORACLE databases. Apple's DAL is also supported.

- *Application Development Environments*
- *Choosing the Right Front-end for Your Needs*

10

Development Front-Ends

I COVERED THE FIRST TWO FRONT-END CATEGORIES IN THE LAST chapter—add-ons to existing products and query/reporting applications. This chapter covers the remaining two categories.

Application development toolkits are used by programmers and application developers to create custom front-ends. Every DBMS vendor has toolkits available that can be used to create front-ends for that vendor's database server. I won't be covering those here; instead, I'll be talking about the third-party application development toolkits that can be used to build front-end applications for a number of popular DBMSs.

Data integration and analysis programs are primarily used to combine information from different sources for analysis purposes. The data sources can be as disparate as databases, spreadsheets, and text applications. They're usually used to create Executive Information System (EIS) and Decision Support System (DSS) applications.

■ Application Development Environments

Application development has become the hot area in the Client/Server market. There's an ever-increasing number of consulting firms and Value-Added Resellers (VARs) creating specialized C/S applications for particular markets. These applications are called *vertical market applications*, because they're created for a particular use, such as inventory control or retail point-of-sale systems.

Application programmers can build their applications from the ground up, using a 3GL and an add-on development library, but there's no point in reinventing the wheel when excellent application development environments are available. Application development environments take care of the bulk of the grunt work (writing code, managing the data, and so on), which leaves the developer free to concentrate on the appearance and functions of the application itself.

Application development environments fall into two broad categories: development toolkits and analysis and integration applications. Application development toolkits are the more generalized of the two, and can be used to create any type of C/S front-end imaginable. Analysis and integration applications are geared toward creating specialized systems for examining data from various sources and making decisions based on that analysis.

Application Development Toolkits

Every Client/Server DBMS vendor has some type of programming toolkit available that can be used with a 3GL such as C or COBOL to create custom front-end applications. Many have also released their own application development products that make it easier to create custom query forms, reports, and user menus; Oracle's SQL*Forms and SQL*ReportWriter, and INGRES/Tools are prime examples. However, these toolkits are usually restricted to creating front-ends for the vendor's DBMS, or for other DBMSs whose vendors have licensed a version of the DBMS vendor's toolkit.

Third-party vendors have filled the gap with application development packages that can be used to create front-ends for a variety of database servers. Some vendors have also released programming libraries that let other vendors's applications access data on a server. And programming language vendors have extended their languages's capabilities to include support for Client/Server databases.

The vast majority of third-party application development toolkits are based on Windows 3.x; its GUI eases the process of creating front-ends. While this can be a problem for many corporate front-end developers whose companies have yet to upgrade to PCs that can run Windows, the basic fact of life is that the computer world is moving to GUIs. The need to create sophisticated GUI-based C/S front-ends can be a compelling reason for an organization to bite the bullet and move to Windows.

SQLWindows

Gupta Technologies Inc. is best known for their SQLBase database server. However, they also sell two popular application development products that support their own RDBMS and others, including the Microsoft and SYBASE versions of SQL Server. Support for SQL Server and other back-end databases is supplied through the various routers and gateways that Gupta sells.

Gupta's main development package is SQLWindows, an application development toolkit that assists programmers in creating Windows 3.x-based client applications. Their other popular package is a query and reporting tool called Quest, which I discussed in Chapter 9.

SQLWindows can be used either as a user query tool or an application development platform. Gupta includes a single-user version of their SQLBase DBMS in the package, which allows developers to create front-end applications without needing access to a full C/S system. SQLWindows isn't limited to only supporting SQLBase, though. It can also be used to create front-ends for both Microsoft and SYBASE SQL Server; Ingres; IBM's OS/2 Database Manager, DB2/2, and SQL/400; NetWare SQL; and Hewlett-Packard's AllBase. Different database servers can be accessed from the same application, which makes SQLWindows useful in a mixed database environment.

SQLWindows's programming environment is object-oriented, but it isn't as tightly integrated as others, such as Powersoft Corp.'s PowerBuilder (discussed in the next section). In addition to supporting direct SQL statements, SQLWindows includes its own SQLWindows Application Language (SAL). There's also support for integrating SQLWindows applications with those created in C; your application code can be converted to C, integrated with other code, and compiled by a number of popular C compilers.

As Figure 10.1 shows, SQLWindows uses a series of windows on the Windows 3.x desktop for designing and creating the application. SQLWindows lets you monitor the programming code that it's creating in a separate window; it adds the appropriate SAL statements to the program each time the developer adds or modifies an object on the design screen.

Figure 10.1

Gupta's SQLWindows is a powerful though not tightly integrated development environment. The main window (titled SQLWindows here) shows you the SAL code being written as you add various objects to the design screen (bottom window).

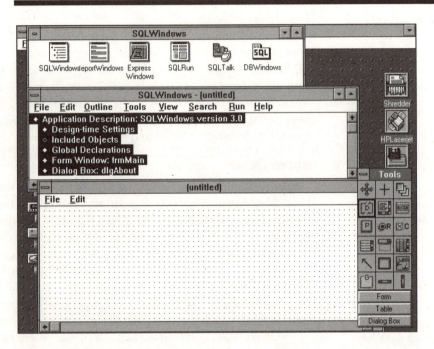

It also has debugging capabilities built in, and the developer can create a run-time application file that's used with the run-time module to execute the application outside of SQLWindows.

SQLWindows includes a couple of modules that let developers and users create front-end applications without writing program code. Express Windows is used to create an on-screen form or table view of the database, and ReportWindows lets the developer create custom reports by painting the design on the screen. SQLWindows also provides Windows Dynamic Data Exchange (DDE) support so that data can be automatically shared with other Windows applications, such as a spreadsheet or a charting program. Version 4.0, which was released in late 1993, added complete support for the new features introduced in Windows 3.1, including the Multiple Document Interface (MDI), which makes it easier to have multiple windows open within the same application, and Object Linking and Embedding (OLE), which provides the ability to include other applications (such as a charting program) or objects directly in a SQLWindows application.

Version 4.0 also added QuestWindow, which adds the quick query functions of Gupta's Quest to SQLWindows. These query functions can be used as a quick prototyping tool by the programmer, to ensure that the SQL statements included in the application are correct and returning the proper results. A QuestWindow browse or edit window can also be included as part of an application to provide the end user with ad-hoc query capabilities.

Version 4.1, which shipped in early 1994, added a new forms-based interface, which supports QBF (query-by-form) applications. It also added the Query Estimator, which application developers and DBAs can use to limit the number of rows that can be accessed in a query. Finally, it included a number of built-in business graphics features, including pie, bar, and line charts.

The Corporate Edition of SQLWindows includes a collaborative programming environment that Gupta calls TeamWindows. TeamWindows makes it easier for a team of application developers to work on the same application by providing an application generator, security features that keep track of which programmer accesses which code module, and source-code version-management and control.

Gupta released Version 5.0 in late 1994. This latest version added two major features: QuickObjects and support for creating C code. QuickObjects are prepackaged objects that make it easy to link data, create automatically updated presentations, and execute external applications based on the analysis of the data. QuickObjects also let you link your application to external e-mail systems and Lotus Notes. Version 5.0 can also translate your SAL code to C. You can then use the C code to add your own modules, and compile the application with any of the popular C compilers.

SQLWindows is only available for systems running Microsoft Windows 3.x. It requires 4Mb RAM. No other versions are available at this time, and Gupta has not publicly stated any plans for supporting other GUIs.

PowerBuilder Enterprise

SQLWindows's closest competitor is Powersoft Corp.'s Windows-based PowerBuilder. Both are very popular among C/S application developers and additional support is available from various user groups.

Powersoft changed how PowerBuilder is marketed with the release of Version 3.0 in 1993. PowerBuilder now consists of six separate components that can be purchased separately or as part of an overall development environment called PowerBuilder Enterprise. The core PowerBuilder product has been renamed PowerBuilder Desktop. The current version is 4.0, which was released in late 1994.

PowerBuilder Enterprise is a powerful object-oriented front-end developer's toolkit that's aimed primarily at the corporate and MIS applications programmer. PowerBuilder Enterprise consists of six separate modules: PowerBuilder Desktop, PowerBuilder Team/ODBC, PowerBuilder Enhanced Database Kit, PowerBuilder Application Library, PowerBuilder Developer Toolkit, and the WATCOM Image Editor. These modules are also available separately so you can start with a basic system and expand as your needs change.

PowerBuilder Desktop is the core program. It's a stand-alone development platform that can access data from the built-in single-user WATCOM SQL engine or from PC-based databases such as dBASE and Paradox through the supplied ODBC driver. PowerBuilder Desktop is the actual application development and execution environment; the other modules tie into it to extend its capabilities.

PowerBuilder Team/ODBC provides capabilities similar to those found in Gupta's TeamWindows. Team/ODBC adds version and quality control to PowerBuilder, which makes it easier for a programming group to work on the same application. It also adds complete support for ODBC access to database servers. You have to have Team/ODBC to access data from an external server.

The PowerBuilder Enhanced Database Kit contains the drivers for all the database servers PowerBuilder supports. The base version of PowerBuilder supports access to dBASE, Paradox, Access, and Watcom SQL databases. In addition to support for all versions of SQL Server, the Enhanced Database Kit adds access support for ORACLE, Gupta's SQLBase, XDB System's XDB-DBMS, INFORMIX, HP's ALLBASE/SQL, IBM's Database Manager and DB2/2 on OS/2, IBM's mainframe-based DB2 through the Micro Decisionware gateway (discussed in Chapter 7), and any other database that supports ODBC.

The PowerBuilder Application Library contains a number of pre-built objects, windows, and functions that developers can include in their own applications. The PowerBuilder Developer Toolkit contains additional development, performance, and database maintenance tools. And the WATCOM Image Editor is a utility for creating icons and bitmaps that can be used in PowerBuilder applications.

PowerBuilder Desktop comes with a single-user version of WATCOM SQL as its native database manager. Like SQLWindows, an application can connect to more than one database server at the same time. It takes full advantage of the Windows 3.1 environment, and includes support for OLE and MDI. All development is done through painters, which is the PowerBuilder name for the various modules that are used to create the database, define the menus and screen appearance, manipulate the data, and develop, debug, and maintain applications (see Figure 10.2). While the module's icons are displayed separately on the main menu, they're also tightly linked, and can be executed from within each other as the need arises.

Figure 10.2

PowerBuilder Desktop
uses application
development tools that
Powersoft calls painters.
They can be accessed
through the PowerPanel
(center) or PowerBar
(top). Developers will find
it a tightly integrated
object-oriented
development environment.

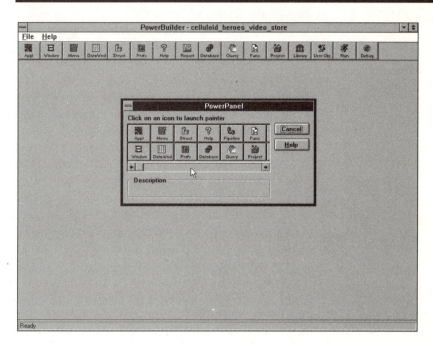

Underlying all the modules and tying the development environment together is PowerScript, PowerBuilder's script language, which resembles a cross between C and Basic. While prior knowledge of C or SQL isn't necessary to create applications in PowerBuilder, an understanding of the event and message-passing nature of Windows applications helps smooth the development process. PowerScript's similarity to C also makes it easier for a 3GL programmer to quickly adapt to its development environment. The included on-line manuals briefly discuss the event, message-passing, and object-oriented concepts, and they include many examples of the proper use of PowerScript statements and functions.

PowerBuilder makes excellent use of Windows graphics throughout the entire development process; for example, a key icon is attached to the appropriate columns on which the table will be indexed, and a view icon is connected to the tables that are part of a view. Bitmap graphic files (created externally or through the Picture Painter) can also be associated with a column in a database, regardless of the database server; the bitmap's file name is stored as the data in the column, and the bitmap is displayed by Power-Builder when the row is retrieved.

The database server can also be administered through PowerBuilder—the developer can enter SQL statements that are sent directly to the server to maintain users, groups, and security, and execute stored procedures (if supported by the particular database server). Direct SQL commands can be entered through the Database Painter.

The DataWindow Painter is the most powerful feature and the heart of PowerBuilder. It's used in combination with SQL statements or PowerScript scripts to retrieve and manipulate one or more rows of data from the database server. However, you don't have to know SQL to create applications with the DataWindow; its point-and-shoot interface lets you pick the data items you want to retrieve or update from dialog boxes and on-screen displays of the structure of the database. DataWindow automatically generates the appropriate SQL and PowerScript commands to perform the query or update.

Data can be displayed in tabular rows, cross tabular forms, or in a freeform window created by Window Painter. SQL statements can be custom-written or built through the Database Painter, and the PowerScript Painter is used to create script files, drawing from over 400 built-in functions. User-defined functions are also supported, and can be created through the Function and User Object Painters. Full DDE and OLE support is included, and external Windows or database server library functions can be called from within a script.

When development is completed, the developer uses the built-in compiler to compile the application into a run-time application file. When combined with the PowerBuilder run-time DLLs, the application can be used independent of the developer environment.

PowerBuilder includes two additional tools to make application development easier. The Library module is used to maintain application libraries, which can be browsed, separated, merged, or regenerated, and it can also create a full report on a library's contents. The Debug module is a full debugger that supports single-step processing and breakpoints. It can be run on its own or from the various painters during the development process.

Powersoft has joined Microsoft in providing technical support files, tips, and the latest PowerBuilder documentation on a CD-ROM, called the Powersoft Infobase CD-ROM. Developers can sign up for a subscription service that sends out updated CD-ROMs on a quarterly basis. PowerBuilder Enterprise is also available on a CD-ROM, which includes the documentation and latest Infobase.

With the release of PowerBuilder 3.0, Powersoft also released two scaled-down database access applications. PowerViewer is a simplified query and reporting tool that's based on the PowerBuilder DataWindow technology. PowerMaker includes the features in PowerViewer, and adds the ability to define databases and create forms, queries, and reports. PowerViewer can best be described as a simplified end-user version of PowerBuilder Desktop.

Currently the only supported platform is Microsoft's Windows 3.1, on a minimum 80386 with 8Mb of RAM. Support for Windows NT is still under development. Powersoft is also considering developing a version of PowerBuilder for OS/2 2.x, but has not announced firm plans or a release date at this time.

Delphi

Borland International, Inc. started out as a 3GL compiler vendor, and has grown to be one of the major vendors of software for Intel-based microcomputers. In late 1994, Borland announced Delphi, its new database application development environment that replaces ObjectVision. Delphi is object-oriented, runs under Windows 3.1 or higher, and comes in two versions.

The standard edition includes a local copy of the Borland Database Engine, which lets you create applications that can access dBASE, Paradox and Local Interbase Server databases. It also supports ODBC. The Client/Server edition includes the Borland SQL Links for direct access to ORACLE, both SYBASE and Microsoft SQL Server, Informix and InterBase database servers.

Delphi has a number of modules that make it easier to create sophisticated programs. The Object Inspector gives the programmer access to all of an application object's properties, and the ObjectBrowser lets the developer view the entire object hierarchy. The Project Manager lets the developer keep track of all the components in the application. The Visual Component Library contains a variety of pre-designed objects that can be used in applications.

Delphi also has a feature called Two-Way-Tools, which is similar in concept to dBASE for Windows command window. The Two-Way Tools let the programmer switch back and forth between the objects being designed and the underlying code; changes in one are automatically reflected in the other.

Delphi compiles the application into a .EXE file that can be distributed royalty-free. Applications can be run under Windows 3.1 or higher, Windows NT, and Windows 95. The upcoming Windows 95 version will create full 32-bit applications. It includes a built-in assembler that can be used to fine-tune the application. Delphi can also create DLLs that can be used by other applications and languages, such as C++, Visual BASIC, Paradox or PowerBuilder.

Delphi has what may be the most sophisticated debugger currently found in C/S application development toolkits. The GUI Debugger supports conditional breakpoints, watchpoints, single-step execution, trace mode, and call stack monitoring. The WinSight utility lets the programmer view the underlying messages being passed in Windows, and the WinSpector utility provides diagnostic tools.

Finally, Delphi includes the ReportSmith report writer. ReportSmith can be used to create both printed reports and on-screen queries. It includes a number of pre-defined report templates and styles.

Delphi requires Windows 3.1 or higher, with 6Mb RAM for the standard edition and 8Mb RAM for the Client/Server version. The standard edition uses 30Mb disk space, and the C/S version 50Mb disk space. It works with any network compatible with Windows 3.1.

Borland has joined the latest trend by only distributing Delphi on a CD-ROM disk. $3^1/2$-inch disks are available direct from Borland for an additional cost.

Object/1

Micro DataBase Systems, Inc. is best known as the vendor of two microcomputer and minicomputer DBMSs, MDBS IV and KnowledgeMan, as well as the expert system development package GURU. MDBS also sells Object/1, an object-oriented graphical database application builder.

Object/1 was originally released as a database development toolkit for the OS/2 Presentation Manager. A version for Windows 3.x has since been released. The base package supports the creation of GUI applications for MDBS's two database products; access to the Microsoft and SYBASE versions of SQL Server is provided through the Object/1 Professional Pack. IBM's Database Manager and DB2/2, and ORACLE are supported through other Professional Packs.

Object/1 is primarily aimed at nonprogrammers, even though it contains a full object-oriented programming language that resembles C++. Its components are all screen-oriented, so the developer only has to create the elements on the screen, and Object/1 will create the appropriate source code. A database engine based on MDBS IV is included in the package, so stand-alone applications can be created in addition to those that access a database server.

The Forms Painter is the primary interface and is used to create all the objects the user will see on the screen. A floating palette lists all the available objects and makes it easy to place them on the form.

Other modules include the System Browser, which lets the programmer search for particular code modules in the source code and edit them. The Project Browser is related to the System Browser; it decomposes a complete application into smaller pieces for testing and editing. A full debugging tool is also included.

Unfortunately, Object/1 doesn't include any type of run-time module, so the whole package is needed to run applications developed under it. The final cost of the application can rise quickly if you have a significant number of users to support, especially when you add in the extra cost for the Professional Packs needed.

Versions of Object/1 and the Object/1 Professional Packs are available for OS/2 and Windows 3.x. The OS/2 version is still based on OS/2 1.3, so it's limited to creating 16-bit applications. However, the OS/2 applications will run under OS/2 2.x, so this limitation isn't very serious.

Q&E Database Editor and Library

Intersolv, the current owners of the Q&E products, has approached the market for database server access modules from a slightly different angle. The Q&E Database Editor for Windows or OS/2 is a query engine that can be used along with other applications to query and import data from a number of database servers, including SQL Server, NetWare SQL, Ingres, DB2, and

Database Manager. The Q&E Database Library for Windows or OS/2 is a collection of function libraries that provide a standard API to be used with 3GLs to incorporate database server access into a programmer's application. Both products provide other vendors with an easy method to add front-end capabilities to their products. The Database Library supports the same back-ends as the Database Editor.

Q&E straddles the line between being a generic add-on and being an application development toolkit. However, the two packages are primarily aimed at providing software vendors and application developers with an easy way to access database servers, so I've included them in this category.

FormFlow

Forms design packages were originally developed to provide a way to design paper forms on a PC. As time went on, the vendors of these applications added the ability to store data with the form, giving on-screen forms the capability to be used in place of paper ones. Delrina's PerForm PRO quickly became one of the most popular and feature-filled forms design packages available.

The increasing popularity of both Windows- and LAN-based electronic mail systems has lead to the development of workflow applications. These applications are designed to take the electronic forms and move them (and the data they contain) through an organization over the network, reducing the need for shuffling paper from one office to another. It wasn't long before the workflow vendors gave their form design applications the ability to access and store data in an external database. Workflow design packages are now sophisticated enough to be used to create front-end applications for a Client/ Server database.

Delrina combined PerForm PRO's form design capabilities with an interface to both e-mail systems and various database formats and servers to create a workflow application called FormFlow. FormFlow Filler is the end-user package, and it runs on Windows 3.x and DOS. The FormFlow Manager Module contains the Windows 3.1-based FormFlow Designer, a copy of Filler, and the Security Administration program.

FormFlow Designer takes full advantage of the Windows 3.1 interface and is very easy to use. It includes a variety of tools that make it easy to recreate paper forms on the screen. FormFlow Designer comes with 100 ready-to-use form templates and seven demo applications that can be modified to fit your company's work style. The form templates cover a range of standard business forms and are easily customized. You can view the forms in a number of ways, including real size, zoomed, fit to the window, or fit to the screen. Figure 10.3 shows the wealth of design tools that FormFlow provides.

Figure 10.3

Delrina's FormFlow is a powerful yet easy-to-use forms design package that gives developers a simple way to create complete workflow and database application systems.

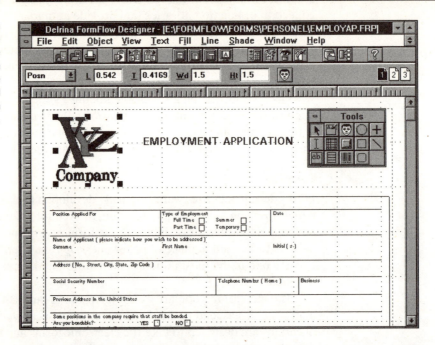

Existing paper forms can be scanned into FormFlow with the PerForm Tracer package. You can then use the scanned images as the basis for designing the electronic forms. FormFlow also has full support for electronic signatures to provide form security. FormFlow includes a script and macro language, called the Intelligent Forms Language (IFL), that lets the designer create complete applications. IFL macros can be assigned to buttons and objects on a form or to the form itself for automating entry and exit functions.

FormFlow includes built-in support for dBASE and Paradox data files and indices. An SQL database server access module that supports the Microsoft SQL Server, ORACLE, and IBM's DB2, OS/2 Database Manager, and DB2/2 was released in early 1994 and will be shipped free to anyone who returns the postcard found in the package. FormFlow lets you mix data from different sources into the same form, which makes it quite capable of being used to design data analysis and display systems. Figure 10.4 shows how different data files are linked in FormFlow Designer.

Delrina sells both DOS and Windows 3.x versions of the FormFlow Filler. The Manager Module requires Windows 3.1. FormFlow provides built-in support for accessing and storing data in dBASE and Paradox files. The SQL server module extends FormFlow's reach to a Microsoft SQL Server database.

Figure 10.4

Creating database links
in FormFlow is as simple
as dragging the key field
icon from one database
file display and dropping
it on another.

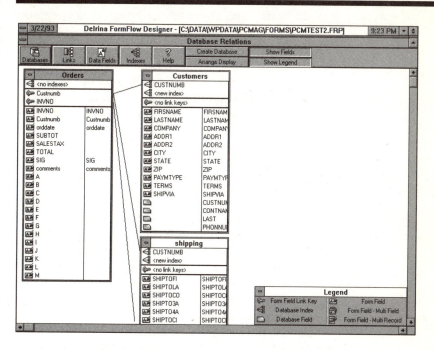

Data Integration and Analysis Applications

The last category of front-end applications covers data integration and analysis tools. Data integration and analysis are actually two parts of the same process—the user first queries data from different sources and then combines the data to analyze what it means.

The most common type of integration and analysis application is called an Executive Information System (EIS). EIS applications are designed to gather data from several different places in an organization and present the information to the organization's managers in a way that helps them make complex business decisions. For example, an EIS might combine data from the inventory, sales order, and personnel databases to help a manager create vacation schedules that have a minimal impact on order fulfillment.

Decision Support Systems (DSS) are a variation on the EIS applications. They're more specialized and are used to provide real-time data to support rapid decision making. Functionally, they're similar to EIS systems, and the two terms are usually used interchangeably to describe the same type of application.

Integration and analysis applications can also be used for statistical or scientific studies, for analyzing stock market trends, or whenever users need to combine and examine data from multiple sources. The proliferation of information in our modern businesses (and even our society) makes it very difficult to distinguish the important data from "background noise" (for lack of a better term), so in some respects, data integration and analysis is the most useful application a computer user can have.

Forest & Trees

Forest & Trees from Trinzic Corp. may be the easiest to use, yet most powerful, data analysis tool available for Windows today. Forest & Trees was originally produced by Channel Computing, Inc., but Channel was purchased by Trinzic in early 1993.

The standard version lets the user combine data from most common PC file formats, including dBASE, Lotus 1-2-3, Novell BTrieve, Excel, Q&A, R:Base, and Paradox. The Client/Server version adds the capability to integrate data from a number of back-ends besides Microsoft's SQL Server, including ORACLE, Gupta's SQLBase, INGRES, Hewlett-Packard's AllBase, NetWare SQL, DB2 (through the Micro Decisionware's Database Gateway), and Digital's Rdb/VMS. It also includes support for Information Builder's EDA/SQL common database access interface. Its biggest limitation is that it's an analysis-only tool that accesses the data sources in read-only mode.

As its name implies, Forest & Trees uses a tree-like metaphor to collect data from various sources into data objects on the screen. Each object is a node in the tree diagram and can contain the results of a query on a particular data source, as shown in Figure 10.5. The objects can then be connected to other objects to create higher-level nodes that are based on formulas that analyze and combine the data from lowerlevel nodes. All the nodes ultimately connect to a top- (root-) level node that contains the complete analysis of the sub-nodes. F&T doesn't have a programming or scripting language, so all data access and analysis is done through objects, pick lists, and dialog boxes.

The easiest way to describe how F&T presents complex data for analysis is by an example. Suppose a business owner wants to look at the business's cash flow. The first step is to create objects that perform the queries to show the different parts of cash flow, such as income received, outstanding invoices, inventory, taxes paid, expenses, cash-on-hand, and investments. Each particular analysis node is created from a query on one data source for the item being examined; for example, the data for income can come from a set of Excel spreadsheets, while the inventory data can come from an SQL Server database. Figure 10.6 shows F&T's data access screen, where the user specifies the data source for a particular node.

Once the lower-level nodes are created, the user creates the second-level nodes that combine the results of the lower nodes into one node for income, and one for money spent. Finally, a top node is created that subtracts expenses from income to show the company's profits.

Figure 10.5

Forest & Trees uses a
tree-like metaphor to
collect and combine data
for analysis from a wide
variety of sources.
Shown here are two
different views of the
interconnections
between the different
data elements.

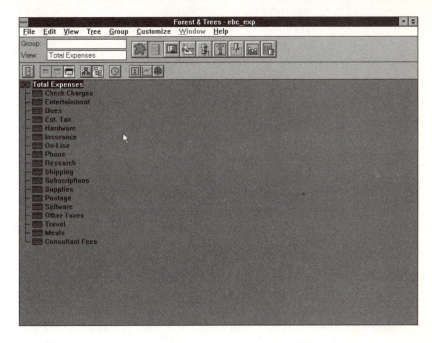

Figure 10.6

Forest & Trees uses a
common dialog box for
accessing different data
sources. It automatically
recognizes the data
source based on the file
or server type.

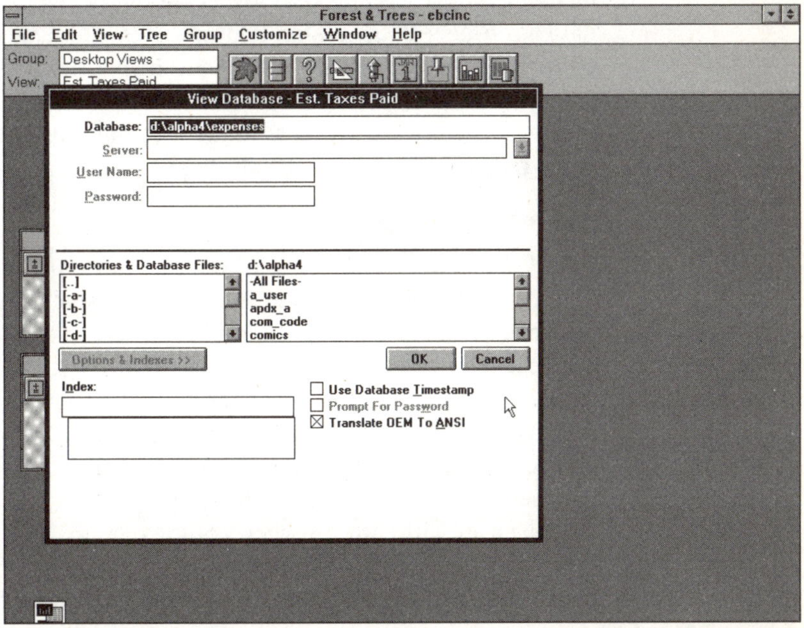

F&T presents all the nodes either as individual data objects, or as a tree with connecting lines showing which lower-level nodes make up which higher-level nodes. Navigating around the tree is easy—each node's display object has button icons that can be used to navigate up and down the tree to examine the data elements that compose the node. Other buttons let the user create a graph or a report on the data the object represents; the user can even add pop-up notes to each node to clarify what the data means, the assumptions behind the data query or calculation, or particular changes to watch for.

Forest & Trees's real power as an analysis tool comes from its ability to provide real-time data results, which let the user examine the data as it changes. This ability comes from F&T's scheduling tool, which lets the application builder create a schedule for when the data in an object is updated. Automatic updating can take place after a set amount of time, such as daily, weekly, monthly, yearly, or after a user-defined period of days, weeks, or months. If the application isn't running during a scheduled time, the updates are automatically performed the next time it's loaded.

F&T can also automatically save a history log of previous results from updates, which lets the user view and analyze the changes in a particular data object over a period of time. This feature is very handy for examining historical trends.

Along with scheduling, F&T lets the user set alarms for particular data conditions in each node. Alarms are indicated through color coding of the data displays in each object, with green meaning the data is okay, yellow meaning the data is approaching a cautionary level, and red meaning the data has triggered the alarm. Pop-up notes can be attached to the alarm to provide further information on what the alarm indicates. Again using our example, an alarm can be set for when expenses exceed 25 percent of total income, bringing the problem to the user's attention by turning the expense value red and popping up the alarm note.

LightShip and Command Center

Pilot Executive Software, Inc. has two applications that qualify as data analysis tools. LightShip is a Windows-based data analysis package that's primarily designed to be used by application developers to create EIS applications. The base package uses DDE as the source for its data, and the optional LightShip Lens module allows LightShip to access data from other PC-based databases, such as dBASE, Excel, and Paradox. LightShip Lens modules are also available for Microsoft SQL Server, ORACLE, and NetWare SQL. Though it allows the user to update the data in the source files, its primary function is to provide the user with different views of the data for analysis.

Command Center is Pilot's high-end EIS development software. It's primarily designed for use on host-based UNIX systems, VAXs, and mainframes, though MS-DOS, Windows 3.x, and Macintosh versions are available. Command Center can be used in a C/S system through the add-on Command Center SQL module, which provides access to SYBASE SQL Server, ORACLE, IBM DB2 and SQL/DS, Rdb/VMS, and Ingres databases. Of the two, LightShip is the product that most users will want to use, so it will be the primary focus of the rest of this section.

LightShip is object-oriented and uses a number of tools to create the different screen and data objects. The tools can either be accessed from the menu or from a floating icon toolbar. LightShip refers to data objects as documents and can place them anywhere on the screen. Each document can display data from only one source.

Standard LightShip uses either directly entered data, a text file, or a Windows DDE link as the source for a document, making it somewhat limited as an analysis tool, particularly if you've not yet moved your databases to Windows. The additional LightShip Lens module is needed to really access LightShip's full power; once it's added to the system, it's automatically available and invoked as a data source when a new document object is created. Queries are easily created through a series of pop-up windows and pick lists that let the user or developer specify the data source, fields, and query conditions.

LightShip also has Hotspot objects, a facility that ties one or more actions to a particular object or to an item in a document. When used in a document, a Hotspot lets the application developer create a pick list of items that the user can click on. The user can then view the document associated with that item in a separate object window on the screen.

One of LightShip's greatest strengths is its integration of screen displays and graphic image objects with data, which Figure 10.7 demonstrates. PCX, BMP, and clipboard images can be added to a screen to be used as backgrounds to highlight different documents in different areas of the screen. A graphic object can also be used as a Hotspot indicator; clicking on the graphic brings up other screens that contain documents associated with the particular data being analyzed. LightShip also gives the developer complete control over the screen palette for each object, which lets the developer highlight particular documents or portions of documents. This is particularly useful for creating data thresholds, where the color of an object can automatically change to reflect its value or status when it exceeds a programmer-defined limit. Data thresholds are similar to, though not as sophisticated and flexible as, the alarms in Forest & Trees.

LightShip is primarily an application-building tool. While novice users can use it to query different data sources, building a complete analysis system isn't a simple process. LightShip is aimed at application developers looking to create a simple-to-use EIS for their clients or upper management. It supports these capabilities by letting the developer create custom menus and screens with Hotspots that shield the user from the underlying program.

Figure 10.7

LightShip uses Windows's graphics capabilities to the fullest; it allows the developer to mix both text and graphics on the same screen.

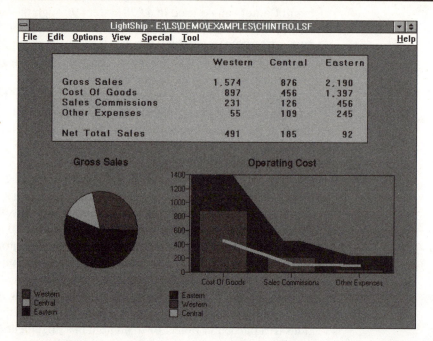

It includes debug facilities that let the developer test-run the application and watch the values of defined variables and the actions being executed through a trace. Debug traces can be saved on disk or printed out to make it easier to correct problems or errors. The debug facility also gives the developer information on any image objects being used and how they're being used.

LightShip's biggest drawback is that it has no easy way to create analysis links or show the relationship between different data documents. The only way to analyze data is by showing different documents on the same screen and manually analyzing the data; data from different documents can't be joined into composite views or results.

Command Center comes in both character mode and GUI versions. It doesn't include LightShip's ability to add graphics to the screen, as it's oriented towards use on terminals. Its built-in database support is limited; the Command Center SQL module is needed to access SQL-based RDBMSs. Command Center is better suited for creating EIS applications on host-based systems; those who are building a mixed host-based and C/S system can use Command Center to create the EIS system for terminal users, and LightShip for the networked C/S clients.

Command Center is available for VAX/VMS, IBM's MVS and VM mainframe operating systems, and numerous versions of UNIX. Versions are also available for Intel-based PCs running DOS or Windows 3.x, and Macintosh systems. The Command Center SQL module is needed to access data stored in SYBASE SQL Server, ORACLE, Ingres, IBM DB2 and SQL/DS, and Rdb/VMS databases.

GQL

Andyne Computing Ltd.'s GQL (for Graphic Query Language) is a combination query, reporting, and analysis tool for GUI systems. Though it has query and reporting functions, I've put it in the data analysis category based on its special features aimed at EIS application developers. GQL is available for the Macintosh, Windows 3.x, and various UNIX GUIs. It can access data from SYBASE SQL Server, ORACLE, Rdb/VMS, IBM's DB2, SQL/DS, and AS/400, Ingres, Informix, and Teradata databases. The Macintosh version can access any database that uses the Apple DAL protocol.

GQL makes heavy use of the point-and-click capabilities of the underlying GUI. Application developers can use pick lists, drag and drop, and dialog boxes to create complex queries. The queries can then be used as the basis for reports or data analysis. Queries can be written in GQL's built-in SQL (GQL automatically does the appropriate translations for different databases) and saved for reuse. Saved queries are interchangeable between the different platforms, so GQL can be used in organizations that have different platforms to support. Users can also use the built-in SQL features to create ad hoc queries.

GQL includes two features similar to those found in LightShip: support for graphics in the on-screen forms, and Executive Buttons, GQL's name for on-screen action spots similar to LightShip's Hotspots. GQL's Executive Buttons can be icons, text, or on-screen graphics. Queries and reports can be associated with the Executive Button and are automatically executed when the user clicks on it. Executive Buttons can also be associated with other GQL forms, providing the user with an easy way to move back and forth between different analysis screens.

GQL's data analysis features include the ability to create dynamic joins from tables in different databases. It uses the GUI's graphics to show the database links on the screen. The Windows version can automatically launch other Windows applications, such as Microsoft's Excel and Word, and pass data to those applications for more detailed analysis.

GQL provides its own security features that work in addition to those found in the underlying database. The built-in security features let the DBA tailor GQL's queries, reports, and analysis features for each individual user.

Intelligent Query (IQ)

IQ Software Corp.'s Intelligent Query (IQ) software is another multi-platform query and reporting tool designed for both the non-technical end-user and the application developer. Its data analysis features come from its capability to combine information from multiple data sources and to format its reports for automatic use by external word processing and spreadsheet software. It's only character mode at this time and versions are available for MS-DOS, OS/2, various versions of UNIX, and Digital's VAX/VMS. IQ can access data from over 60 different DBMSs, including both Microsoft and SYBASE SQL Server, dBASE, ORACLE, Informix, INGRES, Rdb/VMS, and all of IBM's RDBMSs.

IQ is character-mode based, but uses its own graphics capabilities to make it easy for the user to create complex queries and reports. It uses pull-down menus and pop-up windows to guide the user through the process of creating the query. Users create forms and reports directly on the screen through the built-in forms and reports painter.

Its reporting capabilities include cross-tabulation reports and over 30 standard mailing label formats. Reports can be created from multiple data sources. Reports can be automatically formatted for importation into Word-Perfect and Microsoft Word documents, or Microsoft Excel and Lotus 1-2-3 spreadsheets.

IQ started out as a report writer for vertical market application programmers, and it still retains some of its early features. Queries and reports created in IQ can be called from other application development tools as well as from programs written in 3GLs such as C and COBOL.

■ Choosing the Right Front-end for Your Needs

As you can see, a wide variety of front-end applications are available, and more are appearing on the market all the time. The different front-ends also overlap in features and functions, so choosing the right one can be very time consuming. In fact, it may turn out that there isn't just one that solves every problem you have, and you may have to use two or more front-ends depending on the needs of different users.

There are some broad principles you can use as a guide in evaluating front-ends. First, decide if you're going to use character-mode or GUI applications. If you want character-mode front-ends, you're essentially limited to using one of the PC database add-ons or writing your own custom applications in one of the 3GLs, because the majority of the other front-ends are based on Windows.

If you want to program your own applications (or have the resources to do so), and you don't care if they're character- or GUI-based, you may want to use one of the database add-ons or application development tools. If you only want to create GUI front-ends, you should use one of the application development tools or one of the query/reporting tools that have a script language.

If your goal is to combine existing databases with a Client/Server system, you can use either the add-on front-ends or the data integration and analysis front-ends. If most of your data is already in a PC-based database, the add-on would be a better solution for most uses.

The query/reporting tools and integration and analysis tools should be used primarily for users who don't need to modify the data on the server. These tools are much better at retrieving the data than putting it in. You should use one of the add-on or application development front-ends for users that constantly modify the database.

Finally, you should definitely consider using at least one data integration and analysis application. They're the best way to combine and examine all the data in your organization, and they can help you discover relationships between the different parts of your business that you may never have thought existed.

Chart of Front-ends

Table 10.1 summarizes all the different front-ends covered in Chapters 9 and 10. It gives you a handy reference for which products fall into which category and the back-ends they support. Remember that the vendors are constantly adding new capabilities to their products, so you should use this chart as the starting point for your own investigations of the many front-ends available.

Table 10.1

Front-ends and the
Database Servers They
Support

	Supported Environments	Microsoft SQL Server	SYBASE SQL Server	ORACLE
Add-ons				
Access	Windows 3.x	X	X	X
Advance Revelation	DOS, OS/2	X	X	X
Approach	Windows 3.x	X	X	X
Clarion	DOS	X		X
DataEase SQL	DOS	X	X	X
dBase for Windows 5.0	Windows 3.x	X	X	X
Excel	Windows 3.x	X	X	
Lotus 1-2-3	DOS, Windows 3.x, OS/2	X	X	X
Paradox for Windows 5.0	Windows 3.x	X	X	X
PC/Focus & PM/Focus	DOS, OS/2	X	X	
Q&A	DOS	X	X	X
Superbase95	Windows 3.x	X	X	X
Wingz	Windows 3.x, OS/2, Macintosh, Motif, Open Look	X	X	X
App. Development				
FormFlow	Windows 3.x	X		
Object/1	Windows 3.x, OS/2	X	X	X
ObjectVision	Windows 3.x, OS/2	X	X	X
PowerBuilder	Windows 3.x	X	X	X
Q&E	Windows 3.x, OS/2	X	X	X
SQLWindows	Windows 3.x	X	X	

	SQLBase	Watcom SQL	Ingres	Informix	IBM Database Manager
Add-ons					
Access					
Advance Revelation					
Approach					
Clarion	X		X		X
DataEase SQL					X
dBase for Windows 5.0					
Excel		X			
Lotus 1-2-3					
Paradox for Windows 5.0					
PC/Focus & PM/Focus					
Q&A					
Superbase95					X
Wingz				X	
App. Development					
FormFlow					
Object/1					X
ObjectVision					X
PowerBuilder	X	X		X	X
Q&E			X		X
SQLWindows	X		X		X

	IBM DB2/2	XDB-DBMS	NetWare SQL	InterBase	Rdb/VMS
Add-ons					
Access					
Advance Revelation			X		
Approach					
Clarion		X	X		
DataEase SQL	X				
dBase for Windows 5.0				X	
Excel					
Lotus 1-2-3					
Paradox for Windows 5.0				X	
PC/Focus & PM/Focus					
Q&A					
Superbase95	X				
Wingz			X		
App. Development					
FormFlow					
Object/1	X				
ObjectVision	X				X
PowerBuilder	X	X			
Q&E	X		X		
SQLWindows	X		X		

	AllBase	IBM SQL/400	IBM SQL/DS	IBM DB2	EDA/SQL
Add-ons					
Access					
Advance Revelation				X	
Approach				X	
Clarion					
DataEase SQL				X	
dBase for Windows 5.0					
Excel					
Lotus 1-2-3					
Paradox for Windows 5.0				X	
PC/Focus & PM/Focus					X
Q&A					
Superbase95					
Wingz					
App. Development					
FormFlow					
Object/1					
ObjectVision				X	
PowerBuilder	X			X	
Q&E				X	
SQLWindows	X	X		X	

	Supported Environments	Microsoft SQL Server	SYBASE SQL Server	ORACLE
Integration & Analysis				
Command Center	DOS, Windows 3.x, Macintosh, UNIX, VMS		X	X
Forest & Trees	Windows 3.x	X		X
GQL	Windows 3.x, Macintosh, UNIX		X	X
Intelligent Query	DOS, OS/2, UNIX, VMS	X	X	X
Lightship	Windows 3.x	X		X
Query & Reporting				
ClearAccess	Windows 3.x, Macintosh	X	X	X
DataPivot & DataPrism	Windows 3.x, Macintosh		X	X
Impromptu	Windows 3.x			X
Oracle Card	Windows 3.x			X
Personal Access	Windows 3.x	X	X	X
Quest	Windows 3.x	X	X	
Quest Reporter	Windows 3.x	X	X	

	SQLBase	Watcom SQL	Ingres	Informix	IBM Database Manager
Integration & Analysis					
Command Center			X		
Forest & Trees	X		X		
GQL			X	X	
Intelligent Query			X	X	X
Lightship					
Query & Reporting					
ClearAccess					
DataPivot & DataPrism					
Impromptu					
Oracle Card					
Personal Access					
Quest	X		X		X
Quest Reporter	X		X		X

	IBM DB2/2	XDB-DBMS	NetWare SQL	InterBase	Rdb/VMS
Integration & Analysis					
Command Center					X
Forest & Trees			X		X
GQL					X
Intelligent Query	X				X
Lightship			X		
Query & Reporting					
ClearAccess					
DataPivot & DataPrism					
Impromptu				X	
Oracle Card					
Personal Access					
Quest	X		X		
Quest Reporter	X		X		

	AllBase	IBM SQL/400	IBM SQL/DS	IBM DB2	EDA/SQL
Integration & Analysis					
Command Center			X	X	
Forest & Trees				X	X
GQL		X	X	X	
Intelligent Query		X	X	X	
Lightship					
Query & Reporting					
ClearAccess					X
DataPivot & DataPrism					
Impromptu					
Oracle Card					
Personal Access					
Quest	X	X		X	
Quest Reporter	X	X		X	

- *Traditional Database Systems*
- *Client/Server Systems*
- *Object-Oriented Systems*
- *Distributed Processing Systems*

11

Future Trends in DBMS Technology

WRITING THE FIRST EDITION OF THIS BOOK GAVE ME THE OPPORTUNITY to play the prognosticator on trends in DBMS technology. Now three years later, it's time to take a look at what's changed over the past few years, and to predict again where I think the market is going over the next couple of years. Along the way, I'll mention (in passing, of course) how right or wrong I was in my earlier predictions.

Here's how I ended the introduction to this chapter in the first edition of this book:

> This book has focused on the state of dbms technology in general and Client/Server computing in particular during the early 1990s. Both fields are advancing at a rapid pace that shows no signs of slowing down. While I don't own a crystal ball and I can't claim to accurately predict the future, I can make some educated guesses about what advances the next several years will bring in the four major areas of DBMS technology: traditional database systems, Client/Server systems, object-oriented systems, and distributed processing systems. By combining the opinions expressed in this chapter with your own experience, you should be well on your way to judging what the trends are in the DBMS market and how they'll affect your present and future computer system plans.

I was very right about one thing—the field has continued to advance at a rapid pace. And it still doesn't look like it's going to slow down anytime soon. Some vendors left the C/S market, but numerous others have arisen to take their places. Existing database vendors have improved their products, and two new vendors have released C/S database servers. The variety and sophistication of front-end products has also increased over the past three years.

There were a couple of trends I missed, though. The most glaring example was the overwhelming acceptance of and movement to GUI operating environments on the Intel-based PC platforms. Windows 3.0 started the trend, and it became a landslide with the release of Windows 3.1 in 1993. Current estimates are that more than half of all Intel-based PCs run some type of GUI, be it Windows, Windows NT, or OS/2. This has had a tremendous impact on the C/S marketplace, which I'll cover more thoroughly in the rest of this chapter.

Another trend I missed was the rise of the C/S groupware products I covered in Chapter 8 of this edition of the book. Back in 1992, Lotus Notes was the only C/S system available that couldn't quite be classified as a database server. It was expensive, wasn't in widespread use, and to me looked like it was going to turn out to be another failed attempt at creating a market for groupware products. Boy, when I'm wrong, I'm wrong! It took a another year or so, but the groupware concept caught on (with Notes leading the way), to the point where C/S technology is no longer limited to what we traditionally think of as a database.

There's been one very important trend that I didn't see coming three years ago—merger mania. A number of C/S product vendors have merged with other vendors. In some cases (like SYBASE and Powersoft) the merger was between database and front-end vendors. In others (like Computer Associate's acquisition of the Ingres products) it was a merger between a player in the C/S market and a company that didn't have a presence there. I now expect this trend to continue as the market shakes itself out.

In the first edition, I broke this chapter down into four topics: traditional database systems, Client/Server systems, object-oriented systems, and distributed processing systems. There have been advances, retreats, and some surprising changes in all four areas. I'm going to keep the same structure here, and will once again make some educated guesses about where the market is going.

■ Traditional Database Systems

Mainframes haven't vanished in the past three years, but the market for them has stagnated significantly. Few organizations are buying new mainframes, and those that do are doing so mainly to augment or upgrade existing mainframes. Most mainframe databases in use are still based on the Hierarchical or Network models; however, the number of Relational databases has increased, lead by IBM's DB2 and ORACLE7.

The large system emphasis has shifted to the minicomputer market. Minicomputers have continued to increase in power and capabilities. Digital's VAX line, with most of the line now powered by their Alpha chip, continues to be a strong seller. This has kept the VMS versions of the major C/S databases in contention as high-power database servers. ORACLE7, Rdb/VMS, and SYBASE SQL Server 10.0 remain the top three databases for VMS systems. I expect this will remain true for the next couple of years.

IBM's AS/400 minicomputer systems have also surprised almost everyone in the industry by selling as fast as IBM can make them. This has led to the rise of SQL/400 as a popular RDBMS, and in some cases a popular database server. There isn't a lot of third-party support for it yet, but IBM continues to advance their Information Warehouse concept and continues to improve the distributed database and communication capabilities of its various databases.

Overall, the downsizing trend has continued as more and more organizations replace their large data processing systems with minicomputers, UNIX servers, and PC-based C/S systems. In fact, a new term has come out in the last two years that better describes what's been happening—*rightsizing*. Rightsizing is the process of moving your data processing to the proper (right) size system. It may mean moving it down from a large system to a PC-based C/S system. It could also mean moving up from a PC-based system to one that uses UNIX or minicomputer servers. Rightsizing is one of those elegant terms that rarely comes along in the computer industry, and it's the one I now prefer to use.

The real advances have occurred in traditional PC-based databases, though. As I said earlier, I missed the trend toward GUI-based operating environments;

fortunately, the DBMS vendors haven't. Virtually every major PC DBMS vendor now has a Windows version of their product, and a couple of new products have come out that don't even have DOS counterparts.

The biggest news in the past three years has been Borland's release of dBASE for Windows 5.0 (covered in Chapter 9). This product brought dBASE into the 1990s—it combined powerful new features with complete compatibility with previous versions. It also made dBASE a viable platform for developing front-end applications by extending dBASE's reach to a number of C/S database servers. At this point, it looks like dBASE for Windows has breathed new life into the original warhorse of PC databases.

Borland has also upgraded their flagship DBMS Paradox to the Windows platform and improved Paradox's C/S capabilities. In fact, both Paradox and dBASE use the exact same interface to external databases. Both products remain strong sellers in the stand-alone and PC LAN markets; unfortunately, Borland has recently experienced some financial troubles, so only time will tell if the company is going to be able to continue improving these products. It's entirely possible that Borland will have merged with or been acquired by another company before the end of the decade.

Microsoft hasn't been resting on its laurels either. It's moved FoxPro to Windows and has also released two versions of its Windows-only DBMS, Access. Access brought a number of RDBMS capabilities to the desktop, particularly with its built-in support for updatable views and referential integrity features. It's been very well received by the marketplace and continues to increase its market share.

Microsoft's FoxPro has taken over the market as the primary dBASE-compatible programming environment. Computer Associate's Clipper has pretty much faded from the market and is no longer a contender.

There's been no sign of either the Fox database server product or a Microsoft product based on it, though I expect that to change in the near future. I'll be discussing this more in the next section.

Other PC-based DBMS companies have also moved their products to Windows, including Alpha Software (Alpha Five) and Microrim (R:Base for Windows). Lotus acquired the company that made Approach, a Windows-based low-end DBMS, and improved the product to the point where it's a serious competitor in both the nonprogrammable DBMS market and the C/S front-end market.

The trend is unmistakable now. DOS is rapidly approaching the end of its 14-year dominance of the PC operating system market. The GUI platforms have moved to the forefront, particularly Windows 3.1, though both OS/2 and Windows NT have make significant inroads. The major application development is now taking place for the GUI environments, and few DOS products continue to be enhanced and upgraded.

The other shoe will drop with the release of Windows 95, scheduled for August 1995 at the time of this writing (though Microsoft has already missed a couple of ship dates). Windows 95 will be a mostly 32-bit version of Windows that will no longer run under DOS. It will be a complete operating system— like Windows NT and OS/2. Users will boot into Windows 95 and access DOS through a built-in emulator. Assuming that it ships on time, and that it doesn't have any major bugs or incompatibilities with existing hardware, Windows 95 stands to take over the market as the dominant operating system. At that point (and I never thought I'd be writing this), DOS will for all intents and purposes be dead.

■ Client/Server Systems

The C/S market has decidedly heated up in the last three years. Major new versions of existing products have been released, and new products have come out. The biggest trend has been the increase in the quantity, quality, and sophistication of front-ends.

As I mentioned in the previous section, the vast majority of PC-based DBMSs can now be used as front-ends to a database server. This has made them viable alternatives to the dedicated front-end products and will continue to do so.

The application development toolkit market continues to be highly competitive, with both Powersoft and Gupta releasing major new versions of their development products during 1994. The big news here was SYBASE's surprise acquisition of Powersoft, which was announced at Fall Comdex in November 1994. This has the potential to make SYBASE an even bigger part of the marketplace, now that it has excellent technology on both ends of the C/S system. At the least, we should see increased support for the SYBASE SQL Server in PowerBuilder. Other vendors are trying to break into the front-end application development toolkit market, but for the near term I expect Powersoft and Gupta to continue to dominate it.

The RDBMS vendors haven't been sitting back either. Oracle finished releasing ORACLE7, a major upgrade, for all its supported platforms in 1994. SYBASE released its System 10 family of products, spearheaded by SQL Server 10.0. IBM replaced its Database Manager with DB2/2 and continues to improve DB2/2's compatibility and communications capabilities with its other RDBMSs.

While it didn't increase the version number, Microsoft added significant new capabilities to the Windows NT version of its own SQL Server. And Gupta released a major update to its SQLBase as I was writing this second edition.

Speaking of Microsoft, I was unfortunately quite right in one prediction I made back in 1992. In the first edition of this book, I discussed the upcoming release of SQL Server 5.0 (since renumbered 10.0 by SYBASE), and wrote: "However, there's some confusion over which company (Microsoft or SYBASE) will be releasing what operating system versions of the new release or if in fact the relationship between the two companies will continue at all."

I made this statement based on rumors I had heard about troubles in the relationship between the two companies. It didn't take long for me to receive a letter from Microsoft protesting this statement and denying that any problems existed. I wasn't wrong, just very early—Microsoft and SYBASE announced they were going their separate ways in early 1994, just as my book *Client/Server Computing with SYBASE SQL Server* was going to press.

Most of the impact from this split has been felt on the SYBASE side at this point. SYBASE has gone full speed ahead with the release of SQL Server 10.0 for all its supported platforms and is rumored to be working on both OS/2 and Windows NT versions. There's even early talk about the System 11 line of products, though it appears that they're only in the planning stages at this point.

On the other hand, Microsoft has been fairly quiet about their plans for future versions of SQL Server; they haven't even said if they're going to change the name of the product. They have said that they're going to concentrate on enhancing their product's distributed database capabilities. I suspect that the long-rumored Fox database server engine will reappear as at least part of the technology behind future versions of Microsoft's database server product.

I was wrong about Borland's Interbase RDBMS back in 1992—I guessed that it would be released for the PC platform first. In fact, Borland released the initial version as a UNIX product and is working on both OS/2 and Windows NT versions. If the company succeeds in getting back on its feet, we'll probably see these new versions sometime in late 1995 or early 1996.

My award for the most intriguing C/S RDBMS released in the last three years has to go to Watcom SQL. This unassuming database server literally came out of nowhere and got a big boost when Powersoft selected it as the database engine shipped with every PowerBuilder 3.0 package. Watcom's philosophy in designing Watcom SQL was simple—the company wanted to bring both Client/Server and sophisticated relational capabilities to "the masses." They succeeded splendidly, and Powersoft continued that philosophy when they acquired Watcom.

Watcom SQL 4.0 (the latest release) is designed for small and mid-range C/S systems, and it works quite well. It's not a speed demon, but its sophisticated technology and Relational features make it the perfect database server for small groups (under 25 users). The fact that it comes in versions that support all of the standard PC operating systems only adds to its appeal. If you haven't guessed by now, Watcom SQL has become my personal favorite database server.

I was a bit concerned about Watcom SQL's future when I heard that SYBASE had merged with Powersoft—I was afraid that SYBASE would drop Watcom SQL and replace it with a low-end version of SQL Server. Fortunately, I was meeting with some SYBASE representatives shortly after the announcement of the merger, and they said that the company had no plans to drop Watcom SQL. From all I've read and heard since, it looks like SYBASE will continue to market Watcom SQL as their low-end database server. They may even work towards 100-percent code compatibility between Watcom SQL and SQL Server, providing a seamless growth path for Watcom SQL users.

Other than Interbase, no new RDBMSs have come out for the UNIX, minicomputer, and mainframe C/S markets. However, all the vendors continue to enhance their existing products. The general trend in improved technology, though, continues to be in the area of PC and UNIX-based database servers.

One class of products that didn't take off quite as much as I expected them to are the symmetrical multiprocessor (SMP) UNIX systems. Support for SMP has increased with the addition of Windows NT's native SMP support to the mix. IBM is also working on an SMP version of OS/2. But the number of SMP systems in use hasn't significantly increased yet. My gut feeling about why this hasn't happened is that the market hasn't yet hit the capacity limits of standard single processor systems. SMP systems are also still quite expensive, and many potential clients may not be able to justify the price/performance ratio yet. I still expect SMP systems to become the major player in the database server market, but I don't think it'll happen until the end of the decade at the earliest.

One other significant development happened in the last three years—the approval of at least part of the latest ANSI SQL standard. Dubbed ANSI 92 SQL Entry Level, the new SQL standard adds more referential integrity features and support for scrollable cursors. The full standard will be known as SQL Level 3, but there's still no sign of when it will be 100 percent approved and adopted. In the meantime, I expect most of the RDBMS vendors will upgrade their native SQL languages to the ANSI 92 SQL Entry Level specifications.

■ Object-Oriented Systems

By now, the concepts behind object-oriented (OO) systems are commonly known throughout the computer industry. In a nutshell, the OO approach treats everything as an object that can be manipulated or contained in other manipulatable objects. OOP has generated a whole new set of terms that define how objects are handled.

As I predicted in the first edition, the OO principles have had a major impact on the development side of the C/S technology. PowerBuilder and

SQLBase are both object-oriented development platforms. Many of the Windows-based PC DBMSs have OO features. This is natural, as a GUI platform is ideal for object-oriented systems. I fully expect the trend toward OO development environments to continue.

On the other hand, the push for OO databases appears to have receded, if it's not entirely dead in the water. For those who haven't read the first edition, the following was my discussion of OO databases there.

> DBMS theorists and vendors are primarily pursuing two different approaches to applying OO principles; one extends the Relational model by providing OO capabilities, and the other creates a whole new OO database model. Both approaches have their merits, but in my opinion the first will be more successful.

> The Relational model has some weaknesses in handling large, variable data types and null values and is pretty much silent on the concept of user-defined data types. Variable data types are generally designed to accommodate data that doesn't fit into a rigid definition, in particular, large amounts of text and graphic images. RDBMS vendors have already begun to address this weakness with data types that fall under the generic heading of binary large objects, or BLOBs, which usually hold up to 2G of data. No RDBMS available today has a data type actually referred to as a BLOB; the vendors support BLOBs through such implementation-specific data types as LONG VARCHARS or IMAGE. Regardless of the actual name, the concept is the same.

> The other problem with the Relational model lies with user-defined (sometimes referred to as abstract) data types. Current DBMSs define a set number of data types that can be used, such as TEXT, INTEGER, FLOAT, and CHAR. There are situations in which a user needs to store data that just doesn't fit into a rigid format— postal (zip) codes are a prime example. In the USA, all postal codes are composed entirely of numbers, or the more recent format of five numbers, a hyphen, and four numbers. However, in Canada and the U.K., the postal code is a combination of numbers and letters in two sets of three characters separated by a space. If a zip code field in a database has a numeric data type, it will reject Canadian postal codes. If it's defined as character or text, users may not get the results they expect from a sort based on the zip code field.

> A user-defined data type would solve the problem. The database developer could create a new data type known as "zip," and define it as alphanumeric characters in the format of five numbers, or five numbers followed by a hyphen and four numbers, or three mixed characters followed by a space and three more mixed characters. If the user of the database expands operations to another country, the definition of the zip data type can also be expanded to accommodate the format of that country's postal code.

User-defined data types solve a very real business need but present enormous problems for RDBMS developers who must figure out a way to create an index on a user-defined data type. An index is necessary for performance, because the only purpose in having a user-defined data type is that the user needs to query the database based on that field. No currently available RDBMS addresses this problem, but the vendors and theorists are working hard on ways to adapt user-defined data types into the Relational model.

OO database proponents say that the solution is simple: Toss out the Relational model and design an entirely object-oriented database in which every data type is an abstract data type, whether it's built-in or user-defined. This approach sounds appealing, but there are two problems. First, there is as yet no theoretical foundation for an OO database. There's also little agreement on which OO concepts apply to database design or even on what the concepts are. Standard OO terms and concepts will evolve and come into use over time, so this problem will eventually be solved.

The lack of a theoretical foundation is a bigger problem. Every DBMS model has a clear theory behind it; for example, the Network model is based on set theory, and the Relational model is based on mathematical set logic. No such theory yet exists for OO databases. So far, some OO principles treat objects as sets, which is a step backward from the Relational model to the Network and Hierarchical models. OO languages are also more procedural than SQL, which is another step backward for the same reason.

There has been little activity in the area of OO databases in the last three years. No one has released one, and there's simply no agreement on what an OO database should be. I don't expect this situation to change in the near future.

However, the OO situation has improved as far as Relational databases are concerned. Just about every RDBMS now supports user-defined functions, and the vendors are refining the ways in which they deal with them. Every RDBMS now available supports some type of BLOB data type, mainly as a way of storing external objects in the database. Many RDBMS vendors are also adopting OO terms, referring to the tables, views, and stored procedures in their products as objects.

Even so, the big OO activity has been in the front-end area. Microsoft even provides a system administration utility it calls the Object Manager—though all it actually manages is the columns, tables, and views that comprise the database schema.

It seems to me that attempts to create a true OO database have failed over the last three years, and will continue to fail in the near future. No other database model has appeared on the horizon. For the next few years, I fully expect the trend of applying OO principles to the Relational model to continue. And of course, the front-end products will become more and more object-oriented as the GUIs become the dominant operating systems.

■ Distributed Processing Systems

Enormous strides have been made in the area of distributed databases in the last three years. Oracle was one of the first vendors to offer an RDBMS with full built-in distributed capabilities when it released ORACLE7. Other vendors have enhanced their distributed capabilities, improving communications between different servers and providing more complete two-phase commit support.

The move towards distributed systems has also been aided by the almost unanimous adoption of ODBC as the standard API for accessing different DBMSs. ODBC has become sophisticated enough and widespread enough to provide a solid platform for creating applications that mix data from a number of sources, including traditional PC databases, database servers, and nondatabase files. This data integration on the desktop provides a different approach to distributed data that's still mostly transparent to the users.

SYBASE has taken a different, and so far unique, approach to distributed processing with its Replication Server and Navigation Server. The Replication Server is a stand-alone database engine that monitors the primary database server and automatically sends the updated data to one or more secondary servers when the data changes on the primary. That way, the databases on the secondary servers are exact duplicates of the ones on the primary server. Replication Server is event-driven, in that it sends updates as soon as they happen, instead of following a predetermined schedule. It also saves time and increases throughput by just sending the changed portions of the primary server's transaction logs to the secondary sites, instead of sending a copy of the entire database. Because it only sends a copy of the transaction log, the Replication Server can constantly send out updates without interfering with the primary database server's operations.

The Replication Server operates on the asynchronous store-and-forward principle. That way, if a secondary server is down when the Replication Server attempts to contact it, the Replication Server will hold the data changes until the secondary comes back on-line. It then sends all the accumulated changes. If a primary server or Replication Server goes down, the DBA can specify another data site and server as the alternate, to keep the data changes flowing. When the original Replication Server or primary server comes back on-line, the Replication Server automatically synchronizes all the data.

Another Replication Server feature is asynchronous stored procedures. These procedures allow secondary sites to update the data in the primary database. The secondary database thinks it's updating a local database, when in actuality it's executing a stored procedure that sends the data update to the primary server. The Replication Server then passes the changed data back to the secondary database, at which time the database on the secondary server is updated.

Replicated databases are actually an old solution to the problem of keeping distributed databases synchronized. But they've always had the limitation of having to send the entire database, which can be particularly slow when the connection is through modems. Also, users would be prevented from accessing the primary database while the update was going on, to ensure that they weren't making changes to parts that had already been sent. For that reason, replication systems usually operate on a fixed schedule, with the bulk of the data transfers happening overnight.

The SYBASE Replication Server represents an interesting solution to this problem. By sending out the data updates real-time, and by only sending the portions of the data that have been changed, Replication Server solves the major problems with replicating databases. It may well represent a viable alternative to a true distributed database processing system, especially in organizations that need the exact same database in multiple sites. Only time and experience will tell.

The SYBASE Navigation Server represents a different approach to distributed database processing. The Navigation Server is a software extension to SQL Server 10.0 that creates a distributed processing environment by linking multiple SQL Server database servers into a large, virtual database server. The Navigation Server partitions the database across the various servers, giving it the capability to handle much larger databases than any individual database server can handle. The front-end applications talk directly to the Navigation Server instead of to the individual SQL Servers, and the Navigation Server handles all the actual query processing. It takes the user's queries, breaks them up, and sends the various portions to the appropriate database servers.

Navigation Server achieves this capability by running on either a massively parallel processing (MPP) platform, or on a symmetric multiprocessing (SMP) platform, depending on the number of database servers to be managed and the amount of data to be processed. Navigation Server is being jointly developed by NCR and SYBASE, and the initial release runs on NCR's MPP and SMP platforms.

Because it presents a number of database servers as a single, virtual database server, Navigation Server makes it easy for a single DBA to administrate multiple database servers from a single location. The Navigation Server maintains a global directory of the database's partitions and automatically manages the various individual database servers. A GUI-based administration tool is included that lets the DBA manage and monitor the Navigation Server.

The SYBASE Configurator is a related tool that assists the DBA in designing the total Navigation Server database system, by analyzing the various components and making recommendations on how the system should be configured.

Navigation Server represents a distributed database processing solution for situations where organizations need to seamlessly access different databases at the same time. SYBASE's documents on the Navigation Server present an excellent example of such a situation—a travel agency that needs to access different databases containing flight information, hotel reservations, and car rentals. Each separate organization (the airline, hotel, and car rental agency) has its own database server that it uses to maintain its own records. The agents in the travel agency access a Navigation Server that's linked to the other database servers and automatically routes queries and updates to and from the respective servers. The agents would never know that they're accessing different databases that may exist hundreds or even thousands of miles apart; all they'll see is the Navigation Server they're accessing.

The Navigation Server also represents a different approach to distributed database processing. By managing the distributed databases as a large, virtual database, it partially avoids the problems of multiserver two-phase commits, where one user update affects more than one database server. In a regular distributed processing system, a two-phase commit across multiple servers could fail for any number of reasons, including communications failures or an attempt to update a record already being updated by another user. The Navigation Server avoids these problems by handling all the user updates internally and by splitting user updates into multiple parts. It can complete portions of two-phase commit transactions and hold the rest until it's able to complete the entire transaction. Since the Navigation Server monitors all the component databases in real time, it can automatically rollback any changes it made to the different databases if it can't complete the entire transaction.

It appears to me that both the Replication Server and the Navigation Server provide viable alternatives to other distributed processing systems and architectures. Either server can be used to create an enterprise-wide database. The question is, which one will be the best solution for which situation? Based on the current information I've received from SYBASE, I'd say that organizations that need to have multiple copies of the exact same database in multiple locations should choose the Replication Server. An example of this type of organization would be a manufacturing company that has a central warehouse and sales offices scattered around the country. The warehouse's inventory database would be the primary database, and each sales office would have its own secondary database server. With the Replication Server, each remote office would always know the current status of the company's inventory.

The Navigation Server would be ideal for an organization that has a number of different databases residing on servers in different sites, yet needs to provide its users access to data from more than one database. The previously mentioned travel agency is a prime example of this type of organization. The Navigation Server may also be a strong competitor to existing and new mainframe installations and could represent a viable alternative for organizations looking to downsize their existing mainframe-based databases. Again, only time will tell.

There was one other potential bottleneck to distributed processing that I discussed in the first edition—network capacity, reliability, and throughput. Fortunately, the network bottleneck has become less of a problem and will be virtually nonexistent in a few years. There are two technologies that have helped resolve this bottleneck.

The first is the advent of the V.34 standard for 28,800 bit-per-second (bps) modems. These modems represent the height of current technology and provide a very reliable high-speed connection over standard phone lines. The reliability and speed make them ideal for occasional links between different databases in a distributed system.

The second technology that's improved data communication is ISDN. ISDN provides extremely fast data connections between different sites, running at 64kbps (and higher) speeds. ISDN doesn't use standard phone lines, and isn't available in all parts of the U.S. yet, but it's spreading rapidly. At this time, it looks like ISDN will become the long-term solution for reliable high speed connections between different computers.

I can't think of a better way to close this book than the way I did in the first edition. "I hope you've enjoyed this tour through the current and future states of database and Client/Server technologies as much as I've enjoyed playing tour guide. The next step is up to you. Use the information in this book as the basis for your own explorations in how the Client/Server database architecture can best benefit your organization. I'm confident that the right system exists for your needs, and I wish you great success in finding and implementing it."

■ Appendix A

■ Quick Summary Charts

PRODUCT INFORMATION	PCs (Chapter 4)				
Name	Microsoft SQL Server 4.2 (OS/2); Microsoft SQL Server 4.21 (NT)	SYBASE SQL Server 10.0 (NT)	SQLBase 5.2; SQL-Base 6.0	IBM DB2/2	ORACLE7 Server 7.0
Vendor	Microsoft Corporation	SYBASE, Inc.	Gupta Corp.	IBM, Inc.	Oracle Corp.
Operating Systems					
On Database Server	OS/2 1.2 or higher; Windows NT 3.1 or higher	NetWare 3.12 or higher	DOS 3.1 or higher, OS/2 1.3 or higher, Windows 3.1 or higher, Windows NT 3.1 or higher, NetWare 3.11 or higher (5.2); NetWare 3.12 or higher (6.0)	OS/2 2.0 or higher	OS/2 2.0 or higher, Windows NT 3.1 or higher, NetWare 3.11 or higher
On LAN Server	MS LAN Manager, Windows NT Advanced Server, Windows for Workgroups; IBM LAN Server; Novell NetWare; or any other network that supports Named Pipes or NETBEUI	Novell NetWare 3.12 or higher	MS LAN Manager, Windows NT Advanced Server, Windows for Workgroups; IBM LAN Server; Novell NetWare 3.11 or higher; Banyan VINES	MS LAN Manager and Windows NT Advanced Server; IBM LAN Server; Novell NetWare 3.11 or higher; or any network that supports IBM's version of NetBIOS	MS LAN Manager and Windows NT Advanced Server; IBM LAN Server; Novell NetWare 3.11 or higher; or any network supporting NetBIOS, Named Pipes, DEC-Net, or TCP/IP
On Workstations	DOS 3.0 or higher; Windows 3.0 or higher; Windows NT 3.1 or higher; OS/2 1.2 or higher	DOS 3.0 or higher; Windows 3.0 or higher; Windows NT 3.1 or higher; OS/2 1.2 or higher	DOS 3.1 or higher; Windows 3.0 or higher	DOS 3.1 or higher, Windows 3.0 or higher, OS/2 1.3 or higher	DOS 3.1 or higher, OS/2 2.0 or higher, Windows NT 3.1 or higher

PRODUCT INFORMATION	PCs (Chapter 4)				
Name	Microsoft SQL Server 4.2 (OS/2); Microsoft SQL Server 4.21 (NT)	SYBASE SQL Server 10.0 (NT)	SQLBase 5.2; SQL-Base 6.0	IBM DB2/2	ORACLE7 Server 7.0
Minimum Requirements					
RAM on Server	8Mb OS/2; 16Mb Windows NT	32Mb	1Mb Windows, 2Mb DOS, 4Mb OS/2, 8Mb Windows NT and Net-Ware	12Mb	12Mb
RAM on Workstation	640k DOS; 4Mb Windows; 6Mb OS/2; 12Mb Windows NT	640k DOS; 4Mb Windows; 6Mb OS/2; 12Mb Windows NT	640k DOS; 4Mb Windows; 6Mb OS/2; 12Mb Windows NT	640k DOS, 6Mb OS/2	640k DOS; 6Mb OS/2; 12Mb Windows NT
Disk Space on Server	20Mb OS/2; 25Mb Windows NT	30Mb	10Mb	15Mb	30Mb
Utilities Provided					
Administration Utility	Yes	Yes	Yes	Yes	Yes
Interactive User Utility	Yes	Yes	Yes	Yes	Yes
Operating Systems/Environments Supported	DOS 3.0 or higher; Windows 3.0 or higher; Windows NT 3.1 or higher; OS/2 1.2 or higher	DOS 3.0 or higher	DOS 3.1 or higher; Windows 3.0 or higher	DOS 3.1 or higher; OS/2 2.1 or higher	DOS 3.1 or higher, Windows NT 3.1 or higher, OS/2 2.0 or higher
Native Languages					
ANSI SQL	Level 1 with some Level 2 elements	Level 2 with Integrity addendum	Level 2 with Integrity Enhancement	Level 2 with Integrity Enhancement	Level 2 with Integrity Enhancement
DB2 SQL Extensions	No	No	Yes	Yes	Yes
Other SQL Extensions	Yes	Yes	Yes	No	Yes
Non-SQL Language	No	No	Yes (6.0)	No	No

PRODUCT INFORMATION	PCs (Chapter 4)				
Name	**Microsoft SQL Server 4.2 (OS/2); Microsoft SQL Server 4.21 (NT)**	**SYBASE SQL Server 10.0 (NT)**	**SQLBase 5.2; SQL-Base 6.0**	**IBM DB2/2**	**ORACLE7 Server 7.0**
Maximums					
Database Size	Maximum supported by operating system	Maximum supported by operating system	500G	Limited by disk space	Limited by disk space
Column Size	Normally 1,962 bytes; "image" and "text" data types store 2G through pointers to external data	Normally 1,962 bytes; "image" and "text" data types store 2G through pointers to external data	Limited by disk space (LONG VAR-CHAR data type stores 2G)	4,000 bytes, or 32,700 characters in a LONG VAR-CHAR data type	2G
Row Size	1,962 bytes	1,962 bytes	Limited by disk space	4,005 bytes	2G
# of Columns in Row	255 columns	255 columns	250 columns	255 columns	254 columns
# of Rows in Table	Limited by disk space	Limited by disk space	Limited by disk space	Limited by disk space	Limited by disk space
# of Rows per Database	Limited by disk space	Limited by disk space	Limited by disk space	Limited by disk space	Limited by disk space
# of Tables per Database	2 billion	2 billion	Limited by disk space	Limited by disk space	Limited by disk space
# of Views per Database	Unlimited	Unlimited	Unlimited	Limited by disk space	Unlimited
# of Tables per View	Unlimited tables, but only 250 columns per view	Unlimited tables, but only 250 columns per view	Unlimited	15	Unlimited, with maximum 254 columns per view

PRODUCT INFORMATION	PCs (Chapter 4)			RISC & UNIX (Chapter 5)	
Name	Watcom SQL 4.0	XDB-Enterprise Server 4.0	Ingres Server for OS/2 6.4	Ingres Server for UNIX and VAX/VMS	ORACLE7 Server 7.0
Vendor	Watcom International Corp. (a subsidiary of PowerSoft Corp.)	XDB Systems, Inc.	Computer Associates International	Computer Associates International	Oracle Corp.
Operating Systems					
On Database Server	DOS 3.1 or higher, Windows 3.1 or higher, OS/2 2.0 or higher, Windows NT 3.1 or higher, NetWare 3.11 or higher	OS/2 2.0 or higher, Windows NT 3.1 or higher	OS/2 2.0 or higher	30+ versions of UNIX, including AIX, SunOS, AT&T System V; VAX/VMS	VAX/VMS; DG AOS-VS; 30+ versions of UNIX, including AIX, SunOS, ULTRIX, AT&T System V
On LAN Server	MS LAN Manager, Windows for Workgroups, Windows NT Advanced Server; IBM LAN Server; Novell NetWare 3.12 or higher; or any network supporting NetBIOS	MS LAN Manager and Windows NT Advanced Server; IBM LAN Server; Novell NetWare 3.11 or higher; or any network supporting NetBIOS	MS LAN Manager and Windows NT Advanced Server; IBM LAN Server; Novell NetWare 3.11 or higher; or any network supporting NetBIOS	Any network that supports SPX/IPX, NetBIOS, Named Pipes, TCP/IP, or DECNet	Any network that supports DECNet or TCP/IP
On Workstations	DOS 3.1 or higher, Windows 3.1 or higher	DOS 3.1 or higher, OS/2 2.0 or higher, Windows NT 3.1 or higher	DOS 3.1 or higher, OS/2 2.0 or higher, Windows 3.1 or higher	DOS 3.1 or higher, Windows 3.1 or higher, RISC-based UNIX.	DOS 3.1 or higher, OS/2 2.0 or higher, Windows NT 3.1 or higher, RISC-based UNIX (including the Motif GUI)
Minimum Requirements					
RAM on Server	3Mb	16Mb	16Mb	8Mb	Varies by platform
RAM on Workstation	640k DOS; 4Mb Windows	640k DOS; 6Mb OS/2; 12Mb Windows NT	2Mb DOS; 6Mb OS/2; 12Mb Windows NT	2Mb DOS; 6Mb OS/2; 8Mb UNIX	640k DOS; 6Mb OS/2; 12Mb Windows NT; 8Mb UNIX
Disk Space on Server	5Mb	10Mb	100Mb	75Mb	Varies by platform

PRODUCT INFORMATION	PCs (Chapter 4)		Ingres Server for OS/2 6.4	RISC & UNIX (Chapter 5)	
Name	Watcom SQL 4.0	XDB-Enterprise Server 4.0	Ingres Server for OS/2 6.4	Ingres Server for UNIX and VAX/VMS	ORACLE7 Server 7.0
Utilities Provided					
Administration Utility	Yes	Yes	Yes	Yes	Yes
Interactive User Utility	Yes	Yes	Yes	Yes	Yes
Operating Systems/ Environments Supported	DOS 3.1 or higher, Windows 3.1 or higher	DOS 3.1 or higher, Windows NT 3.1 or higher, OS/2 2.0 or higher	OS/2 2.0 or higher; DOS versions available as part of the client-side package	UNIX or VAX/VMS; DOS versions part of client-side package	DOS 3.1 or higher, Windows NT 3.1 or higher, OS/2 2.0 or higher, RISC-based UNIX
Native Languages					
ANSI SQL	Level 2 with Integrity Enhancement	Level 2 with Integrity Enhancement	Level 2 with Integrity Enhancement	Level 2 with Integrity Enhancement	Level 2 with Integrity Enhancement
DB2 SQL Extensions	No	Yes	Subset	Subset	Yes
Other SQL Extensions	Yes	Yes	Yes	Yes	Yes
Non-SQL Language	No	No	Yes, QUEL	Yes, QUEL	No
Maximums					
Database Size	2G per file, 12 files per database	Limited by disk space	Limited by disk space	Limited by disk space	Limited by disk space
Column Size	No limit for individual columns; tables limited to 2G in a single file	4,056 bytes	2,000 bytes	2,000 bytes	2G
Row Size	Limited by table size	32,767 bytes	2,008 bytes	2,008 bytes	2G
# of Columns in Row	999 columns	400 columns	127 columns	127 columns	254 columns
# of Rows in Table	Limited by table size	Limited by disk space	Limited by disk space	Limited by disk space	Limited by disk space
# of Rows per Database	Limited by disk space	Limited by disk space	Limited by disk space	Limited by disk space	Limited by disk space

PRODUCT INFORMATION	PCs (Chapter 4)		RISC & UNIX (Chapter 5)		
Name	Watcom SQL 4.0	XDB-Enterprise Server 4.0	Ingres Server for OS/2 6.4	Ingres Server for UNIX and VAX/ VMS	ORACLE7 Server 7.0
Maximums					
# of Tables per Database	32,767 tables	Unlimited	Limited by disk space	Limited by disk space	Limited by disk space
# of Views per Database	Unlimited	Unlimited	Limited by disk space	Limited by disk space	Unlimited
# of Tables per View	Unlimited	Unlimited, with maximum 400 columns per view	Unlimited, with maximum 127 columns per view	Unlimited, with maximum 127 columns per view	Unlimited, with maximum 254 columns per view

PRODUCT INFORMATION	RISC & UNIX (Chapter 5)				Proprietary Minicomputers (Chapter 6)
Name	SYBASE SQL Server 10.0	SQLBase 5.2; SQL-Base 6.0	INFORMIX-OnLine 6.0	InterBase 4.0	Rdb/VMS Version 6.0
Vendor	SYBASE, Inc.	Gupta Corp.	Informix Software, Inc.	Borland International, Inc.	Digital Equipment Corp. (DEC)
Operating Systems					
On Database Server	VAX/VMS; most major versions of UNIX, including AIX, NeXT MACH, AT&T System V, and Sequent Dynix	SunOS 4.1.1 or higher	SunOS 4.1.1 or higher, AIX, ULTRIX, XENIX, AT&T System V, HP-UX	Some versions of UNIX, including Alpha OSF1, SunOS and Solaris, and HP-UX	DEC OpenVMS
On LAN Server	Any network that supports DECNet or TCP/IP	Any network that supports TCP/IP	Any network that supports TCP/IP	Netware 3.11 or higher; Windows NT Advanced Server 3.1 or higher; any network that supports TCP/IP	DEC Pathworks (DEC version of MS LAN Manager)

PRODUCT INFORMATION	RISC & UNIX (Chapter 5)				Proprietary Minicomputers (Chapter 6)
Name	SYBASE SQL Server 10.0	SQLBase 5.2; SQL-Base 6.0	INFORMIX-OnLine 6.0	InterBase 4.0	Rdb/VMS Version 6.0
Operating Systems					
On Workstations	DOS 3.0 or higher; Windows 3.0 or higher; Windows NT 3.1 or higher; OS/2 1.2 or higher; RISC-based UNIX (including the Open Look and Motif GUIs)	DOS 3.1 or higher; Windows 3.0 or higher; SunOS 4.1.1 or higher	DOS 3.1 or higher; RISC-based UNIX	Windows 3.1 or higher	PC/MS-DOS; ULTRIX; OpenVMS
Minimum Requirements					
RAM on Server	Varies by platform	4Mb	8Mb	250k	Varies depending on platform
RAM on Workstation	640k DOS; 4Mb Windows; 6Mb OS/2; 12Mb Windows NT; 8Mb UNIX	640k DOS; 4Mb Windows; 6Mb OS/2; 12Mb Windows NT; 4Mb SunOS	640k DOS; 8Mb UNIX	4Mb Windows	640k DOS
Disk Space on Server	Varies by platform	10Mb	5Mb	6Mb	Varies depending on platform
Utilities Provided					
Administration Utility	Yes	Yes	Yes	Yes	Yes
Interactive User Utility	Yes	Yes	No	Yes	Yes
Operating Systems/ Environments Supported	DOS 3.0 or higher; RISC-based UNIX	DOS 3.1 or higher; Windows 3.0 or higher; SunOS 4.1.1 or higher	SunOS 4.1.1 or higher, AT&T System V, HP-UX	Windows 3.1 or higher	PC/MS-DOS; ULTRIX; OpenVMS

PRODUCT INFORMATION	RISC & UNIX (Chapter 5)				Proprietary Minicomputers (Chapter 6)
Name	**SYBASE SQL Server 10.0**	**SQLBase 5.2; SQLBase 6.0**	**INFORMIX-OnLine 6.0**	**InterBase 4.0**	**Rdb/VMS Version 6.0**
Native Languages					
ANSI SQL	Level 2 with Integrity addendum	Level 2 with Integrity Enhancement	Level 2 with Integrity Enhancement	Level 2 with Integrity Enhancement	Level 2 with Integrity Enhancement
DB2 SQL Extensions	No	Yes	Yes	No	No
Other SQL Extensions	Yes	Yes	Yes	No	Yes
Non-SQL Language	No	Yes (6.0)	No	GDML for backwards compatibility	RDML
Maximums					
Database Size	Limited by disk space	Limited by disk space	Limited by disk space	Limited by disk space	Varies depending on platform
Column Size	Normally 1,962 bytes; "image" and "text" data types store 2G through pointers to external data	Limited by disk space (LONG VARCHAR data type stores 2G)	32,767 bytes; BLOB stores 2G	32,767 bytes; BLOB stores 2G	32,767 bytes; LIST data type up to 2G
Row Size	1,962 bytes	Limited by disk space	65,271 bytes	65,271 bytes	65,291 bytes
# of Columns in Row	255 columns	250 columns	2,000	16,000	2,000
# of Rows in Table	Limited by disk space	Limited by disk space	Limited by disk space	Limited by disk space	Limited by disk space
# of Rows per Database	Limited by disk space	Limited by disk space	Limited by disk space	Limited by disk space	Limited by disk space
# of Tables per Database	2 billion	Limited by disk space	4,096	64,000	4,096
# of Views per Database	Unlimited	Unlimited	4,096	64,000	4,096
# of Tables per View	Unlimited tables, but only 250 columns per view	Unlimited	4,096	64,000	4,096

PRODUCT INFORMATION	Proprietary Minicomputers (Chapter 6)		Mainframes (Chapter 7)		
Name	AllBase/SQL	SQL/400	Database 2, Version 4.0	SQL/Data System (SQL/DS) Version 3, Release 3	ORACLE7 Server 7.0
Vendor	Hewlett-Packard Company	IBM, Inc.	IBM	IBM	Oracle Corp.
Operating Systems					
On Database Server	MPE/XL, HP-UX	OS/400	MVS/XA, MVS/ ESA, MVS/SP	VM/SP, VM/XA, VSE/AF, VSE/VSAM	MVS, VM, AIX
On LAN Server	Any LAN that supports TCP/IP	IBM LAN Server or any network that supports APPC; TCP/IP support optional	Any network that supports APPC or an appropriate gateway	Any network that supports APPC or an appropriate gateway	Any network supporting APPC, DEC-Net, or TCP/IP
On Workstations	PC/MS-DOS; Windows; HP-UX	OS2 2.0 or higher	OS/2 2.0 or higher, with IBM's DB2/2; other operating systems through an appropriate gateway	OS/2 2.0 or higher, with IBM's DB2/2; other operating systems through an appropriate gateway	Any operating system supported by ORACLE7 front-ends
Minimum Requirements					
RAM on Server	3Mb	8Mb	Varies based on platform and number of users	Varies based on platform and number of users	Varies depending on platform and operating system
RAM on Workstation	640k DOS, 4Mb HP-UX	8Mb OS/2	16Mb under OS/2	16Mb under OS/2	640k DOS; 6Mb OS/2; 12Mb Windows NT; 8Mb UNIX
Disk Space on Server	10Mb	10Mb	Varies based on platform	Varies based on platform	Varies depending on platform and operating system
Utilities Provided					
Administration Utility	Yes (terminal-based)	Yes (terminal-based)	Terminal-based	Terminal-based	Terminal-based

PRODUCT INFORMATION	Proprietary Minicomputers (Chapter 6)		Mainframes (Chapter 7)		
Name	**AllBase/SQL**	**SQL/400**	**Database 2, Version 4.0**	**SQL/Data System (SQL/DS) Version 3, Release 3**	**ORACLE7 Server 7.0**
Utilities Provided					
Interactive User Utility	No	No	No; OS/2 DB2/2 needed	No; OS/2 DB2/2 needed	Terminal-based
Operating Systems/ Environments Supported	HP-UX, MPE/XL	OS/2 2.0 or higher	MVS; OS/2 2.0 or higher for DB2/2	VM, DOS/VSE; OS/2 2.0 or higher for DB2/2	MVS, VM, AIX, or any platform supported by ORACLE7 front-ends
Native Languages					
ANSI SQL	Level 2 with Integrity Enhancement	Level 2 with Integrity Enhancement (98% compatible)	Level 2 with Integrity Enhancement	Level 2 with Integrity Enhancement	Level 2 with Integrity Enhancement
DB2 SQL Extensions	No	Compatible	Yes	Yes	Yes
Other SQL Extensions	No	No	No	Yes	Yes
Non-SQL Language	Image	RPG/400	No	No	No
Maximums					
Database Size	Varies depending on platform	Varies depending on platform	Varies according to system capacities	Varies according to system capacities	Limited by disk space
Column Size	Not available	4,000 bytes, or 32,700 characters in LONG VARCHAR	4,056 bytes; 2G in various LONG data types	4,056 bytes; 2G in various LONG data types	2G
Row Size	Not available	4,005 bytes	32,767 bytes	32,767 bytes	2G
# of Columns in Row	Not available	255 columns	750	750	254 columns

PRODUCT INFORMATION	Proprietary Minicomputers (Chapter 6)		Mainframes (Chapter 7)		
Name	AllBase/SQL	SQL/400	Database 2, Version 4.0	SQL/Data System (SQL/DS) Version 3, Release 3	ORACLE7 Server 7.0
Maximums					
# of Rows in Table	Limited by disk space	Limited by disk space	Limited by disk space	Limited by disk space	Limited by disk space
# of Rows per Database	Limited by disk space	Limited by disk space	Limited by disk space	Limited by disk space	Limited by disk space
# of Tables per Database	Not available	Limited by disk space	Unlimited	Unlimited	Limited by disk space
# of Views per Database	Not available	Limited by disk space	Unlimited	Unlimited	Unlimited
# of Tables per View	Not available	15	Unlimited tables, but only 750 columns per view	Unlimited tables, but only 750 columns per view	Unlimited, with maximum 254 columns per view

■ Appendix B

■ Listing of Vendor Information

The following is an alphabetical list of all the Client/Server vendors mentioned in this book: Each listing includes a representative sampling of the vendor's products. This list is for information purposes only, and the presence or absence of a product or company in no way implies a recommendation or endorsement.

Andyne Computing, Ltd.
552 Princess St.
2nd Floor
Kingston, ON, CD K7L 1C7
(613) 548-4355, (800) 267-0665
Products: GQL

Borland International, Inc.
P.O. Box 660001
100 Borland Way
Scotts Valley, CA 95067-0001
(408) 431-1000, (800) 245-7367
Products: ObjectVision, ObjectVision SQL Connection, Paradox for Windows, Borland SQL Link, dBASE for Windows, InterBase

Brio Technology, Inc.
444 Castro St.
Suite 700
Mountain View, CA 94041
(415) 961-4110, (800) 486-2746
Products: Datapivot, Dataprism

Cognos Corp.
67 S. Bedford St.
Suite 200W
Burlington, MA 01803-5164
(617) 229-6600, (800) 4-COGNOS; (800) 267-2777 (Canada)
Products: Impromptu

Computer Associates International, Inc.
One Computer Associates Plaza
Islandia, NY 11788-7011
(516) 342-5224, (800) 225-5224
Products: Clipper, Realizer, INGRES Server, INGRES/Star, INGRES/Gateway,
INGRES/Tools, INGRES/Net

DataEase International, Inc.
7 Cambridge Drive
Trumbull, CT 06611
(203) 374-8000, (800) 243-5123
Products: DataEase, DataEase for Windows, DataEase SQL Connect

Delrina Corp.
895 Don Mills Rd.
500-2 Park Centre
Toronto, ON, CD M3C 1W3
(416) 441-3676, (800) 268-6082
Products: FormFlow

Digital Communications Associates, Inc. (DCA)
1000 Alderman Dr.
Alpharetta, GA 30202-4199
(404) 475-8380, (800) 348-3221
Products: DCA OpenMind

Digital Equipment Corporation (DEC)
146 Main St.
Maynard, MA 01754-2571
(508) 493-5111, (800) 344-4825
Products: VAX/VMS, Rdb/VMS, ULTRIX, DECNet; DECStations, MicroVAX,
MiniVAX, and VAX computer systems

Extended Systems, Inc.
5777 North Meeker Ave.
Boise, ID 83713
(208) 322-7575, (800) 235-7526
Products: ExtendBase for NetWare 386, Advantage XBase Server

Fusion Systems Group, Ltd.
225 Broadway
24th Floor
New York, NY 10007
(212) 285-8001
Products: Wingz DataLink for Oracle, Wingz DataLink for SYBASE

Gupta Technologies, Inc.
1060 Marsh Rd.
Menlo Park, CA 94025
(415) 321-9500, (800) 876-3267
Products: SQLBase, SQL Windows, Quest, Quest Reporter

Hewlett-Packard Company
3000 Hanover St.
Palo Alto, CA 94304
(415) 857-1501, (800) 752-0900
Products: AllBase/SQL, AllBase/4GL, AllBase/Query, MPE/XL, HP-UX; Apollo
workstations, HP3000 and HP9000 series

IBM Corporation
Old Orchard Rd.
Armonk, NY 10504
(914) 765-1900, (800) 426-3333
Products: OS/2 2.1, OS/2 Warp (3.0), DB2/2, ImagePlus/2, DB2, SQL/DS, SQL/
400, AIX, MVS/XA, DOS/VSE, PC-DOS; PCs, minicomputers, and mainframes

Information Builders, Inc.
1250 Broadway
30th Floor
New York, NY 10001-3782
(212) 736-4433, (800) 969-INFO
Products: EDA/SQL, Focus, PC/Focus

Informix Software, Inc.
4100 Bohannon Dr.
Menlo Park, CA 94025
(415) 926-6300, (800) 331-1763
Products: INFORMIX-SE, INFORMIX-OnLine, INFORMIX-OnLine/Secure,
INFORMIX-STAR, INFORMIX-Net, Wingz, Wingz DataLinks

Intersolv, Inc.
3200 Tower Oaks Blvd.
Rockville, MD 20852
(301) 230-3200, (800) 547-4000
Products: Q+E Database Editor, Q+E Database Library, Q+E Database Library for Windows, Q+E Database/VB for Windows

IQ Software Corp.
3295 River Exchange Dr.
Suite 550
Norcross, GA 30092-9909
(404) 446-8880, (800) 458-0386

Lotus Development Corporation
55 Cambridge Pkwy.
Cambridge, MA 02142
(617) 577-8500, (800) 343-5414
Products: 1-2-3 for Windows, DataLens Driver for SQL Server, Approach, Notes

Micro Decisionware, Inc.
3035 Center Green Dr.
Boulder, CO 80301
(303) 443-2706, (800) 221-3634
Products: Database Gateway for DB2, Database Gateway for SQL/DS, Database Gateway for DBC/1012, PC/SQL-Link

Microsoft Corporation
One Microsoft Way
Redmond, WA 98052-6339
(206) 882-8080, (800) 426-9400
Products: Windows 3.1, Windows for Workgroups 3.11, Windows NT 3.5, MS-DOS 6.2, Windows NT Advanced Server 3.5, MS SQL Server, FoxPro for Windows, Access, Excel, Visual BASIC, MS C 7.0

Novell, Inc.
122 East 1700 South
Provo, UT 84606-6914
(801) 429-7000, (800) 453-1267
Products: NetWare

Oracle Corporation
500 Oracle Pkwy.
Box 659308
Redwood Shores, CA 94065
(415) 506-7000, (800) 633-0596
Products: ORACLE7 Server Version 7.0, ORACLE Card, ORACLE for 1-2-3
DataLens, SQL*Forms, SQL*ReportWriter, SQL*Plus

PC DOCS Inc.
124 Marriott Dr.
Suite 101
Tallahassee, FL 32301
(904) 942-3627, (800) 933-3627
Products: PC DOCS Open

Pilot Software, Inc.
1 Canal Park
Cambridge, MA 02141
(617) 374-9400, (800) 944-0094
Products: LightShip, LightShip Lens, Command Center

Powersoft Corporation
561 Virginia Rd.
Concord, MA 01742-2732
(508) 287-1500, (800) 273-2841
Products: PowerBuilder Desktop, PowerBuilder Enterprise

Quadbase Systems, Inc.
2855 Kifer Rd.
Suite 203
Santa Clara, CA 95051
(408) 982-0835
Products: QuadBase-SQL, QuadBase-Server/NLM

Revelation Technologies, Inc.
181 Harbor Dr.
Stamford, CT 06902
(203) 973-1000, (800) 262-4747
Products: Advanced Revelation, DB2 Bond, ORACLE Server Bond, SQL Server
Bond

Saros Corp.
10900 Northeast 8th St.
700 Plaza Center Bldg.
Bellevue, WA 98004
(206) 646-1066, (800) 827-2767
Products: Mezzanine, Saros Document Manager

Sequent Computer Systems, Inc.
15450 S.W. Koll Pkwy.
Beaverton, OR 97006-6063
(503) 626-5700, (800) 854-0428
Products: Symmetry series multiprocessor superservers

ShareBase Corporation (Subsidiary of Teradata Corp.)
2055A Logic Dr.
San Jose, CA 95124
(408) 369-5500
Products: SQL Server/8000 series multiprocessor superservers

Superbase Inc.
800 Orville Dr.
Bohemia, NY 11717
(516) 244-1570, (800) 315-7944
Products: Superbase95

SYBASE, Inc.
6475 Christie Ave.
Emeryville, CA 94608
(510) 596-3500, (800) 879-2273
Products: SYBASE SQL Server, SYBASE System 10

Symantec Corporation
10201 Torre Ave.
Cupertino, CA 95014-2132
(408) 253-9600, (800) 441-7234
Products: Q&A

TechGnosis, Inc.
5 Burlington Woods Dr.
Suite 202
Burlington, MA 01803
(617) 229-6100, (800) 321-0543
Products: SequeLink, SequeLink Engine

TopSpeed Corp.
150 E. Sample Rd.
Pompano Beach, FL 33064
(305) 785-4555, (800) 354-4444
Products: Professional Clarion

Trinzic Corp.
101 University Ave.
Palo Alto, CA 94301
(415) 328-9595, (800) 845-2466
Products: Forest & Trees for Windows

WATCOM International Corp.
415 Philip St.
Waterloo, ON, CD N2L 3X2
(519) 886-3700, (800) 265-4555
Products: Watcom SQL 4.0, Watcom C++

XDB Systems, Inc.
9861 Broken Land Pkwy.
Columbia, MD 21046
(410) 312-9300, (800) 488-4948
Products: XDB-Server, XDB-LINK for DB2, XDB-Workbench for DB2

■ Appendix C

■ Suggestions for Further Reading

The fields of database and network technology are enormously complex and cover a broad range of theories and real-world experience. Though I've tried to present as complete an overview as possible, no one book can cover it all. Here are some suggestions for further reading in the areas of databases (general and specific), SQL, and local area networks, with a brief description of what's covered in each book or article.

Database Theory

Codd, E.F., "A Relational Model of Data for Large Shared Data Banks," *Communications of the ACM*, Volume 13, No. 6, June 1970. This is Codd's first paper, which laid the groundwork for the Relational model.

Codd, E.F., "Is Your DBMS Really Relational?," *Computerworld*, October 14, 1985; "Does Your DBMS Run by the Rules?," *Computerworld*, October 21, 1985. This two-part article first laid out the now-famous "12 Rules" for determining how closely a DBMS fits the Relational model.

Codd, E.F., *The Relational Model for Database Management, Version 2*, Addison-Wesley Publishing Company, 1990. This book details Codd's latest revision of the Relational model, based on further study and real-world experiences.

Date, C.J., *An Introduction to Database Systems, Volume I, Sixth Edition*, Addison-Wesley Publishing Company, 1995. This book thoroughly covers the entire range of database models and theory. It also contains some interesting discussions on Date's disagreements with Codd over the practicalities of the Relational model. Date is the cofounder of Codd and Date International.

Flores, Ivan, *Data Base Architecture*, Van Nostrand Reinhold Company, Inc., 1981. Though somewhat dated and mainframe-oriented, this book has very clear and detailed explanations of the theory behind data management, as well as the Relational, Hierarchical, and Network models.

Pascal, Fabian, *SQL and Relational Basics*, M&T Books, 1990. Aimed primarily at PC users, this book provides a detailed explanation of the Relational model through the "12 Rules" plus the basics of SQL. Of particular interest are the chapters that evaluate how well PC-based databases follow the Relational model.

C/S Databases

Salemi, Joe, *Client/Server Computing With ORACLE*, Ziff-Davis Press, 1993. Covers ORACLE Server 6.0, with specifics on front-ends and specialized applications. Includes some details on the changes in ORACLE7.

Salemi, Joe, *Client/Server Computing With SYBASE SQL Server*, Ziff-Davis Press, 1994. Covers SYBASE SQL Server 4.9 and System 10, and Microsoft SQL Server, with specifics on front-ends and specialized applications.

SQL

ANSI, "American National Standard for Information Systems—Database Language—SQL with Integrity Enhancement," Publication ANSI X3.135-1989, American National Standards Institute, October 1989. This ANSI booklet details the 1989 version of the SQL standard, otherwise known as the ANSI Level 2 with Integrity Enhancement, or ANSI-89, standard. Though it's somewhat dry reading, anyone evaluating a SQL-based RDBMS should have a copy.

Date, C.J., *A Guide to the SQL Standard, Third Edition*, Addison-Wesley Publishing Company, 1993. This book translates the ANSI Standards document into a more readable form and provides practical examples.

Hursch, Dr. Carolyn and Dr. Jack, *SQL—Structured Query Language, Second Edition*, Windcrest Books, 1991. This book is an advanced and theoretical discussion of SQL. It includes details on some commercial implementations and what's required to make them conform to the standard.

Networks

Derfler, Jr., Frank J., *PC Magazine Guide to Connectivity, Third Edition*, Ziff-Davis Press, 1995. Derfler is the senior networking editor for *PC Magazine*. His book is the best available introduction to the subject of PC-based networks.

Derfler, Jr., Frank J., *PC Magazine Guide to Linking LANs*, Ziff-Davis Press, 1992. Another excellent book by Derfler that covers the different aspects of using bridges, gateways, and routers to link networks.

■ Glossary

ANSI Level 2 Integrity addendum   The portion of the ANSI Level 2 SQL standard document that describes how referential integrity should be implemented.

ANSI Level 2 with Integrity Enhancement   The 1989 American National Standards Institute (ANSI) standard for the SQL language. Sometimes referred to as the ANSI-SQL 89 standard; replaced the previous Level 1 version, the ANSI-SQL 86 standard.

ANSI-SQL 92 Entry Level   The first portion of the 1992 American National Standards Institute (ANSI) standard for the SQL language. The full standard, still under development, will be referred to as SQL Level 3.

application prototyping utility   A type of code generator that assists programmers in designing and testing the screens, reports, and so on for an application before they write the program code. The utility may also contain a code generator, or it may just outline the final application (called a skeleton code).

asymmetrical multiprocessing   A multiprocessing system in which each CPU is responsible for a different task. For example, one CPU handles the operating system while another runs the DBMS.

back-end   Common term for the database server or application in a Client/Server system.

bridge   A hardware/software combination connecting two LANs using the same or different topologies and the same network protocol. A bridge simply combines two or more smaller LANs into one large LAN and passes all network traffic through to both parts. Some modern bridges also have the ability to filter network traffic or route different protocols between the individual LANs. Bridges that also have these routing features are usually referred to as bridge/routers or brouters.

bus   The part or subsystem of a computer that connects peripherals to the main CPU. Also known as the data bus.

business rules   SQL statements and commands that enforce a user's rules specifying the values for one or more columns in a database. A business rule's values are usually more restrictive than the domain of the column. For example, the domain of a salary column may be "$0 to $99,000," but the business rule may restrict the maximum value according to the employee job classification.

character coding   A standard method of translating characters such as alphabetical letters, numbers, and symbols into a binary code for storage and manipulation on a computer. The two current standards are ASCII and EBCDIC.

Client/Server database   A database system in which the database engine and database application reside on separate intelligent computers that communicate with each other through a network. In this system, the processing power is split between the two CPUs. The user's workstation is the client, and the DBMS runs on the server.

clustered index   A method of indexing a database in which the data in a table is physically arranged on the disk to closely match the index order. This reduces the delay in accessing data from large tables.

clustering   The linking of two or more DEC VAX/VMS systems to automatically share CPUs and resources and to create a larger computer complex. The linked computers appear as one system to users.

coaxial cable   An electrical networking cable that has an insulated center core surrounded by an exterior braid and additional layers of insulation. Cable TV system cabling is a familiar example.

code generator   An application development tool (usually menu-driven) that helps users create DBMS applications without writing programming code. Users lay out the steps they want an application to take, and the code generator writes the code that carries out those steps.

cost-based optimization   An advanced method of optimizing SQL statements before execution. In a cost-based system, the DBMS analyzes the amount of CPU time and resources needed to fulfill a particular SQL statement using various methods. The DBMS then determines the "least costly" method and executes the statement accordingly.

daisy chain   A network topology, usually thin Ethernet, in which the cable runs from node to node of the network in a chain-like configuration.

data compression   Reduces the size of data packets for storage or transmission, using one of a number of methods. A compression algorithm shrinks the data to the smallest size possible without losing or damaging it.

data integrity (DI)   The overall guiding principle behind the Relational model and the specific sections of the model that define how the database protects the data it contains, and how it prevents inadvertent or unexpected modifications or damage to that data.

data integrity rules   The SQL statements or commands in a particular RDBMS that provide DI services.

data redundancy   The duplication of data in a database or application. Undesirable within a single database because data redundancy decreases available disk storage space and usually slows down data access. Desirable when duplicating an entire database on a different device in order to provide backup and database integrity services. This type of data redundancy is also known as fault tolerance.

database   A set of information, defined by the user's criteria, that is electronically organized, stored, accessed, and updated.

database administrator (DBA)   The technical support person who typically assigns user IDs and data access permissions, creates new databases, removes databases no longer in use, and monitors the database's disk storage usage and performance.

database application   A computer program designed to provide user access to the data in a DBMS, through data entry forms, query forms, and reports.

database dictionary   A specific type of system table that stores information about the structure of a particular database. Primarily used in relational DBMSs to store the names and data types of the tables and columns in a database.

database engine   The portion of a DBMS that stores and manipulates the data according to commands issued from a database application.

database integrity   The general theory of protecting and preserving data in a database that is realized in particular hardware and/or software methods. Database integrity may be implemented by the DBMS itself, or through administrator intervention, such as tape backups.

database management system (DBMS)   A computer application designed for the specific purpose of collecting and storing data. It always includes a database engine and may include an application programming language or interface for users to create applications.

database server   A computer in a Client/Server system that primarily runs the DBMS and processes user queries.

declarative referential integrity   The most advanced type of referential integrity (RI), which requires that rules for handling deletions be declared in the table definition, instead of being implemented through stored or precompiled SQL procedures by the application programmer.

disk duplexing   A method of providing database integrity whereby the application or platform automatically writes the data to two different disks on the same controller at the same time. If the primary disk fails, the system automatically switches to the duplexed disk and continues operating. Duplexing provides no protection against failure of the controller card.

disk mirroring   A method of providing database integrity whereby the application or platform automatically writes the data to two different disks on two different controller cards at the same time. If one disk or card fails, the system automatically switches to the mirror disk and continues operating.

distributed database   A database that resides on two or more servers, yet appears to users as a single large database.

distributed database communications   The means by which two or more databases pass queries or data between themselves.

distributed database dictionary   A database dictionary that is stored on two or more database servers and is automatically updated when any changes are made to any of the databases associated with it.

distributed processing   A method of sharing application processing between two or more computer systems. Client/Server databases are a basic form of distributed processing.

distributed query optimization   A method of SQL command optimization designed to speed queries on distributed databases.

distributed transactions   Database transactions that are split between two or more databases in a distributed system. All portions of the transaction must be successfully completed before the whole transaction can be considered successful.

domain (data domain)   The permitted range or set of values of a particular data item in a particular field or column. For example, the domain of a column of last names could be, "Words containing the characters A to Z in upper- and lowercase."

domain integrity   A principle of the Relational model that governs how the DBMS ensures that each value in a column fits in the domain of the column.

downsizing   A computer industry buzzword that describes the process of moving applications from large systems (usually mainframes) to smaller, less expensive systems (usually PCs or superservers). Gradually being replaced by *rightsizing*.

dynamic optimization   A type of SQL statement optimization developed by DEC for their Rdb/VMS DBMS. It dynamically changes the type of search it performs on a table based on information or statistics gathered while performing the query.

encrypted file storage   A method of coding a file to prevent access by those who don't have the proper password or decoding "key."

Enhanced Industry Standard Architecture (EISA)   A 32-bit data bus developed as an enhancement to the ISA bus and an alternative to the MCA bus. The EISA bus is backward-compatible with ISA cards.

entity integrity   A term used by some DBMS vendors to refer to domain integrity.

fiber-optic cable   Networking cable that consists of one or more clear fiber threads inside a protective insulator. Fiber-optic cables use intense light or lasers instead of electrical currents to transmit the signal. Fiber-optic cables suffer less from signal strength loss than do electrical cables and are generally immune to outside interference.

field   One specific piece of information or item of a database, such as a manufacturer's part number or an employee's Social Security number; referred to as a column in the Relational model.

file server   A computer (usually a PC) that provides the primary shared resources on a LAN that can be used by all the workstations or nodes on the LAN. Shared resources usually include hard-disk space and printers.

forms-based development tool   An application development tool that lets the programmer develop user interface screens by painting a data entry form on the screen.

fourth generation language (4GL)   An advanced computer programming language designed for creating a particular type of application, such as a database application. Examples of 4GLs include SQL and the dBASE-compatible programming languages.

front-end application   An application that runs on a client system and is designed primarily to serve as an interface between a database user and the database itself.

front-end processor (FEP)   A hardware system that handles communications with nonstandard devices, usually for a mainframe. The FEP is primarily used for dial-in access through modems and LAN attachments.

gateway systems   A hardware and software system used to link two or more networks that use different protocols. Gateways are usually used to link PC-based LANs to a mainframe.

Graphical User Interface (GUI)   A general term used to define a class of operating systems or operating environments that base their user interface on graphics instead of text. Examples include Windows 3.1 and Windows NT, the Workplace Shell in OS/2 2.0 and later, and the interface on the Apple Macintosh.

hard-disk subsystem   The combination of one or more hard disks and the controller card that connects them to the rest of the computer.

hashed clustered index   Hashing is a method of creating a smaller index by substituting binary values for common elements in the index. A hashed clustered index combines a hashed index with clustered data.

host   Another term for a central computer system, such as a minicomputer or mainframe, that runs all the user and database applications. Users generally communicate with the host through terminals.

index   A method used to speed up access to individual data items by creating a separate construct that only contains information on one or more fields in the database, sorted in a user-defined order. The index is searched, and a pointer leads the DBMS or application to the particular record the index refers to.

index file   Some DBMSs store the index as a separate file on the disk, instead of storing it as part of the file that holds the database's records.

index pointer   A programming construct that's included in the index. It's used by the DBMS to find the particular data record on the disk that the indexed item refers to.

Industry Standard Architecture (ISA)   A term used to describe the data bus pioneered by IBM in the PC-AT systems that has since become the standard 16-bit bus in the industry.

Information Warehouse   IBM's marketing term for their concept of a distributed processing system in which data can be stored on and accessed from any computer on a network.

interface card   A hardware card that plugs into a PC's bus and connects the CPU to peripheral devices. Examples include the disk interface card (commonly called the disk controller) for connecting the CPU to the hard disks, and a parallel interface card for connecting the PC to a printer.

interprocess communications   Data communications among different processes running on the same computer system. A process can be a user application, a system function, or even different functions within the same application.

leaf   In the Hierarchical model, a leaf is the very last data node on the lowest level of a database tree.

library   A collection of programming routines that can be included in custom-written applications to provide specific functions or to speed the process of application development.

local area network (LAN)   A combination of hardware (such as interface cards and cabling) and software that lets two or more computers (usually PCs) communicate with each other to share resources.

Location Independence   An IBM term distinguishing the ability of DB2 users to access data residing in any accessible database that can participate in the Information Warehouse concept, regardless of the database system's location on the network.

Management Information Systems (MIS)   The usual name of the corporate department in charge of supporting computer resources. Sometimes shortened to Information Systems (IS).

MicroChannel Architecture (MCA)   A 32-bit data bus invented by IBM for their third-generation microcomputers (the PS/2 series). MCA was developed to enhance and replace the ISA bus and is not backward-compatible with ISA cards.

motherboard   A generic term that describes the primary circuit board in a computer. The motherboard usually contains the support circuitry for the CPU, external ports, and data bus. Other terms commonly used for the motherboard are the system board and the planar board.

multiprocessing system   A computer system with two or more CPUs that share processing duties.

multitasking operating system   An operating system designed to perform one or more computer tasks, such as running different applications, at the same time. OS/2, Windows NT, and UNIX are examples.

multithreaded operating systems   A type of multitasking operating system that supports threads of execution that let applications multitask within themselves. OS/2 and Windows NT are examples.

multiuser operating system An operating system designed for running applications that are accessed by multiple users simultaneously through terminals and that are usually run on minicomputers and mainframes. UNIX, VAX/VMS, and IBM's MVS are examples.

NetWare Loadable Module (NLM) A program or application that executes on a file server running under the Novell NetWare 3.11 and higher LAN operating system.

network administrator The technical support person responsible for maintaining the network. Usual administration tasks include assigning network user IDs, monitoring disk space and network traffic, and ensuring that network backups are performed properly.

Network Interface Card (NIC) An interface card designed to attach a PC to a LAN through the PC's bus. Software drivers that tell the PC how to "talk" to the card and the network are usually provided with the card or with the network software.

network topology The cabling scheme used for a computer network, consisting of the type of cables and the way the cables are interconnected. Ethernet and Token Ring are two types of network topologies.

network traffic The amount of data that passes through a network during an arbitrary period of time. The traffic indicates the network's workload versus its capacity.

node In the Hierarchical and Network models another term for a particular data item or field. Node is also used in networking to describe a single computer on the network.

normalization Used in the Relational model to describe the process of designing a database's structure to reduce the amount of duplicated data. There are five levels of normalization commonly used, with each level reducing the amount of duplication over the previous level.

off-the-shelf software A generic term used to describe any commercial software package that can be purchased in a software store or by mail order; distinct from those applications that are custom-written for a single company or industry.

one-to-many relationship A term from database theory that identifies the structure of the relationship between one data item and multiple different data items. For example, a department supervisor has a one-to-many relationship with the employees in the department.

one-to-one relationship A term from database theory that identifies the structure of the relationship between a data item that only relates to one other data item. For example, there's a one-to-one relationship between an employee's name and Social Security number.

open systems Refers to operating systems that will run on any of a class of computer hardware, regardless of vendor. PC/MS-DOS, OS/2, Windows NT, and UNIX are examples of open systems.

parallel-processing system An advanced form of multiprocessing in which a task is divided among different CPUs for processing. Each CPU handles a portion of the computations, and the final result is derived by combining all the separate calculations.

parent-child relationship A database term that defines how two pieces of data relate to or depend on each other in a particular database. A child record contains data that's also contained in the parent record.

platform A general term that refers to the hardware/software combination that a particular application runs on. Specifically, the platform consists of the computer hardware and operating system.

plug compatible A term used to describe third-party hardware systems that are compatible with IBM mainframes. Called plug compatible because they use the same input/output plugs as IBM hardware.

population A term that describes the specific group of information contained in the database. For example, the population of an employee database is "All the people who work for the company."

POSIX A U.S. federal government standard for computer operating systems sharing the same Application Programming Interface (API). The goal of POSIX is to allow programmers to write one application that can then be compiled and run on any POSIX-compliant system.

precompiled procedure An SQL procedure that's compiled and stored on the same computer system as the DBMS and that can be used by any application accessing the database. Unlike a stored procedure, it's not part of a particular database. Precompiled procedures are executed on the client system instead of the server.

preoptimized procedure A precompiled or stored procedure that's optimized prior to use. Preoptimization saves CPU time and increases DBMS performance by eliminating the need to optimize a statement each time it's executed by a client application.

program analyst   A senior applications programmer who determines the end user's application needs and designs the program to fill those needs. The analyst then gives the design to the application programmers for development.

proprietary operating systems   Computer operating systems designed to run only on a specific vendor's hardware. Digital Equipment Corporation's VAX/VMS is an example of a proprietary operating system.

record   A record is comprised of all the fields that contain information about a particular individual item in a database; also referred to as a row in the Relational model.

Reduced Instruction Set Computer (RISC)   A type of CPU designed to perform high-speed processing by reducing the number of internal instructions the CPU must process to carry out a computation task. RISC CPUs are usually found in UNIX-based workstations and superservers.

referential integrity (RI)   A principle of the Relational model. Referential integrity is the part of data integrity that specifies how the DBMS should respond to a user's attempt to delete a parent row (record) in one table that has dependent (child) rows in another table. A proper implementation of RI ensures that child rows are never orphaned.

referential integrity rules   The SQL statements or commands in a particular RDBMS that provide RI services.

replication   The process where one or more exact copies of a database are made and maintained on remote servers. Replication is a limited form of distributed processing.

report writer   An application or application development tool primarily designed to assist the user or programmer in creating reports from a database. Report writers usually let the user or programmer create the report layout by painting it on the screen.

rightsizing   A new buzzword that's gradually replacing downsizing. Rightsizing refers to the concept of moving a database to the proper platform, regardless of whether the database is moved up from PCs or down from larger systems.

router   A hardware/software combination that joins two or more LANs. A router can link LANs using different topologies and protocols. Routers also reduce network traffic by only passing the data destined for the interconnected LAN(s), while filtering out data that should remain on the source LAN.

scalability   The characteristic of applications or databases that run on multiple platforms of varying sizes; for example, an ORACLE database can run on a PC or a VAX.

scrollable cursor   An SQL construct that allows the user to browse forward and backward through all the data returned in response to a query, instead of receiving and viewing the query results one row at a time.

sibling relationship   The characteristic of two or more pieces of information that are related to one another and are equal in importance. It's another way of describing the fields in a record; for example, the name, address, and phone number of an employee are each in sibling relationships with one another and with any data describing that employee.

Small Computer Standard Interface (SCSI)   A standard method for connecting data peripherals to a microcomputer, usually used for storage devices such as disks, tape drives, and CD-ROMs.

star configuration   A type of network topology in which the cables that connect the nodes to the network emanate from a central hub, with one cable per node. Sometimes referred to as a *hub-and-star* configuration.

stored procedures   SQL procedures that are stored as part of the database and executed entirely on the back-end system. Using stored procedures allows more of the database processing to be moved from the client to the server.

supercomputers   High-speed, high-powered computers predominantly used for intense scientific calculations, such as weather predictions and engineering design.

symmetrical multiprocessing (SMP)   A multiprocessing system in which processing tasks are divided between various CPUs. Each new task is routed to the CPU with the lowest workload at the time of processing.

syntax-based optimization   The original method of optimizing SQL statements whereby the DBMS analyzes the commands for the most logical order of executing them, without regard to the CPU time and resources needed. Syntax-based optimizers are generally slower and more resource intensive than cost-based optimizers.

system tables   A special database used by some DBMSs to store information about the whole database system; for example, it identifies which individual databases are contained in the system and records user security access information. Primarily used in DBMSs that follow the Relational model.

terminal controllers   A hardware subsystem that handles the communications between terminals and the central host. Usually used with minicomputers and mainframes, a terminal controller can connect up to 64 terminals to the host through a single host connection.

terminal, dumb   A dedicated system connected to a central host that typically consists of only a display screen and keyboard. It sends keystrokes to the host and displays the screen information sent back from the host.

terminal, intelligent   A type of terminal connected to a central computer host that has its own CPU for handling some of the processing, such as screen drawing and network communications; it may or may not be a dedicated system. A PC is an example of an intelligent terminal when it's connected via a specialized peripheral board to a mainframe.

third generation language (3GL)   A general-purpose computer programming language used to create any type of application. Examples of 3GLs include BASIC, COBOL, C, and Pascal.

third-party add-on   A hardware or software product developed by one vendor to work with and enhance another vendor's product.

thread   A process within an application that carries out a particular operation or task. Single-threaded applications can only do one task at a time. Multithreaded applications can do multiple tasks at the same time, such as sorting a database while printing a report. The ability to perform multiple threads within an application is usually provided by the operating system.

transaction recovery logs   Log files maintained by a DBMS that keep a record of every recent transaction performed on a database. Provides data integrity services when a transaction fails or the system crashes by helping the DBMS return the database to a consistent state. Often, simply referred to as the transaction logs.

triggers   A particular type of stored procedure that is automatically executed when certain SQL commands (usually those that modify the data) are issued. Called rules by some vendors, triggers usually implement referential integrity (RI) in systems that don't support declarative RI.

twisted-pair cable   Electrical network cable consisting of two or more pieces of insulated wire twisted together and covered with one or more insulation layers. Round telephone wire is a familiar example.

two-phase commit   A form of transaction processing on multiple databases (or multiple tables within a database) that ensures that modifications made to every database involved in a transaction are successful before the transaction itself is considered successful.

upsizing   Moving an application from a smaller system to a larger one as the need for disk storage space and processing power grows. Usually refers to moving a PC-based database to a UNIX-based superserver. Gradually being replaced by *rightsizing*.

user-transparent   A characteristic of systems in which data processing actions are taken without the user either being aware of them or manually performing them. For example, a user sends a query to a local database server, and the server automatically passes the query on to another server where the data actually resides but the user is unaware of the transfer.

value-added reseller (VAR)   A vendor or consultant who sells a complete system and application solution that usually includes all the necessary hardware and software.

vertical market application   A specialized application designed for a specific market, such as schools, government, etc. Vertical market applications are usually programmed and sold by VARs.

virtual memory (VM)   A method whereby an operating system swaps inactive data and code to available disk space, freeing up working RAM for active applications. The data and code is swapped to the disk in pages (the size of the page is dependent on the CPU), so the process is sometimes referred to as virtual memory paging, or simply paging. OS/2, Windows NT, and UNIX are examples of operating systems that use virtual memory.

wide area network (WAN)   A network that connects computer systems from more than one building. A WAN generally consists of one or more LANs in separate locations that are interconnected with each other directly or through a central host.

■ Index

Ziff-Davis Press Survey of Readers

Please help us in our effort to produce the best books on personal computing. For your assistance, we would be pleased to send you a FREE catalog featuring the complete line of Ziff-Davis Press books.

1. How did you first learn about this book?

Recommended by a friend . . . . ☐ -1 (5)

Recommended by store personnel . . . . ☐ -2

Saw in Ziff-Davis Press catalog . . . . ☐ -3

Received advertisement in the mail . . . . ☐ -4

Saw the book on bookshelf at store . . . . ☐ -5

Read book review in: _____ ☐ -6

Saw an advertisement in: _____ ☐ -7

Other (Please specify): _____ ☐ -8

2. Which THREE of the following factors most influenced your decision to purchase this book? (Please check up to THREE.)

Front or back cover information on book . . . ☐ -1 (6)

Logo of magazine affiliated with book . . . . . . ☐ -2

Special approach to the content . . . . ☐ -3

Completeness of content . . . . ☐ -4

Author's reputation. ☐ -5

Publisher's reputation . . . . ☐ -6

Book cover design or layout . . . . ☐ -7

Index or table of contents of book . . . . ☐ -8

Price of book . . . . ☐ -9

Special effects, graphics, illustrations . . . . . . ☐ -0

Other (Please specify): _____ ☐ -x

3. How many computer books have you purchased in the last six months? _____ (7-10)

4. On a scale of 1 to 5, where 5 is excellent, 4 is above average, 3 is average, 2 is below average, and 1 is poor, please rate each of the following aspects of this book below. (Please circle your answer.)

Depth/completeness of coverage	5	4	3	2	1	(11)
Organization of material	5	4	3	2	1	(12)
Ease of finding topic	5	4	3	2	1	(13)
Special features/time saving tips	5	4	3	2	1	(14)
Appropriate level of writing	5	4	3	2	1	(15)
Usefulness of table of contents	5	4	3	2	1	(16)
Usefulness of index	5	4	3	2	1	(17)
Usefulness of accompanying disk	5	4	3	2	1	(18)
Usefulness of illustrations/graphics	5	4	3	2	1	(19)
Cover design and attractiveness	5	4	3	2	1	(20)
Overall design and layout of book	5	4	3	2	1	(21)
Overall satisfaction with book	5	4	3	2	1	(22)

5. Which of the following computer publications do you read regularly; that is, 3 out of 4 issues?

Byte . . . . ☐ -1 (23)

Computer Shopper . . . . ☐ -2

Home Office Computing . . . . ☐ -3

Dr. Dobb's Journal . . . . ☐ -4

LAN Magazine . . . . ☐ -5

MacWEEK . . . . ☐ -6

MacUser . . . . ☐ -7

PC Computing . . . . ☐ -8

PC Magazine . . . . ☐ -9

PC WEEK . . . . ☐ -0

Windows Sources . . . . ☐ -x

Other (Please specify): _____ ☐ -y

Please turn page.

6. What is your level of experience with personal computers? With the subject of this book?

	With PCs	With subject of book
Beginner	☐ -1 (24)	☐ -1 (25)
Intermediate	☐ -2	☐ -2
Advanced	☐ -3	☐ -3

7. Which of the following best describes your job title?

Officer (CEO/President/VP/owner) ☐ -1 (26)
Director/head ☐ -2
Manager/supervisor ☐ -3
Administration/staff ☐ -4
Teacher/educator/trainer ☐ -5
Lawyer/doctor/medical professional ☐ -6
Engineer/technician ☐ -7
Consultant ☐ -8
Not employed/student/retired ☐ -9
Other (Please specify): _____ ☐ -0

8. What is your age?

Under 20 ☐ -1 (27)
21-29 ☐ -2
30-39 ☐ -3
40-49 ☐ -4
50-59 ☐ -5
60 or over ☐ -6

9. Are you:

Male ☐ -1 (28)
Female ☐ -2

Thank you for your assistance with this important information! Please write your address below to receive our free catalog.

Name: _____

Address: _____

City/State/Zip: _____

Fold here to mail.

3105-04-19